Cuneiform in Canaan

Cuneiform in Canaan

The Next Generation

SECOND EDITION

Wayne Horowitz
Takayoshi Oshima
Seth L. Sanders

Yigal Bloch, Janet Safford, E. Jan Wilson, Peter Zilberg

EISENBRAUNS | University Park, Pennsylvania

Library of Congress Cataloging-in-Publication Data

Names: Horowitz, Wayne, 1957– author. | Oshima, Takayoshi, author. | Sanders, Seth L., author.
Title: Cuneiform in Canaan : the next generation / Wayne Horowitz, Takayoshi Oshima, Seth L. Sanders.
Description: Second edition. | University Park, Pennsylvania : Eisenbrauns, [2018] | Includes bibliographical references and index.
Summary: "Presents the full corpus of all 91 cuneiform tablets and inscribed objects that have been recovered from the Land of Israel, including cuneiform tablets from the Bronze Age cities of Canaan, texts from the cities of the Philistines, and inscriptions from the Kingdoms of Judah and Israel"—Provided by publisher.
Identifiers: LCCN 2018007175 | ISBN 9781575067919 (cloth : alk. paper)
Subjects: LCSH: Cuneiform inscriptions. | Israel—Antiquities. | Palestine—Antiquities.
Classification: LCC PJ3701 H67 2018 | DDC 492/.1—dc23
LC record available at https://lccn.loc.gov/2018007175

Printed in the United States of America
Published by The Pennsylvania State University Press,
University Park, PA 16802-1003

Eisenbrauns is an imprint of The Pennsylvania State University Press.

The Pennsylvania State University Press is a member of the Association of University Presses.

It is the policy of The Pennsylvania State University Press to use acid-free paper. Publications on uncoated stock satisfy the minimum requirements of American National Standard for Information Sciences—Permanence of Paper for Printed Library Material, ANSI Z39.48–1992.

For the fathers of Israeli Assyriology from us their Assyriological children, and now grand-children, in memory of

HAYIM TADMOR

AARON SHAFFER

ANSON RAINEY

and

ITAMAR SINGER

CONTENTS

Acknowledgements	ix
Part I: The Corpus	
Introduction	3
The History of Cuneiform in Canaan	10
Part II: The Sources	
Aphek	27
Ashdod	37
Ashqelon	40
Beer Sheva	42
Ben Shemen	44
Beth Mirsim	45
Beth Shean	46
Beth Shemesh	49
Gezer	50
Tel Hadid	59
Hazor	63
Hebron	89
Tel el-Ḥesi	93
Tell Jemmeh	96
Jericho	97
Jerusalem	99
Tel Keisan	101
Khirḅet Kusiya	103
Megiddo	105
Mikhmoret	112
Tel en-Naṣbeh	114
Qaqun	115
Samaria	116
Sepphoris (Ṣippori)	122
Shechem	125
Shephela	130

Taanach 132
Tabor 156
Wingate 157

Part III: Alphabetic Cuneiform Texts
Beth Shemesh 1 161
Taanach 15 165
Tabor 1 168

Abbreviations 173
Bibliography 175
Index of Personal Names in the Sources 191
Index of Divine Names in the Sources 197
Index of Geographical Names in the Sources 199
Index of Sumerian and Akkadian Words Discussed 201
Index of Subjects 203
Hand Copies 207
Photographs 223
Appendix A: New Hand Copies 241
Appendix B: New Photographs 245

ACKNOWLEDGEMENTS

For the First Edition

As director of the Cuneiform in Canaan Project and co-author of the project's final product, the *Cuneiform in Canaan* volume, I take it upon myself to acknowledge the many colleagues, friends, teachers, students and institutions around the globe who participated in the project and gave aid of all sorts since the project began with a generous grant from the Israel Academy of Sciences and Humanities in 1997.

First and foremost, I would like to thank Takayoshi Oshima for all his seen and unseen contributions to this project. Takayoshi was part of the project from beginning to end, starting as a M.A. level research assistant and ending as a newly minted Ph.D. with numerous responsibilities in the project, including that of chief epigraphist. Seth Sanders made numerous important contributions to the project, both during a one year stay in Jerusalem as a research fellow in the project and afterwards. His editions of the alphabetic texts in Part III of the volume are but the most visible product of Seth's endeavors.

A special thank you is due to Elnatan Weissert, who provided us with advance knowledge of the contents of the Qaqun stele, and to my colleague Nathan Wasserman for a number of academic courtesies, great and small. On the archaeological side, thanks are due to Amnon Ben-Tor for entrusting us with the publication of the most recent tablets from Hazor, and to all the faculty and staff of the Hebrew University Institute of Archaeology for ongoing support throughout the project and the preparation of the book. Gabi Laron of the Institute of Archaeology produced most of the photographs of tablets published in the book.

Contributions were also made by a number of Hebrew University students, in particular Uri Gabbay, who contributed to the editions of the tablets from Tel Hadid, James Ford and others who served terms as research assistants in the project, including Yehudah Kaplan. From the Rothberg International School Bryan Kovach and Jennifer Kaufman should be singled out.

The project also enjoyed the aid of numerous colleagues at universities, museums and other institutions. Osnat Misch-Brandl, Michal Dayagi-Mendels and others at the Israel Museum, Jerusalem, provided prompt and repeated access to tablets in the museum's collections. Veysel Donbaz of the Arkeoloji Müzeleri, Istanbul, was a gracious host to myself and to Takayoshi Oshima during a visit to the museum in 2004. Gary Beckman of the University of Michigan, Ann Arbor, and Robin Meador-Woodruff of the Kelsey Museum of Archaeology, Ann Arbor, provided access to the texts from Sepphoris, as well as a photograph of Sepphoris 1. Hussein Alhaib of the Hazor Museum at Kibbutz Ayelet Hashachar helped us locate and study what came to be Hazor 4 in our study. Chava Katz and the staff of the Israel Antiquities Authority were helpful throughout the project.

We would like to formally thank the Israel Museum, the Instititute of Archaeology of the Hebrew University, the Israel Antiquities Authority, the Arkeoloji Müzeleri, Istanbul, and the Kelsey Museum of Archaeology, Ann Arbor, for permission to study and publish materials held in their collections.

Other scholars and institutions from around the world helped the project in many ways. Shlomo Izre'el of Tel Aviv University was a true friend of the project, and offered keen insights on both textual and technical matters. Anson Rainey made available his copies of Glock's notes to the Taanach tablets and offered his continuous support to the project. Nadav Na'aman too allowed us to make use of his knowledge and experience with the texts in our group, and Yuval Goren provided us with data from his petrographic analysis of tablets in our study. Long before his recent troubles, Oded Golan of Tel Aviv allowed us to study the lexical fragment Hazor 6, which he found at Tel Hazor while visiting the site as a boy.

Overseas, John Huehnergard of Harvard University provided us with an advance copy of his edition of the Ashqelon lexical tablet (Ashqelon 1). Sam Paley and Ira Spar made available study materials relating to Mikhmoret 1, and Prof. Paley also made available his materials regarding our Khirbet Kusiya 1. Andrew George, Ed Greenstein, Richard Hess, Dennis Pardee and Gus van Beek also made unpublished materials available to the project.

I benefitted from the insights of a number of colleagues in the spring of 1998, while a research fellow at what is now the Center for Advanced Jewish Studies of the University of Pennsylvania. On behalf of Seth Sanders, I would like to thank the following scholars who assisted him in his study of the alphabetic cuneiform texts: Thomas Douza, Richard Jasnow, Ed Greenstein, Alan Millard, Dennis Pardee, Christopher Rollston and Aslahan Yener.

Finally, on the academic side, the scholars to whom the book is dedicated, Hayim Tadmor and Aaron Shaffer of the Hebrew University. Hayim Tadmor provided valuable insights, wisdom, and inspiration throughout the course of the research project, and we are saddened that his recent passing will not allow us the honour of presenting him his copy of *Cuneiform in Canaan*. Aaron Shaffer, who became ill and passed away during the preparation of the volume, was sorely missed even though we were able to benefit from his great knowledge through writings made available to us by his wife Ethel.

Our thanks are extended to the Israel Exploration Society and to its Director, Joseph Aviram, who agreed to undertake the publication of this book. We are indebted to the Dorot Foundation and to its President, Professor Ernest S. Frerichs, whose generous grant made this publication possible.

Thanks are extended to Avraham Pladot, for the layout and design of the volume, and to Marzel A.S. for the typesetting.

The authors are indebted to Tsipi Kuper-Blau for editing and guiding the book to publication, from manuscript to its final form.

Last but not least, I would like to acknowledge the families ofTakayoshi, Seth and myself: Sabina, Marie, Lilach Lisa, Mikhael, and Liam.

Much of what is good in this volume comes from the generous contributions of those listed above, and many others who answered the occasional question and supported the project in countless ways. I regret that space and memory does not allow me to thank each and every one by name. As director of the project, all errors of omission or commission remaining in the book after all our endeavours is ultimately my responsibility and mine alone.

Wayne Horowitz
Kfar Adumim, January 2006

For the Second Edition
In the decade since the completion of the 2006 *Cuneiform in Canaan* book, the participants in the original Cuneiform in Canaan research project and authors of the volume have gone their separate ways. Some of the junior scholars acknowledged on p. ix of that volume have gone on to grown-up careers in Ancient Near Eastern Studies: Uri Gabbay is now my colleague at the Institute of Archaeology at the Hebrew University, James Ford is at Bar-Ilan University, and Yehuda Kaplan is curator of the Bible Lands Museum Jerusalem. My two co-authors too have moved on to bigger and better things. Seth L. Sanders is now at the University of California, Davis, and Takayoshi Oshima is at Leipzig University. Takayoshi has also remained active in the Cuneiform in Canaan project, co-authoring with myself most of the *new* tablets that have been recovered or identified since the publication of the 2006 volume, including Hazor 16–18 and Jerusalem 1–2. Since 2006, the project has continued on a more informal basis and a new generation of Assyriology students has risen and taken their turn as assistants, then colleagues, and now named co-authors of the book. I thank these new colleagues and friends, my own Ph.D. students Peter Zilberg, Yigal Bloch, and Janet Safford for all their seen and unseen contributions to *Cuneiform in Canaan: The Next Generation.* Also deserving of mention is an old friend of the project, Jan Wilson, who reappeared in Jerusalem after two decades of absence and served as the catalyst for completion of the volume. His work in identifying outstanding problems in the manuscript, and his editing work, provided the final push needed to bring this book to print. To paraphrase what I wrote at the end of the acknowledgements of what is now the first edition of *Cuneiform in Canaan*, much of what is good in both volumes comes from the generous contributions of others, and I regret that time, space, and memory do not allow me to thank each and every one of them formally. However, as director of the project, I can take full responsibility for all old errors of omission or commission remaining from the first edition, and all manner of error and/or foolishness in this the second edition.

Finally, some personal reflections and a look forward. The publication of the second edition of *Cuneiform in Canaan* now brings my own formal participation in the project to an end. I now turn over the project to my students Yigal Bloch and Peter Zilberg, and wish them well and bless them that they may be the generation to finally have the opportunity to study and publish the royal archives of Hazor, and other archives, tablet collections, and inscribed objects that we have yet to even dream about. I would like to thank all my Assyriological friends and colleagues here in Israel and abroad for all their help with the project over the years. There are too many to name them all individually, if for no other reason than that I am sure I will forget to thank someone yet again, but will close with a word of thanks and remembrance to Itamar Singer and Anson Rainey, who were good friends of the project from its inception and are no longer with us. Of course we continue to mourn the fathers of Israeli Assyriology, Hayim Tadmor and Aaron Shaffer, who left us a legacy of fine scholarship and love of the place of the cuneiform text tradition in the long and often tortured history of the Land of Israel.

Wayne Horowitz
Jerusalem, 2017

PART I

The Corpus

Introduction

The ancient land once known as Canaan, bordered by the Mediterranean in the west, the Negev Desert in the south, Syria and the Lebanon in the north, and the Jordan River in the east, has been called by many names over the millennia, and has served as the homeland of many different nations, who shared their civilization with their neighbors beyond the land's borders.[1] The Cuneiform in Canaan project is the first examination of one of the most important manifestations of the cultural heritage of the land in ancient times, namely, the use of cuneiform script from the Middle Bronze Age down into the Iron Age. Unlike Egypt to the west, and Syria and Mesopotamia to the north and east, our region of study has yet to produce any large collection of cuneiform texts. Over the past century or so, archaeologists and others have recovered 97 cuneiform objects,[2] scattered in space and time from diverse sites and periods. This book and its predecessor bring together these objects, which include cuneiform tablets from the Bronze Age cities of Canaan, texts from the cities of the Philistines, and inscriptions from what once were the Kingdoms of Judah and Israel, with critical editions of the published material, and bibliographies for all the known sources.

Due to the uneven pace of discovery and the changing political and academic realities in our region, in modern times these materials were never published as a group before the first edition of *Cuneiform in Canaan*. In fact, the only published attempt to provide a comprehensive list of the relevant material was that of K. Galling in *Textbuch zur Geschichte Israels* in 1968.[3] Thus, in the late 1990s, when we started work on the project, there was no comprehensive edition or bibliography of the texts in our corpus. In fact, there was not even an accurate list of the sources, and consequently, the materials were largely inaccessible to most scholars.

1. For the purpose of our discussion, Canaan includes the areas currently under the jurisdiction of the State of Israel and the Palestinian Authority.

2. The 91 objects known at the time of the first edition of *Cuneiform in Canaan* in 2006, Hazor 16–18, Jerusalem 1-2, and Megiddo 6.

3. Galling 1968: 13–14, 61. Demsky 1990 and Rothenbusch 2000: 481–86 discussed many of the texts from the second millennium, and Van der Toorn 2000 provided an even broader general discussion. A number of scholars have compiled lists over the years for their personal use. We would like to thank N. Na'aman of Tel Aviv University and D. Pardee of the University of Chicago in particular for sharing information with us.

In 1997, the Cuneiform in Canaan project was founded with a generous grant from the Israel Academy of Sciences and Humanities. The mandate of this project was to seek out and identify those cuneiform sources that belonged to our group, with the ultimate goal of publishing these sources together in book form. The Cuneiform in Canaan research team began its work by searching for sources and bibliography in the numerous works relating to the archaeology and history of the land that have appeared since the late nineteenth century. Most of the cuneiform sources were well known, well documented, and easy to find, but others proved to be nearly forgotten, particularly the still lost fragment Shechem 3, which is only known by way of an aside at the end of the archaeological discussion by L. E. Toombs in Campbell et al. 1971: 16.

Once we were able to compile a list of cuneiform sources and to collect documentary evidence for the tablets, including photographs, copies, and collations, the subsequent stage of research was to prepare preliminary editions for those sources which we had permission to publish in full. At the same time, we compiled an up-to-date bibliography for all the sources. This we first made available to the academic community (Horowitz, Oshima, and Sanders 2002). The first edition of *Cuneiform in Canaan* was published soon after in 2006. Since then we have continued to check, recheck, and update our sources, editions, and bibliographies, and we now feel ready to publish an updated version of the book with the results of our research updated to December 2016.[4]

THE SOURCES

The Cuneiform in Canaan corpus now includes 97 objects from 29 sites (table 1; map 1). These objects come in many forms and belong to a wide variety of genres. In addition to cuneiform tablets of various sizes, shapes, and states of preservation, the corpus includes numerous inscribed objects: royal stelae, cylinder seals, clay liver models, an inscribed vessel, a fragment of a stone bowl, a bronze ringlet, and even a jar stopper. The tablets include literary texts, letters, administrative texts, royal inscriptions, private dedicatory inscriptions, lexical lists, school exercises, mathematics, a magical/medical text, and recently discovered fragments from a law collection at Hazor reminiscent of *The Laws of Hammurabi* from Babylon.

More than a third of the inscribed objects come from three sites: Hazor (18), Taanach (17), and Aphek (8). For Samaria we list seven items, but Samaria 5–7 are fourth-century coins for which multiple exemplars exist. Megiddo has yielded six objects, but only two of these are cuneiform tablets; the other four are three cylinder seals and an inscribed jar stopper. We list five items for Gezer, but the fifth (our Gezer 5$^{?}$) is of uncertain origin.

4. Reviews of the first edition include Charpin 2007, Cogan 2007, Cohen 2008, Niehr 2011, and Sigrist 2008.

Table 1. Sources classified by site, period and genre

Site	Total[a]	By Period					By Genre								
		Second Millennium BCE			First Millennium BCE										
		Middle Bronze/OB	Late Bronze/MB	Uncertain[b]	Neo-Assyrian	Late	Administrative Docs	Letters	Royal Inscriptions	Private Inscriptions	Academic Tablet[c]	Miscellaneous	Cylinder Seals	Law Collection	Alphabetic Cuneiform
Aphek	8	—	8	—	—	—	2	1	—	—	2	3	—	—	—
Ashdod	4	—	—	1	3	—	—	—	3	—	—	—	1	—	—
Ashqelon	1	—	1	—	—	—	—	—	—	—	1	—	—	—	—
Beer Sheva	1	—	—	—	1	—	—	—	—	—	—	—	1	—	—
Ben Shemen	1	—	—	—	1	—	—	—	1	—	—	—	—	—	—
Beth Mirsim	1	1	—	—	—	—	—	—	—	—	—	—	1	—	—
Beth Shean	2	1	1	—	—	—	—	1	—	—	—	—	1	—	—
Beth Shemesh	1	—	1	—	—	—	—	—	—	—	—	—	—	—	1
Gezer	5	1	—	1	2(1)	—	3	1	—	—	—	1	—	—	—
Hadid	2	—	—	—	2	—	2	—	—	—	—	—	—	—	—
Hazor	18	10	6	2	—	—	6	3	—	3	5	—	—	1	—
Hebron	1	1	—	—	—	—	1	—	—	—	—	—	—	—	—
el-Ḥesi	1	—	1	—	—	—	—	1	—	—	—	—	—	—	—
Jemmeh	1	1	—	—	—	—	—	—	—	—	—	—	1	—	—
Jericho	3	—	1	2	—	—	1	—	—	—	—	—	2	—	—
Jerusalem	2	—	2	—	—	—	—	2	—	—	—	—	—	—	—
Keisan	1	—	—	—	1	—	1	—	—	—	—	—	—	—	—
Khirbet Kusiya	1	—	—	—	1	—	1	—	—	—	—	—	—	—	—
Megiddo	6	—	6	—	—	—	1	—	—	1	1	—	3	—	—
Mikhmoret	1	—	—	—	—	1	1	—	—	—	—	—	—	—	—
en-Naṣbeh	1	—	—	—	—	1[d]	—	—	—	1	—	—	—	—	—
Qaqun	1	—	—	—	1	—	—	—	1	—	—	—	—	—	—
Samaria	7	—	—	—	4	3	2	—	1	—	—	3	1	—	—
Sepphoris	4	—	—	—	—	4[e]	3	—	1	—	—	—	—	—	—
Shechem	3	1	1	1	—	—	1	1	—	—	—	1	—	—	—
Shephela	1	—	—	—	1	—	—	—	—	—	1	—	—	—	—
Taanach	17	—	17	—	—	—	6	9	—	—	—	—	1	—	1
Tabor	1	—	1	—	—	—	—	—	—	—	—	—	—	—	1
Wingate	1	—	—	—	1	—	—	—	—	—	—	—	1	—	—
Total	**97**	**16**	**46**	**7**	**18(1)**	**9**	**31**	**19**	**7**	**5**	**10**	**8**	**13**	**1**	**3**

[a]The number of items that may belong to either the first or second millennium BCE are indicated in parentheses.

[b]Second-millennium BCE items which are most likely Late Bronze Age, but for which a Middle Bronze Age date cannot be totally excluded.

[c]These include: the Lamaštu plaque, lexical lists, literary texts, liver models, mathematical texts, school tablets, and the Hazor law fragments.

[d]Either Neo-Assyrian or later.

[e]Sepphoris 1 is from the Persian period. Sepphoris 2-4 are either Neo-Assyrian or later.

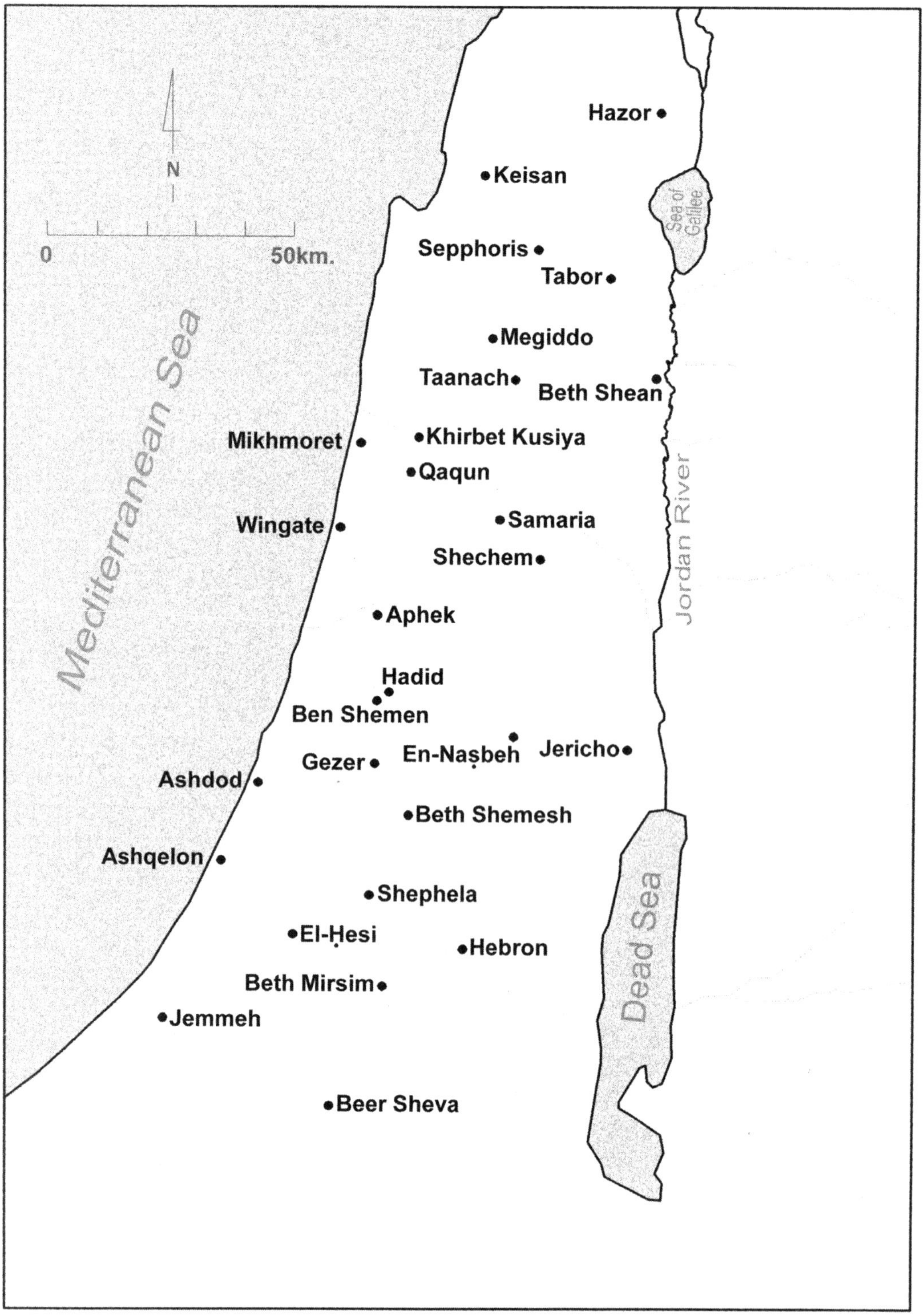

Map 1. The Late Bronze Age

No other site has provided more than four items, and most sites have yielded only one or two. Sites that have yielded epigraphic finds range from Hazor in the north to Beer Sheva in the south, and from Ashqelon and Ashdod on the Mediterranean coast to Jericho and Beth Shean by the Jordan River. Although most of the items were recovered in controlled archaeological excavations, a number of items are chance finds. For example, the Megiddo Gilgamesh tablet (Megiddo 1) was discovered by a kibbutz shepherd on his rounds with his flocks (Goetz and Levy 1959:121).

Items in our corpus date from the second and first millennia BCE. The earliest texts are the ones from Hazor, which can be associated with the archives of Mari and the Middle Bronze Age II cities of Syria. Hazor 12, in fact, names the cities of Mari and Ekallatum.

Just over half of the tablets can be dated with certainty to the Late Bronze Age, in many cases on the basis of clear epigraphic and linguistic similarities to the fourteenth-century BCE Amarna archive in Egypt. Beth Shean 2 even names two figures familiar from the Amarna letters: Tagi and Lab'aya. A smaller number of texts date from the first millennium, including at least 17 belonging to the Neo-Assyrian period.[5] These may be divided into two main groups: (1) royal stelae left behind by Assyrian kings; and (2) administrative documents from the time of the Assyrian occupation. A few isolated texts date from the late Babylonian or Persian periods. These include a vase fragment with part of an inscription of an Artaxerxes (Sepphoris 1).

Most of the texts are written in Akkadian of one type or another, ranging from the standard Akkadian of the Mesopotamian homeland to local dialects with West-Semitic features. The local West-Semitic language(s) are directly represented in our corpus in lexical lists, glosses, and by three texts inscribed in a "southern" version of the alphabetic cuneiform script best known from Ugarit (see Part III). A few academic texts and short inscriptions on cylinder seals are written in Sumerian. One text—the aforementioned fragment Sepphoris 1—bears part of the name Artaxerxes in Elamite. The texts also include a wide variety of personal names representing diverse languages and cultures, including Babylonian/Assyrian, Hurrian, Egyptian, Indo-Iranian, and various West-Semitic languages, including Hebrew.[6] We did not include objects inscribed in other scripts, even if found in our area of interest.

Most of the items are now in collections in Jerusalem (Israel Museum, Rockefeller Museum, the Institute of Archaeology of the Hebrew University of Jerusalem), while some pieces are stored by the Israel Antiquities authority in Beth Shemesh. Others are held in museums and private collections in Tel Aviv, Istanbul, and Ann Arbor, among other places. The present whereabouts of some items remain unknown.

5. Beer Sheva 1 most likely dates from the Neo-Assyrian period. Tel en-Naṣbeh 1 and Sepphoris 2–4 may be Neo-Assyrian or later.

6. Note, for example, Gezer 4:1: ^{m}*Na-tan-ia-u*.

THE ORGANIZATION OF THE BOOK

Our presentation of the objects is arranged by site in alphabetical order.[7] The discussion of each site begins with a list of objects found, and continues with the study of each object in numerical order, generally beginning with the earliest published tablets. Each entry typically contains three parts: (1) general information and bibliography; (2) transliteration and translation; and (3) commentary. On occasion we offer a preliminary discussion before our editions. For those objects for which we cannot provide an edition, we offer as much information as possible.

The general information, provided in petit font at the beginning of each entry, includes, whenever available, the following details: basic information about the object (material, form, dimensions); registration number and current location; date; language; and find information. The classification of the language does not take into consideration the language(s) of personal names.

A bibliography is also provided, divided into primary editions and additional studies. Primary editions usually offer hand copies and/or photographs of the text, with transliterations, translations, and discussion. Studies offer additional epigraphic, linguistic, and historical observations.[8]

Towards the end of the book indices are provided for personal names; geographical names; divine names; Sumerian and Akkadian words discussed; and subjects. Maps and tables documenting the geographical distribution of sources by period and genre are included in this introduction. New copies and photographs of objects prepared in the course of this project are presented at the end of the book.

This Cuneiform in Canaan volume, although by far the most comprehensive study of the subject, is not intended for use by itself. Our project began with the aim of addressing the pressing need to provide easy access to all the cuneiform sources from our geographic region, in as timely a manner as possible. We believe that this aim is best achieved by the format we offer here, a kind of super *Handbuch*, which provides all previous bibliography for each item and offers the reader basic text editions for all the published materials. Thus, our editions are intentionally minimalistic in nature, offering only the briefest discussion and commentary. For example, in our commentaries, we seek to explain how we came to new translations or interpretations of the material, but we do not survey previous studies or indulge in critical analysis of earlier works. Hence, in many cases, previous readings and interpretations are left without comment. Nor do we purport to offer a comprehensive

7. We disregard the word "Tel": thus, Tel Aphek, for example, appears under A.

8. For example, in the case of Taanach 1–2 and 5–6 we consider Rainey 1999 to be a primary edition because it contains transliterations and translations based on personal collations of the original tablets, although neither copies nor photographs are offered. On the other hand, we consider Glock 1983 to be a study even though it is based on and includes valuable personal collations, since Glock does not offer complete editions of the texts. The mere mention of a document in the secondary literature does not normally constitute a "study."

review of the labors of all those who came before us, or to offer the final word on the sources. We see ourselves as collectors of the work which came before us and hopefully facilitators of studies to come. Readers wishing to obtain a full overview of any source must therefore make use of the previous editions and studies cited in the bibliographies.

In the following essay, we offer an overview of the history of the cuneiform writing system in our region of study.

The History of Cuneiform in Canaan

THE MIDDLE BRONZE AGE

The earliest evidence for cuneiform in Canaan is, from a Mesopotamian point of view, relatively late. The earliest phases of cuneiform script in the West are attested in the upper Euphrates region in northern Syria in the fourth millennium BCE (e.g., Jebel Aruda and Habuba Kabira), and an important archive is found in western Syria at Ebla, dating from the middle of the third millennium.[9] Nonetheless, there is no mention of Canaan or any of its cities in the third-millennium cuneiform texts, which suggests that our region still lay beyond the horizon of Mesopotamian geographical knowledge at this time.[10]

The earliest sources in our corpus date to the Middle Bronze Age II,[11] the time of the international system best known to us from the Mari archives. At this time, Hazor is mentioned at Mari as one of a number of trading partners to the west of Mari, and a king of Hazor, Ibni-Addu, appears as a contemporary of Zimri-Lim of Mari and Hammurabi of Babylon. Tablets associated with this time span in the Hazor corpus display scribal features best known to us from the Mari archives. For example, personal names in Hazor 7 include the theme vowel *u* for *šapāṭu (išpuṭ)* instead of standard Akkadian *išpiṭ*, and utilize the reading *ṭà* for HI, features typical of Mari (Horowitz and Shaffer 1992a: 22). Likewise, the letter fragment Hazor 8, which is written in an exceptionally fine hand suitable for a royal letter, may bear part of King Ibni-Addu's name; the mathematical tablet Hazor 9 shares a feature with a parallel from Mari (*ARM* 9, no. 299; see below *sub* commentary to Hazor 9); and Hazor 12 explicitly refers to Mari and Ekallatum; the former of which was destroyed by Hammurabi:[12]

9. For a summary of the early epigraphic finds from Syria, see Klengel 1992: 21–25; for Jebel Aruda and Habuba Kabira, in brief, see Nissen et al. 1993: 129–30.

10. Third-millennium royal inscriptions refer to the far west in most general terms, for example, "The Upper Land," i.e., the lands by the Upper Sea = the Mediterranean (see, e.g., *RGTC* 1: 120, 203–4; 2: 83 and "The Cedar Mountain" (*RGTC* 1: 49). An exception is Byblos, whose name occurs with the name of its ruler in Ur III administrative documents (see *RGTC* 2: 66).

11. The absolute chronology of the Middle Bronze Age is still in dispute. For a review of the problem, see Charpin 2004: 35–38.

12. See Horowitz and Wasserman 2004 for the dating and historical background of this tablet, which appears to be from the generation before Zimri-Lim and thus may be the earliest item in our corpus.

Table 2. Sources from the Middle Bronze Age / Old Babylonian period, classified by genre

Site	Total	Administrative documents	Letters	Private Inscriptions	Academic Documents	Law Collection	Cylinder Seals
Beth Mirsim	1	—	—	—	—	—	1
Beth Shean	1	—	—	—	—	—	1
Gezer	1	1	—	—	—	—	—
Hazor	11	2	3	1	4	1	—
Hebron	1	1	—	—	—	—	—
Jemmeh	1	—	—	—	—	—	1
Shechem	1	—	1	—	—	—	—
Total	**17**	**4**	**4**	**1**	**4**	**1**	**3**

> let them send to me quickly to Mari. Some mishap might happen! After I have arrived at the city of Mari, I intend to go to Ekallatum to perform sacrifices and celebrations.
>
> Hazor 12: 20'–25'

To these texts may be added the law collection fragment Hazor 18 and Hazor 5, particularly if ^{m}*Ir-pa-*⸢*a*⸣*-du* in Hazor 5:1 is the same person as in Hazor 8:2: ^{m}*Ir-p*[*a*. . . . Hazor 1, and possibly Hazor 4, also belong to this group. All tablets in this group include only Semitic personal names—either West Semitic or Akkadian.[13]

The letter Hazor 12 also includes two scribal features consistent with the Mari archives (Horowitz and Wasserman 2004: 337–38), but also bears features elsewhere foreign to the Mari tradition. Most important, the name of Mari is written *Má-ri*^{ki} here, a writing that is not in use in the Old Babylonian period Mari archives, but is more typical of Babylonia (Horowitz and Wasserman 2000: 174; 2004: 336). Similarly, line 14' of this tablet includes a writing DU_8.ŠI.A for *duhšûm/dušû*,[14] which is attested at Qatna, but not at Mari. The tablet also includes a number of other Sumerograms that are realized in a slightly different manner than at Mari (Horowitz and Wasserman 2004: 336). Yet these apparent anomalies cannot be used to access the nature of Hazor's own local scribal tradition since the sender of Hazor 12 appears to be a visitor at Hazor, rather than a resident, as is apparent in the passage quoted above.

No text from any site other than Hazor shows evidence of contact with the Mari tradition. Moreover, there is no epigraphic or archeological evidence for any of the texts from Canaan being earlier than the Middle Bronze Age II. Thus, based on the available evidence, we hypothesize that cuneiform was introduced into Canaan by way of Mari around the time of Ibni-Addu, Zimri-Lim, and Hammurabi, primarily

13. See, e.g., Horowitz and Shaffer 1992a: 22–23.

14. Explained by Dalley 2000 as referring to beadwork. See Horowitz and Wassermann 2000: 173; 2004: 337.

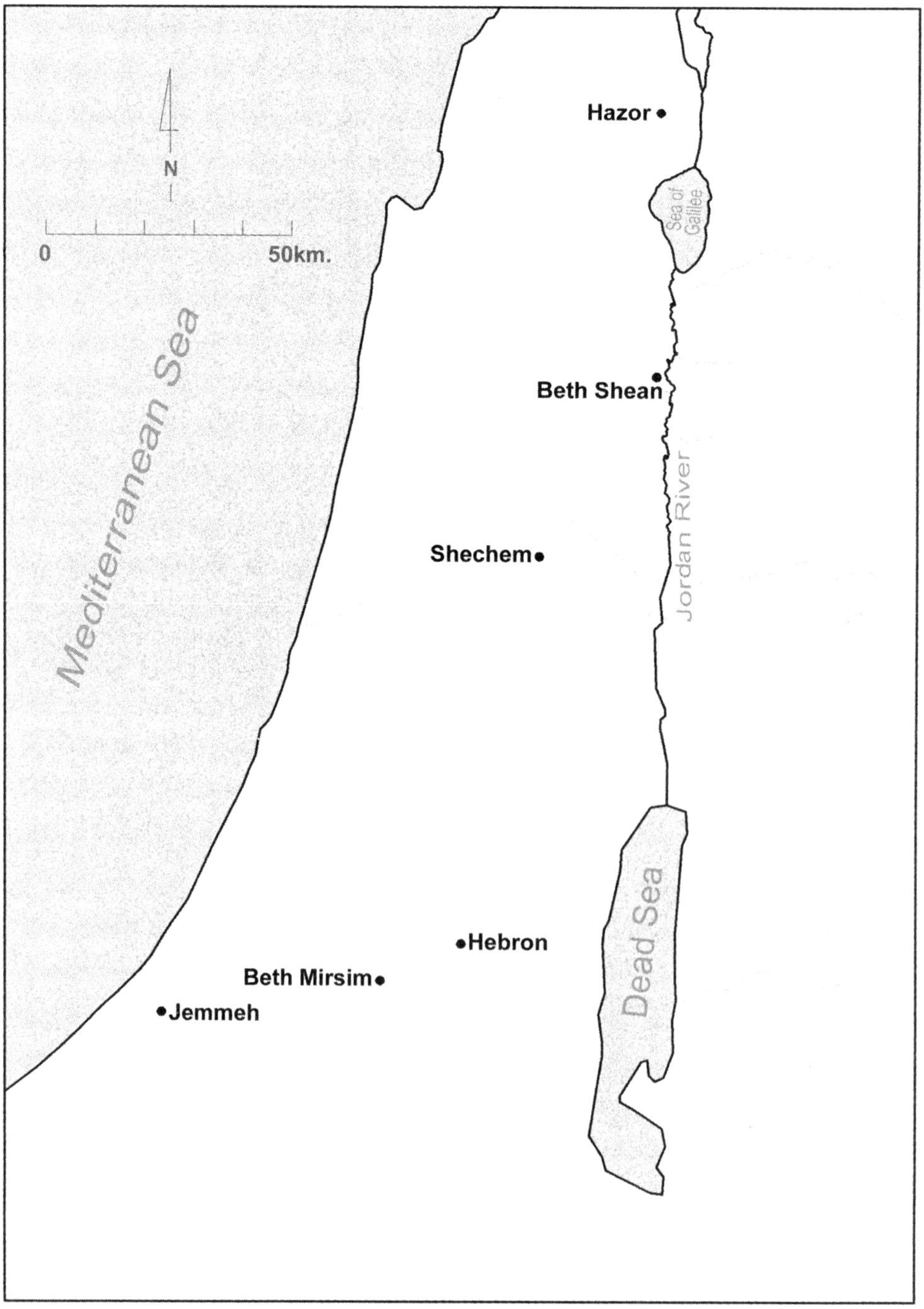

Map 2. The Middle Bronze Age

to facilitate trade between Hazor and the cities of Syria and Mesopotamia. It is likely that this led to the formation of a scribal community at Hazor whose interests were not strictly limited to commerce and administration; this would account for the law collection Hazor 18 and mathematical prism Hazor 9, which, as mentioned above, shares a feature with a parallel from Mari. Unfortunately, the available evidence does not allow us to determine whether this community could have supported a scribal school in which local Hazorians might have been trained as scribes by foreign experts from Mari and/or other sites.[15]

The Middle Bronze Age materials in our corpus include a second group, consisting of materials that show signs of a scribal tradition influenced by the local linguistic environment of Canaan and the cuneiform west. Such works appear to be later than the time of the Hazor-Mari contacts, but are certainly older than our Late Bronze Age sources, most notably Taanach and the materials associated with the Amarna period. Texts belonging to the later Middle Bronze Age group maintain the basic linguistic structure of good Old Babylonian Akkadian (the verb appearing at the end of the sentence, etc.), as well as the Old Babylonian sign forms, but begin to show signs of later developments characteristic of the Late Bronze Age groups.

Further, these tablets preserve the first appearances of non-Semitic personal names. This is of particular importance since it is an indicator of the population change that occurs between the time of the Mari-Hazor contacts, when all the personal names are Semitic, and the Late Bronze Age in Canaan, when non-Semitic names represent approximately one-third of the personal name repertoire.[16] An example is Hebron 1, which is written in a hand familiar with Old Babylonian Mesopotamia, but includes a nominal form without mimmation (rev. 4': *mu-ša-di-na-ti*) and the personal names of the Hurrian type *In-ti* and *Su-ku-hu* (Hebron 1:8). The letter Shechem 1, addressed to a man bearing the Hurrian-type name *Pí-ra-aš-še/-x,* appears to be even later than Hebron 1. Here we find a number of Old Babylonian signs and verbal forms, but on the other hand, *inūma* and *u* are used in the same way as in the Amarna archives.[17] The Hazor liver models Hazor 2–3 and 17 also appear to belong to this group.

The only other materials in our corpus that we can assign to the Middle Bronze Age are the inscribed cylinder seals Beth Mirsim 1, Beth Shean 1, and Tell Jemmeh 1. Ashdod 1, Gezer 1,[18] and Jericho 2–3 might also date from the later part of the Middle Bronze Age.

15. The presence of a later scribal school at Hazor is suggested by the school tablet Hazor 6, which is apparently from the Late Bronze Age, and by the liver model fragments Hazor 2–3 and 13, which can best be dated to the late Old Babylonian period / Middle Bronze Age.

16. See the detailed discussion of the transition from the Middle to the Late Bronze Age in Na'aman 1994, with reference to the presumed late Middle Bronze tablets listed in the Index of Geographical Names. We take the element Hanuta in personal names in Hazor 5 (the legal document) to be Semitic.

17. For the late Middle Bronze date of Shechem 1 and Hebron 1, also see Rainey 1999: 154*–55*.

18. For the dating of Gezer 1 on the basis of the sign forms and Hurrian personal names to the seventeenth century, see Shaffer 1970: 111.

We suggest that the phenomena outlined above were the result of a gradual loosening of the cultural and academic ties that bound the scribes of Middle Bronze Age Canaan with their colleagues in Syria and Mesopotamia. This process may have started as early as the time that cuneiform was first introduced into Canaan, which, as suggested above, seems to have been proximate to the time of the Hazor-Mari contacts. This would account for the fact that Hazor 5, which we tentatively dated above to the earlier period on the basis of a possible shared personal name with Hazor 8, already preserves an example of dropped mimmation (a writing É-*ti*, apparently for *bīti*). Similarly, Horowitz and Shaffer 1992a: 33 observed an innovative feature in Hazor 7, although this tablet includes significant Marian scribal features.

We imagine that the separation of the cuneiform tradition of Canaan from that of the Mesopotamian homeland was a process that took generations. Our very limited corpus gives us only snapshots of this process, and there is no way to be sure that this process occurred in a linear, temporal manner. Thus, the criteria employed above to classify the Middle Bronze Age tablets into two groups cannot guarantee complete success and accuracy. In fact, what we classify as early and late may in some cases be due to a well-trained scribe writing in the classical tradition as opposed to a more amateurish scribe who allowed features of the local West-Semitic language(s) of Canaan to penetrate into his Akkadian. Such problems cast doubt on our ability to offer anything akin to a reliable chronology for the Middle Bronze corpus of Cuneiform in Canaan based on our small sample of texts; this problem is compounded by the fact that none of the Hazor tablets discussed above was recovered in a secure Middle Bronze archaeological context.

The one thing we are sure about is the end result of the process. By the time of the Taanach tablets in the fifteenth century, the Akkadian of Canaan was radically different from that of the Middle Bronze Age, as well as from that of the contemporary Late Bronze Age / Middle Babylonian / Middle Assyrian tablets in Syria and Mesopotamia. Nevertheless, as observed by Rainey 1999: 155*–56*, the Akkadian of Taanach, Aphek, and the Amarna letters, although radically different from that of the Middle Bronze Age, remained firmly rooted in the language of the Middle Bronze Age / Old Babylonian period.[19] Thus, what we have here is an example of a rule taught to us by our teacher, Aaron Shaffer: the cuneiform periphery is, at one and the same time, both innovative and conservative.

THE LATE BRONZE AGE

The cuneiform remains from the Late Bronze Age can be divided into four groups: (1) the mini-archive from Aphek; (2) the mini-archive from Taanach; (3) materials

19. Here we should note A. George's observation that the Megiddo Gilgamesh fragment (Megiddo I) "is likely to be a descendant of an Old Babylonian recension" (George 2003: 343).

Table 3. Sources from the Late Bronze Age/second millennium BCE, classified by genre[a]

Site	Total	Administrative Documents	Letters	Private Inscriptions	Academic Tablets	Misc.	Cylinder Seals	Alphabetic Cuneiform
Aphek	8	2	1	—	2	3	—	—
Ashdod	0/1	—	—	—	—	—	0/1	—
Ashqelon	1	—	—	—	1	—	—	—
Beth Shean	1	—	1	—	—	—	—	—
Beth Shemesh	1	—	—	—	—	—	—	1
Gezer	1	—	1	—	—	—	—	—
Hazor	6/2	3/1	1	1/1	1	—	—	—
El-Ḥesi	1	—	1	—	—	—	—	—
Jericho	1/2	1	—	—	—	—	0/2	—
Jerusalem	2	2	—	—	—	—	—	—
Megiddo	6	1	—	1	1	—	3	—
Shechem	1	1	—	—	—	—	—	—
Taanach	17	6	9	—	—	—	1	1
Tabor	1	—	—	—	—	—	—	1
Total	**47/5**	**16/1**	**14**	**2/1**	**5**	**3**	**4/3**	**3**

[a]The number following the slash indicates sources for which a Late Bronze Age date is most likely, but not certain.

with definite affinities to the El-Amarna archives; and (4) miscellaneous. Chronologically, the Taanach group is the earliest. Consensus has long held that the Taanach materials can best be dated to the late fifteenth century (e.g., Rainey 1999: 153*–54*), although no direct evidence points to any precise date. The earliest tablets in the Amarna archives, which include letters of Amenophis III (1386–1349 BCE) and Amenophis IV (1350–1334 BCE),[20] are at least a generation or two later than the Taanach materials. The Tel Aphek tablets are even later, dating from the second half of the thirteenth century (cf. Singer 1999: 716). The tablets in the Amarna period group include some that actually name people known at Amarna as well. See, for example, Šipṭi-Baʿlu and Zimrida in Tel el-Ḥesi 1,[21] and Tagi and Labʾaya in Beth Shean 2 (see Hess 1993: 102–3; 153–55). More generally, the repertoire of personal names in the Late Bronze materials reflects the change in population that has occurred since the time of the Mari-Hazor contacts. For example, at Taanach, where we have a sample of more than 75 names, roughly one third are Hurrian or Indo-Aryan; this is approximately the same proportion as we find in the Amarna letters from Canaan (see Naʾaman 1994: 177, Pruzsinszky 2006).

Taanach, Amarna, and Aphek can serve as chronological signposts for dating the remaining texts. For example, Shechem 2 seems to have more in common with the Taanach personal name lists than with later materials, and the Late Bronze Age

20. Dating and spelling follow Moran 1992: xxxix.

21. See Hess 1993: 143–44, 169–70 for these names in both EA 333 (= Tel el-Ḥesi I) and the el-Amarna tablets.

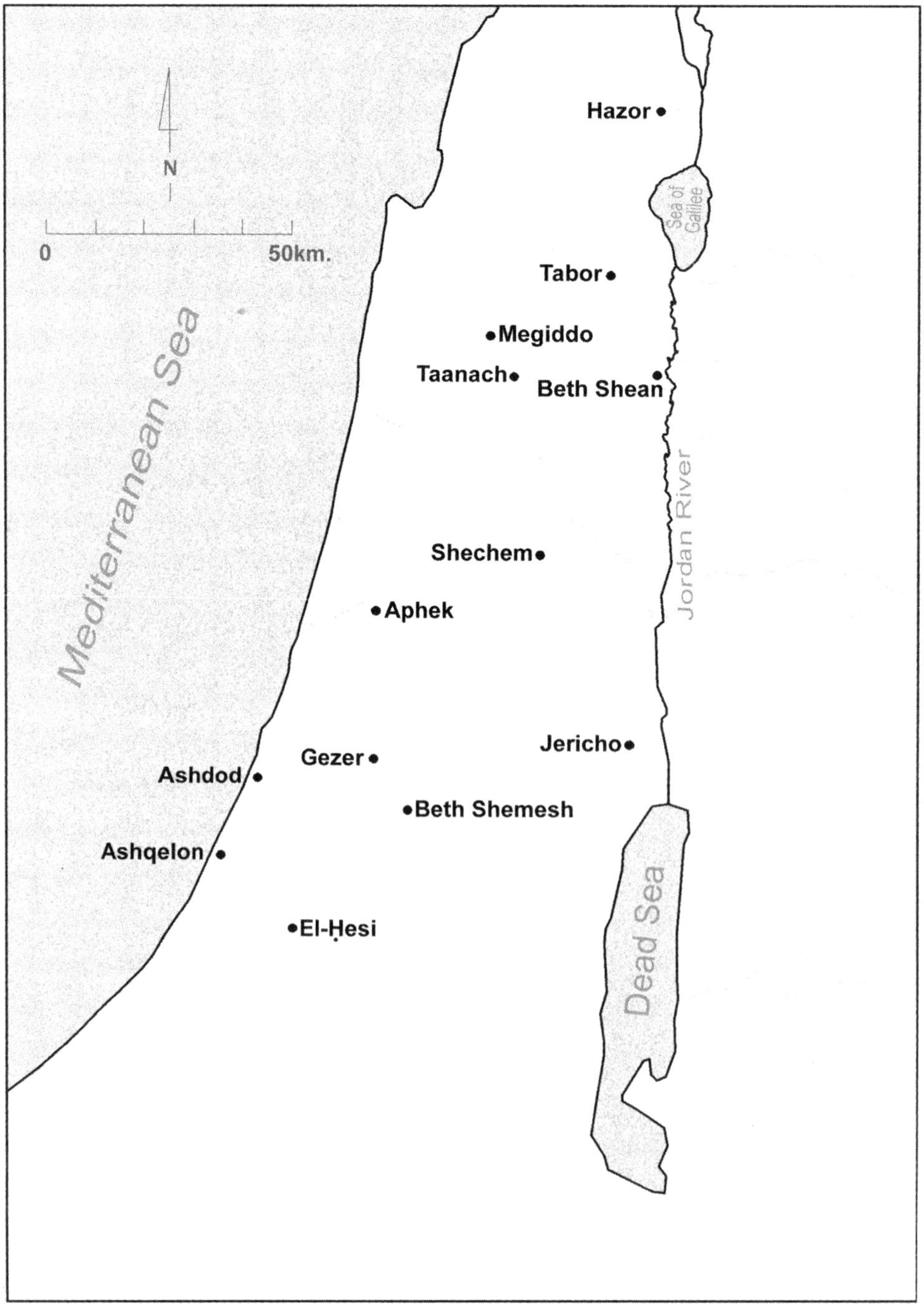

Map 3. Sites where cuneiform finds were discovered.

tablets from Hazor (Hazor 6, 10–11, 13–14, 16, and maybe 15) also seem to us to be earlier rather than later in the Late Bronze Age. The same could be said of Jericho 1. The archaeological context of the lexical fragment Ashqelon 1 is the thirteenth century, but the tablet itself could be slightly earlier (Huehnergard and Van Soldt 1999: 184). We do not presume to try to assign an exact date for the Megiddo Gilgamesh fragment, which was found in a secondary context, but note the presence of Akkadian literary works at Amarna itself, including Adapa, Nergal, and Ereshkigal, and "Sargon, King of Battle" (*Šar tamḫāri*). The date of the surface find Gezer 2, which seems to be written in a Mesopotamian hand from the Late Bronze Age, is uncertain, as are the exact dates of the three alphabetic tablets Beth Shemesh 1, Taanach 15, and Tabor 1. The two very tiny fragments Jerusalem 1–2 are too small to provide any useful information about Jerusalem in the Late Bronze Age on their own.

In terms of the writing system, the Late Bronze age cuneiform tablets exhibit true independence from Mesopotamia. The hand of almost all the tablets shows affinities with the hand of the Amarna archives, suggesting close contacts with the scribal traditions of the Egyptian Empire, rather than with Kassite Babylonia, Middle Assyria, or even the areas of Syria under Hittite (earlier Hurrian) control. Generally speaking, the verbal system of the Late Bronze Canaan materials also displays western phenomena of the type found at Amarna and described in Izreʾel 1998a and Rainey 1996. The glosses in Hazor 10:19–22 and Aphek 7:40 are particularly reminiscent of those at Amarna (see Gianto 1995; Izreʾel 1995, and 1998b). Given that Canaan was under Egyptian rule during the Late Bronze Age, all this should not be surprising.

The academic tradition of the materials, on the other hand, shows signs of ongoing contact with developments in the Mesopotamian scribal tradition, as well as some more local features. The lexical fragments Hazor 6 and Ashqelon 1 are in the classical Mesopotamian tradition, with Ashqelon 1 preserving parts of a West-Semitic tradition of the original Sumerian-Akkadian lexical series Urra = *ḫubullu*.[22] Megiddo 1 preserves part of none other than the most popular Akkadian literary work, the Gilgamesh Epic (cf. George 2003). Yet this is not necessarily proof of direct contact with Babylonian and Assyrian scribes. Rather, it is more likely that the developments in Mesopotamia were transmitted to the scribes of Canaan through intermediaries in the west, for example, the scribal community at Ugarit, where traditional Sumerian-Akkadian lexical lists often occur with added translations into West-Semitic, Hittite, and/or Hurrian.[23] Aphek 7, a letter from the governor of Ugarit to an official at Aphek, may offer indirect evidence of such contacts.

In contrast, some sources represent a tradition not known from Mesopotamia or Syria. For example, Aphek 1 and 3, which offer West-Semitic equivalents to selected

22. Hazor 6 preserves only a Sumerian column, although it might have originally had additional columns for other languages as well.

23. The best examples are the materials published in *Ugaritica* V. For discussion, see Greenfield 1991: 173–74.

Sumerian-Akkadian words, are totally noncanonical. The same mix of Mesopotamian and local scribal tradition characterizes Amarna too, where one finds copies of the Akkadian epics noted above, standard Mesopotamian lexical lists, including S[a] and Diri, but also the totally noncanonical Egyptian-Akkadian vocabulary EA 368 (cf. Izre'el 1997: 77–81).

This methodology, comparing our smaller corpus of materials in Canaan with the larger corpus at Amarna in Egypt, although currently unavoidable, is in a sense misleading. The Amarna archive almost certainly reflects what is happening in the cuneiform southwest, including Canaan in the Late Bronze Age, rather than setting a Pharaonic royal standard for the cuneiform traditions of Canaan and the rest of the Egyptian Empire. First of all, most of the letters found at Amarna were written in Canaan or other Egyptian possessions, and there is a geographical logic to a proposition that most, if not all, cuneiform traditions that reached Egypt passed through Canaan on their way westwards. Thus, when more extensive tablet collections are recovered from Canaan, we may find that it is Amarna that is like Canaan, rather than Canaan being like Amarna.

Finally, some remarks in the realm of historical geography are warranted. By the Late Bronze Age cuneiform had truly become a feature of the local social and cultural landscape. The cuneiform script was no longer an extension of the culture of the east, which had apparently entered into Canaan through the portal of Hazor. Now, in the Late Bronze Age, we find local activities documented by means of cuneiform letters and administrative tablets throughout the land, with cuneiform serving as the main means of communication with Egypt as well. More telling is the fact that the local language now came to be represented in the alphabetic form of the cuneiform script. This was the heyday of cuneiform script in Canaan.

This state of affairs came to an end with the end of the Late Bronze Age, which also marked the disappearance of cuneiform from the local landscape. In the Iron Age, alphabetic scripts dominated in the west, while cuneiform was apparently only reintroduced at the time of the Assyrian conquest; first in the royal inscriptions of the conquerors, and later for more mundane use by those segments of the population most closely associated with foreign rule. Thus, cuneiform in Iron Age Canaan was in a sense no longer a local writing system but an extension of foreign hegemony in the land, particularly during the height of the Neo-Assyrian Empire.[24]

THE NEO-ASSYRIAN PERIOD

The Neo-Assyrian period items in our corpus come from Philistia (Ashdod), the Assyrian period at Samaria, and from scattered sites on the periphery of the Judean

24. In this context, note that not a single cuneiform letter has been found to date from the first millennium BCE, in contrast to 17 such finds from the second millennium BCE.

Table 4. Sources from the Neo-Assyrian period, classified by genre

Site	Total	Administrative Documents	Royal Inscriptions	Academic Documents	Cylinder Seals
Ashdod	3	—	3	—	—
Beer Sheva	1	—	—	—	1
Ben Shemen	1	—	1	—	—
Gezer	2	2	—	—	—
Hadid	2	2	—	—	—
Keisan	1	1	—	—	—
Khirbet Kusiya	1	1	—	—	—
Qaqun	1	—	1	—	—
Samaria	4	2	1	—	1
Shephela	1	—	—	1	—
Wingate	1	—	—	—	1
Total	**18**	**8**	**6**	**1**	**3**

and Israelite homelands: Beer Sheva, Ben Shemen, Gezer, Tel Hadid, Tel Keisan, Khirbet Kusiya, Megiddo, Qaqun, the southern Shephela (Shephela 1), and the central coastal plain (Wingate 1). These materials can be classified into two main groups: (1) stelae and stela fragments commemorating the Assyrian conquest; and (2) administrative documents and a few other miscellaneous items documenting the Assyrian occupation.

The surviving datable stela materials are from the reigns of Sargon II and Esarhaddon. The three stela fragments Ashdod 2–4 most likely mark Sargon II's conquest of the city in 712 BCE. Ben Shemen 1 is also dated to the reign of Sargon II (by Tadmor 1973: 72). We concur and surmise that the stela fragment from Samaria (Samaria 4) dates to early in the reign of Sargon II, soon after the fall of the northern kingdom and its reorganization into an Assyrian province. Given that we have only a small fragment of the stela, however, we cannot be certain of this. We presume that the presence of the Esarhaddon stela fragment Qaqun 1 commemorates one of Esarhaddon's campaigns. To date, no stela marking the conquests of Tiglath-Pileser III or Sennacherib has been recovered, despite the numerous mentions of places in our region of study in their royal inscriptions.[25]

The Assyrian occupation of Israel and parts of Judah is represented in our corpus by the other Neo-Assyrian finds. Assyrian administration is indicated by the documents found at Gezer, Tel Hadid, Tel Keisan, Khirbet Kusiya, and Samaria. Among these only four can be dated on the basis of internal evidence: three from the time of Assurbanipal (Hadid 2, ca. 664; Gezer 3, ca. 651; and Gezer 4, ca. 649), and one from the time of Sennacherib (Hadid 1, ca. 698). The range of dates at Tel Hadid demonstrates that the Assyrian administration at that site lasted for more

25. See, e.g., the various listings in Parpola 1970, with Judah on p. 182 and Samaria on pp. 302–3.

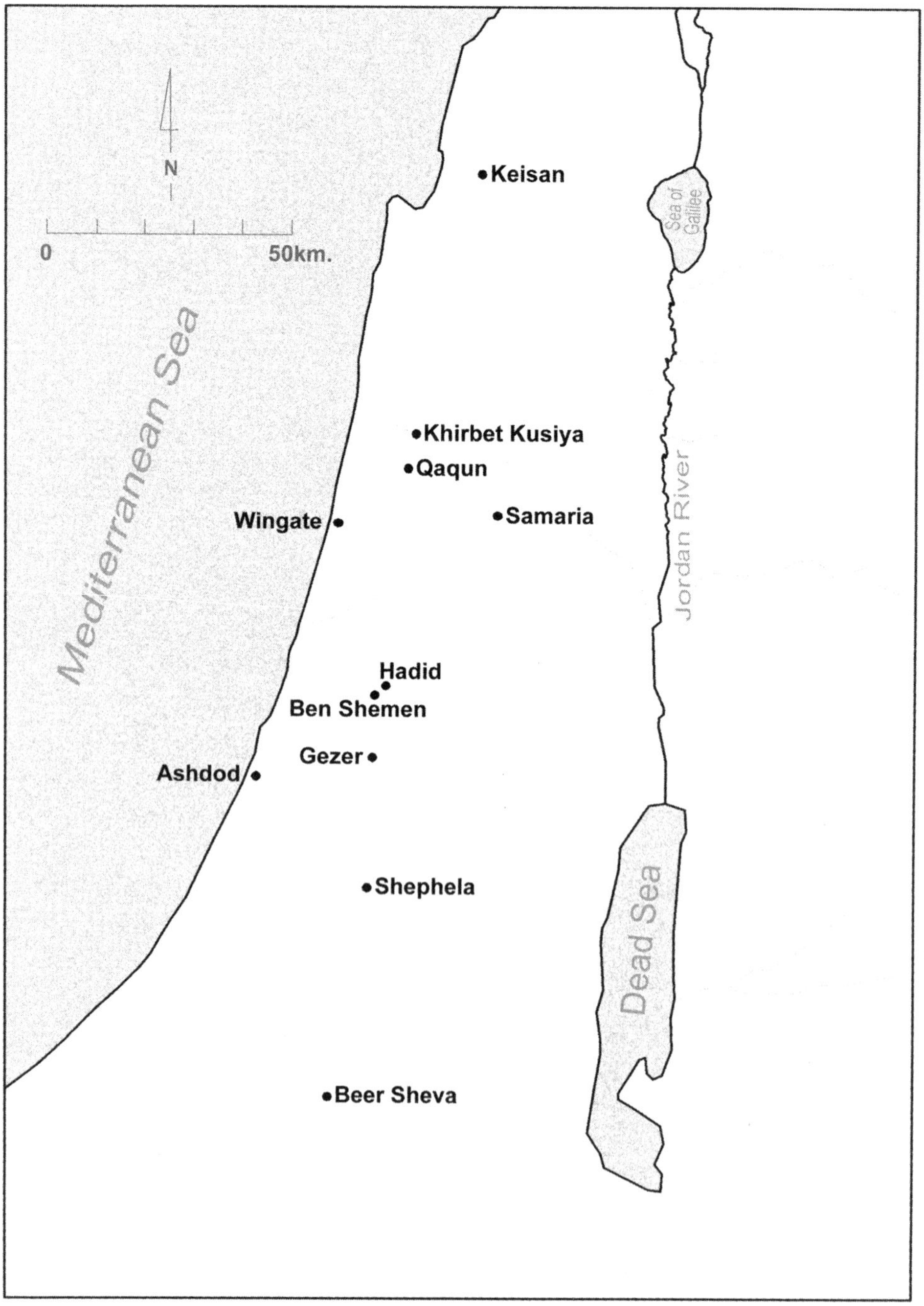

Map 4. The Neo-Assyrian Period

than a generation. Keisan 1, Khirbet Kusiya 1, and Samaria 1–2 are also administrative documents, but they cannot be dated.[26]

Despite the small number of items in our corpus, an examination of the personal names yields some interesting results. The names in the administrative documents are for the most part Babylonian,[27] but Gezer 3–4 and Hadid 2 include West-Semitic names which most likely belong to members of the local population. Gezer 3 (*Mannu-kī-Arbaʾil*)[28] and Samaria 1 (^{md}A[Š+ ŠUR-x-(x)-*i*]*n*)[29] even preserve Assyrian names, with the gentleman in Gezer 3 listed as a witness in a land sale.

It is usually assumed that all Babylonians named in the documents are deportees (or their offspring in the case of a second generation), but this need not necessarily be the case, particularly given the presence of the Assyrian names. It is possible that at least some of the Babylonians mentioned relocated voluntarily to serve in the Assyrian administration. In this light, we suggest that the Lamaštu plaque Shephela 1, the votive cylinder Samaria 3 (with a Babylonian PN and DNs), and the cylinder seal Wingate 1 may have belonged to expatriate Mesopotamians in the service of the crown, or who perhaps lived in the west voluntarily for some other reason.[30] The fact that Keisan 1 is written in a poor Babylonian script is yet another indicator of Babylonian presence.

Gezer 3–4, the two Gezer administrative tablets (ca. 651 and ca. 649), are the latest dated Neo-Assyrian items in our corpus. Here we find a combination of Babylonian and apparently local West-Semitic personal names. This is also the case in Hadid 2, dated to ca. 664. In contrast, in Hadid 1, which is dated to ca. 698, we find only Akkadian names, with the exception of one name which might be Aramaic (Naʾaman and Zadok 2000: 169). This may be evidence of greater social and economic contact between the immigrant population and the indigenous population as time progressed, but one should be wary of coming to such far-reaching conclusions on the basis of four administrative documents spread over half a century. Furthermore, personal names are not always a true indicator of ethnic origin. Thus, our sample of Neo-Assyrian period finds described above is unfortunately too small and too scattered in time and place to reach any definite conclusions about the chronology and nature of the Assyrian occupation of Philistia, the former territory of the northern kingdom, and parts of Judah. The information that may be gleaned from our materials must be interpreted in relation to what is known elsewhere about the Assyrian presence in the west and Assyrian administrative practices in conquered

26. Tel en-Naṣbeh I and Sepphoris 2–4 might also date from the Neo-Assyrian period.

27. For another Babylonian, *Nabû-duru-uṣur*, in a Neo-Assyrian period letter referring to Samaria, see *SAA* 1 220. Cf. *SAA* 1 255.

28. For this name, cf. *PNAE* 685–88.

29. Perhaps for *A*[*ššur-iddi*]*n*.

30. See Cogan 1995: 161, but note Tadmor and Tadmor 1995: 353–54, who suggest that both Wingate 1 and Beer Sheva 1 arrived in the west in secondary use. The votive cylinder Beer Sheva 1 may present the more complicated situation of a father with a West-Semitic name, his son bearing an Akkadian name, and a dedication to a western deity.

territories in general. Na'aman and Zadok 2000 represent an important first step in this direction.

THE NEO-BABYLONIAN, PERSIAN, AND HELLENISTIC PERIODS

There are few finds in our corpus which can be dated with certainty to the periods following the fall of the Neo-Assyrian Empire. Even in the Neo-Assyrian period, Aramaic and local languages written in alphabetic script had already replaced Akkadian in cuneiform as the main medium for written communication in the west, and this process continued after the fall of Assyria.

Five items in our corpus can be dated with certainty to the Persian period: the economic tablet Mikhmoret 1, the fragment of an inscribed Achaemenid royal vessel Sepphoris 1, and the small group of coins from Samaria that we list as Samaria 5–7. The first two bear the name of a Persian monarch: Cambyses at Mikhmoret (in the date formula) and one of the Artaxerxes at Sepphoris. The stone vessel fragment from Sepphoris is one of a number of such finds which are spread throughout the Persian Empire from Greece to Susa, and which have even been found as far afield as southern Russia (Stolper 1996: 167). The coins from Samaria are dated to the middle of the fourth century, but before the time of Alexander the Great.

In contrast, there are no cuneiform texts that can be dated positively to the period of Babylonian rule over Judah and its neighbors, the only candidates being four finds of uncertain date: Tel en-Naṣbeh 1 and Sepphoris 2–4.

Tel en-Naṣbeh 1 is from a bronze ringlet preserving a private dedicatory inscription. Since its script is Neo-Babylonian, it seems to attest to a Babylonian presence at this site, biblical Mizpah, where the Babylonian appointee Gedaliah is placed in 2 Kings 25 after the fall of Jerusalem to Nebuchadnezzar II. The exact date of the piece, however, is most uncertain: the Neo-Babylonian script remained in use from the Neo-Assyrian period down into Persian times, and the archaeological context of

Table 5. Sources from the Neo-Assyrian / Neo-Babylonian or Persian period[a]

Site	Total	Administrative Documents	Royal Inscriptions	Private Inscriptions	Miscellaneous (Coins)
Mikhmoret	1	1	—	—	—
En-Naṣbeh	0/1	—	—	0/1	—
Samaria	3	—	—	—	3
Sepphoris	1/3	0/3	1	—	—
Total	**5/4**	**1/3**	**1**	**0/1**	**3**

[a]In entries with slashes, the number preceding the slash indicates sources that are definitely from the Neo-Babylonian or Persian period, while the number following the slash indicates sources in Babylonian script that could possibly be from the Neo-Assyrian period.

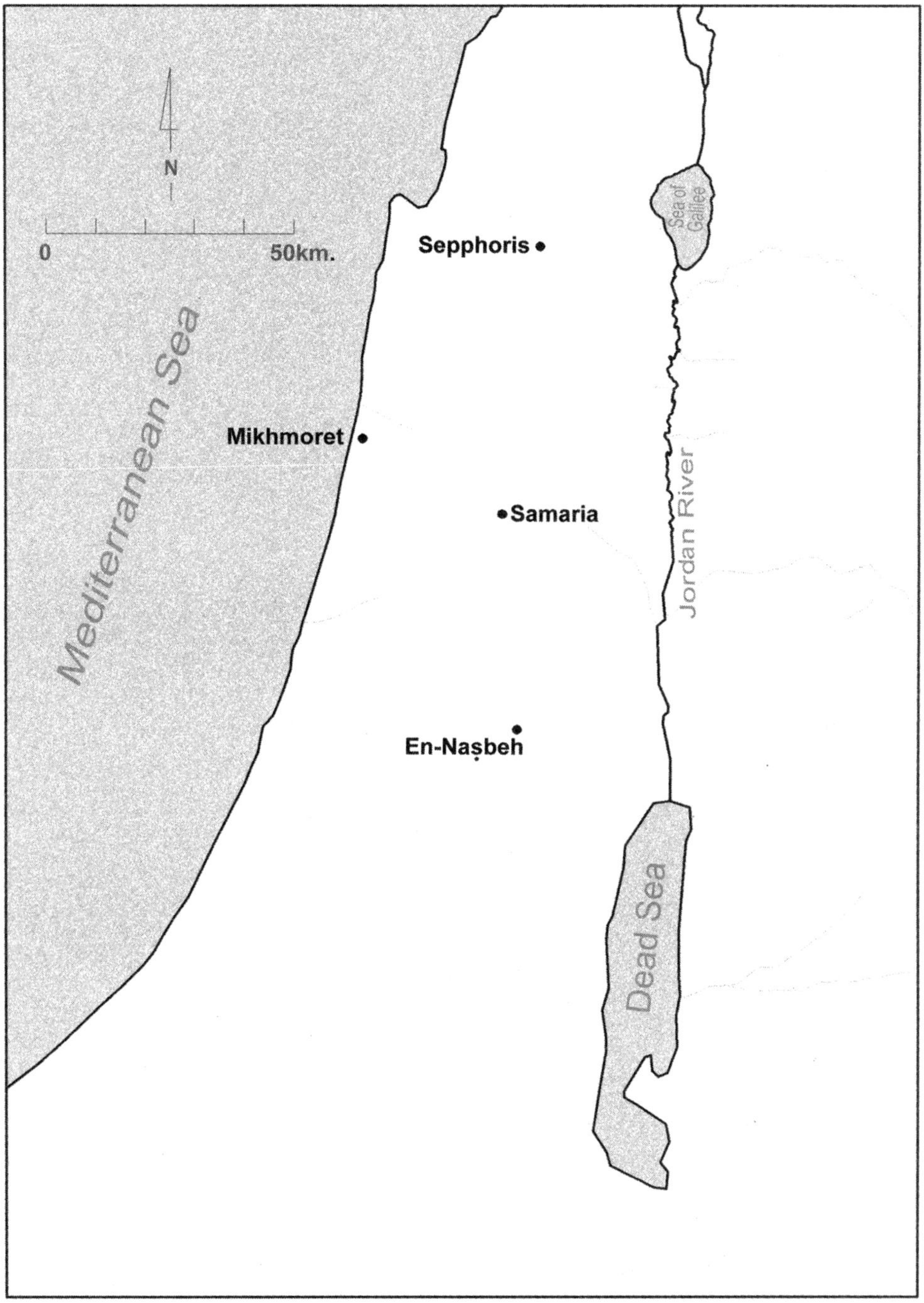

Map 5. The Neo-Assyrian, Neo-Babylonian, and Persian Periods

the find is inconclusive as to its date. Furthermore, the dedicatory inscription gives no indication whatsoever of any specific connection between the item and Mizpah. Thus, the piece cannot be used to demonstrate that Mizpah served as a center for Babylonian administration (Horowitz and Vanderhooft 2002: 323–25; Vanderhooft 2003: 253). Sepphoris 2–4 are too fragmentary for dating purposes. Thus, in contrast to the Neo-Assyrian period, the Neo-Babylonian period has so far yielded no royal monuments commemorating the Babylonian conquest, nor administrative tablets documenting a Babylonian administration of Judah. Is this lack of cuneiform finds from the time of Nebuchadnezzar and his successors merely an accident of archaeological chance, particularly given the relative short chronological lifetime of the Neo-Babylonian Empire, or did the Babylonians indeed fail to impose an administrative presence in their far west, as has been suggested (see, e.g., Vanderhooft 2003, with further bibliography)? The cuneiform evidence in our corpus cannot answer this question. In any case, it is clear that by the Persian period the long history of the use of cuneiform in the west was coming to a close. In Jordan, only two finds are found after the fall of Assyria: a Neo-Babylonian inscribed rock relief, certainly of Nabonidus, found in the vicinity of Petra (Dalley and Goguel 1997), and an administrative tablet from the same area from the reign of one of the Persian kings named Darius (Dalley 1984).[31] For western Syria, the last important collection of tablets is the small family archive from Nērebu near Aleppo from the time of Neriglissar to Darius I (*RlA* 9 215). There are no cuneiform finds from the Land of Israel that can be dated to the Hellenistic period or later, although cuneiform continues in Babylonia proper down into Roman times.[32]

31. For a review of epigraphic finds from Jordan, including cuneiform, see Bienkowski 1991: 135–48.
32. For the latest stages of cuneiform and the death of cuneiform script, see Geller 1997.

PART II

The Sources

Aphek

1. Lexical$^{?}$ Fragment
2. Administrative Fragment
3. Fragment of Trilingual Lexical Text
4. Fragment
5. Fragment
6. Fragment
7. The Governor's Letter
8. Administrative Fragment

Aphek, with eight cuneiform texts, is the third-largest group in our corpus. This group has been dated to ca. 1230 on the basis of archaeological evidence (e.g., Owen 1981: 1; Hallo 1981: 18; Singer 1999: 716). For an earlier list of the Aphek tablets, see Hallo 1981: 21–23, with a list of sign forms, and *NEAEHL* 68. A provenance study of the Aphek tablets is available in Goren, Na'aman, Mommsen, and Finkelstein 2006.

APHEK 1: LEXICAL$^{?}$ FRAGMENT

Basics: Clay tablet, 5.8 × 5.7 × 1.7 cm; hand copy, p. 208, photo, p. 224
Reg. Nos.: IAA 90/251, Aphek 5837/1 (present location: Israel Museum)
Primary Publication: Rainey 1975: 125–28 (photo, pl. 24)
Studies: Kochavi 1977: 65–66 (photo), 1981: 79; Edzard 1985: 251; Demsky 1990: 161–62; Van Soldt 1991, *passim* and index, p. 783; Van der Toorn 2000: 105; *NEAEHL* 69 (photo); Von Dassow 2004: 670; Goren, Na'aman, Mommsen, and Finkelstein 2006: 162–63; Cohen 2008: 85
Date: Late Bronze Age, ca. 1230 BCE
Language: When complete, most likely Sumerian, Akkadian, and West-Semitic entries
Find Information: Aphek, Area 10, Locus 1137; see Rainey 1975: 125.

Edition

	Col. i'	*Col. ii'*
1'	. . .]	AN [. . .
2'	. . .]	ŠU : [. . .
3'	. . .]	UR$_{4}^{?}$/ŠÀ$^{?}$: [. . .
4'	. . .]	^{d}UTU-*ši* : [. . .
5'	. . .]	APIN.ME : [. . .

6'	. . . *NA*]*M*	GIŠ [. . .
7'	. . .]	GIG.MEŠ : [. . .
8'	. . .] *IG*	^{giš}MAR : *gi-*[*dim-mu*]
9'	. . .]	^{lú}KÚR : *ta-á*[*r-gi-gu*]
10'	. . .] × *KA*	GU$_4$: *al-p*[*u* . . .

Translation

Col. i'		***Col. ii'***
1'		god/heaven
2'		hand
3'		to harvest$^?$/heart$^?$
4'		my Sun / my Majesty
5'	*Too fragmentary*	plows
6'	*for translation*	*tree*$^?$
7'		wheat
8'		spade
9'		evildoer
10'		ox

Commentary

Aphek 1 preserves the bottom left corner of a writing surface which may very well have belonged to a prism of some sort. The left edge of the tablet is straight and appears to have been cut intentionally, while the clay tablet was still soft (a fingerprint survives on the fragment's left edge; see photo).[1] What remains appears to be the bottom of a noncanonical lexical text with double dividing lines between two surviving columns. Col. i' is cut in the middle and preserves the last signs of only three entries. Col. ii' appears to preserve 10 lines of Sumerian terms, followed by *Glossenkeile* and then Akkadian equivalents. Upon closer examination, however, it becomes clear that the tablet is not part of the traditional Sumero-Akkadian lexical list genre. First, in cols. ii' 4' and 8'–9', determinatives are written to the left of the column; second, entries in lines 5' and 7' are plural; and third, the writing ^{d}UTU-*ši* with the phonetic complement in line 4' suggests an Akkadian reading *Šamši*, "my Sun / my Majesty" (see Rainey 1975: 126), rather than a Sumerian reading ^{d}UTU (= *Šamaš*). Thus, it seems most likely that col. ii' presents logographic writings of the Akkadian words followed by phonetic writings, either in Akkadian or in the local West-Semitic language. If so, *alpu* in line 10' could represent the West-Semitic cognate of Akkadian *alpu*, "ox," rather than the Akkadian word itself. Aphek 1 may

1. Cf. T. Jacobsen's comments in Rainey 1975: 127, line 9'.

very well belong to the same tradition as the trilingual (Sumerian, Akkadian, and West-Semitic) lexical fragment Aphek 3.[2]

Line 7′

GIG.MEŠ. In Mesopotamia proper we might expect an equation with *marṣū*, "sick" (pl.), perhaps referring to sick people. At Aphek, however, cf. GIG.MEŠ, "wheat," as in Aphek 7:13–14, 19, 23 (the Governor's Letter).

Line 8′

This reconstruction is suggested in Cohen 2008. See CAD G 65 for possible parallels.

APHEK 2: ADMINISTRATIVE FRAGMENT

Basics: Clay tablet; 4.3 × 4.3 × 1.5 cm; copy, p. 208; photo, p. 224
Reg. Nos.: IAA 90/252, Aphek 5936/1 (present location: Israel Museum)
Primary Publication: Rainey 1975: 128 (photo, pl. 24)
Studies: Kochavi 1977: 65; Edzard 1985: 252; Demsky 1990: 163; Goren, Na'aman, Mommsen, and Finkelstein 2006: 164
Date: Late Bronze Age, ca. 1230 BCE
Language: Akkadian
Find Information: Aphek, Area 10, Locus 1137; see Rainey 1975: 125

	Edition	Translation
1'	1 *li-im* [. . .	1 thousand [. . .
2'	4 *me-at* × [. . .	4 hundred . [. . .
3'	2 *me-at* × [. . .	2 hundred . [. . .
4'	5 ⸢*li*⸣-*i*[*m* . . .	5 thousa[nd . . .

Commentary

Line 2′

Perhaps read G[IG for "wheat." Cf. Aphek 1:7' and commentary.

APHEK 3: FRAGMENT OF TRILINGUAL LEXICAL TEXT

Basics: Clay cylinder fragment; 5.9 × 5.4 × 2.4 cm; outer circumference: 7.3 cm; copy, p. 208; photo, p. 224
Reg. Nos.: IAA 90/254, Aphek 8151/1 (present location: Israel Museum)

2. In contrast, the lexical fragment Ashqelon 1 preserves part of a western parallel to Urra with West-Semitic equivalents.

Primary Publication: Rainey 1976: 137–39 (photo, pl. 9, nos. 1–3)
Studies: Kochavi 1977: 66 (photo); 1981: 79 (photo); Edzard 1985: 251; Demsky 1990: 161–62; Dalley 1998: 59 (copy); Izre'el 1998b: 426; Rainey 1998: 240; Rothenbusch 2000: 485; Van der Toorn 2000: 105; Von Dassow 2004: 669–70; Goren, Na'aman, Mommsen, and Finkelstein 2006: 163–64
Date: Late Bronze Age, ca. 1230 BCE
Language: When complete, most likely Sumerian, Akkadian, and West-Semitic entries
Find Information: Aphek, Area 10, Locus 1137; see Rainey 1976: 137

	Edition	**Translation**
1'	. . . A].MEŠ : *ma-wu* : *mu-mi*	water
2'	. . . GEŠTI]N.MEŠ : *ka-ra-nu* : *ye-nu*	wine
3'	. . . : ⸢*ša*?⸣-*am-nu*	oil
4'	. . . : . . . :] × ×	. . .
5'	. . . : *di-iš-pu*:] ⸢*du*?-*uš*⸣-*bu*	honey

Commentary

The fragment preserves at least parts of five lexical entries in three languages for standard everyday items: water, wine, oil, honey, as well as a fifth item now represented by traces in line 4'. The first language appears to be Sumerian, the second Akkadian, and the third a West-Semitic language. In line 3' the West-Semitic space is left blank, presumably because the Akkadian and West-Semitic words for "oil" were considered to be identical. The text would appear to belong to the same tradition as Aphek 1.

APHEK 4: FRAGMENT

Basics: Clay tablet; 1.4 × 2 × 1.5 cm
Reg. No.: Aphek 8552 (location unknown)
Primary Publication: Rainey 1976: 139 (photo, pl. 10, no. 1)
Studies: Goren, Na'aman, Mommsen, and Finkelstein 2006: 164
Date: Late Bronze Age, ca. 1230 BCE
Find Information: Aphek, Area 10, Locus 1137; see Rainey 1976: 139

Rainey 1976: 139 reports that the fragment belonged to the upper left-hand corner of the original tablet.

Edition (from photo)

1'	× [. . .	*Too fragmentary for translation*
2'	*MU* [. . .	

APHEK 5: FRAGMENT

Basics: Clay tablet; 2.95 × 2.7 × 0.85 cm
Reg. No.: Aphek 8436 (location unknown)
Primary Publication: Rainey (1976) 140 (photo, pl. 10, no. 2)
Studies: Goren, Na'aman, Mommsen, and Finkelstein 2006: 164
Date: Late Bronze Age, ca. 1230 BCE
Find Information: Aphek, Area 10, Locus 1137; see Rainey 1976: 139

Rainey 1976: 140 reports that the fragment looks as though it belongs to the right-hand side of the original tablet.

Edition (from photo)

1'	. . .] × [(. . .	
2'	. . .] × *EN* [(. . .	*Too fragmentary for translation*
3'	. . . .] *AK* [(. . .	
	] [	

APHEK 6: FRAGMENT

Basics: Clay tablet; 4.0 × 5.2 × 1.8 cm; copy, p. 208; photos, p. 225
Reg. Nos.: IAA 90/212, Aphek 27386/1 (present location: Israel Museum)
Primary Publication: Hallo 1981: 18–20 (photo, pl. 3, nos. 1–2; copy, p. 19); reprinted in Owen et al. 1987: 18–20
Studies: Kochavi 1997: 66 (photo); Goren, Na'aman, Mommsen, and Finkelstein 2006: 165–66
Date: Late Bronze Age, ca. 1230 BCE
Language: Akkadian
Find Information: In alley adjoining Building 1104 on the east; see Hallo 1981: 18

The present fragment is flat on both sides, so it is not certain which side is the obverse and which is the reverse. Side A presents 8 lines of text in one column. Side B preserves six lines with a vertical ruling between B col. i'–ii'. No signs are currently preserved in B i', which is now represented by open space to the left of the ruling. B ii' is very narrow, containing no more than three signs per line, ending at the right edge of the tablet. The physical format of the tablet and the fact that many of the signs are crudely executed both suggest that Aphek 6 is a school text. Side A seems to preserve an excerpt from an administrative tablet or legal document. Side B is of uncertain content.

Edition	Translation
Side A	
1' . . .] × × × [×]	. . .] . . . [.
2' . . . *-l*]*i-i-ia-*⸢*šu*⸣	. . .] . . . .
3' . . . *š*]*a*! ŠÀ ITI-*ḫu*	. . . wh]ich in the course of a month
4' . . . *-a*]*t-ti-ka* É GÁN	. . .] . . . home (and) field
5' . . .] ×*-ka-am*	. . .] . . .
6' . . .] *IM DA*	. . .] . .
7' . . .] × *MI* DUGUD	. . .] . . heavy
8' . . .]-⸢*din-nu*⸣	. . .] . .

Side B

Col. i'

No surviving signs

Col. ii'

1' [(×)]×	[(.)]
2' [*i*]*q*?*-qir*	[i]s expensive?
3' × (×) *AK*	. . .
4' × *LUM SU*	. . .
5' *ZI NAM*	. . .
6' *SI* [×]	. [.]

Commentary

Due to the lack of any clear context, many different restorations for various lines are possible, some of which are offered in the edition of Hallo 1981.

Side A, line 4'

See Hallo 1981: 20 for a parallel in Hazor 5:4–5: É*-ti ú* ^{giš}KIRI$_6$ *i+na* URU *Ha-ṣú-*⸢*ra*⸣, "a home and a garden in the city of Hazor."

Side B, col. ii', line 2

Perhaps from a western variant (*y*)*aqāru* (see Hallo 1981: 20). Also possible is [*i*]*k-kir*, "became hostile," from *nakāru*.

APHEK 7: THE GOVERNOR'S LETTER

Basics: Clay tablet; 9.4 × 6.3 × 1.3 cm; photos, p. 225 (collated)

Reg. No.: Aphek 52055/1 (present location: Israel Museum)

Primary Publication: Owen 1981: 1–15 (photo, pls. 1–2, no. 1; copy, pp. 2–3), reprinted in Owen et al. 1987: 1–15

Studies: Kochavi 1981: 80; Singer 1983: 3–25; 1999: 698, 716; Edzard 1985: 251; Zadok 1996: 114; Hallo 2002: 243–44; Hess 2003: 44–45; *NEAEHL*: 69 (photo); Goren, Na'aman, Mommsen, and Finkelstein 2006: 164–65; Cohen 2008: 85
Date: Late Bronze Age, ca. 1230 BCE
Language: Akkadian
Find Information: Aphek, Area X, Building 1104, also known as "government house"; see Owen 1981:1

The historical background and immediate circumstances of this letter are discussed in depth in Singer 1983 with a later short summary in Singer 1999: 716.

	Edition	**Translation**
	Obverse	
1	*a-na* ^{m}*Ḫa-a-ia* LÚ.GAL	To Haya, the Great Man,
2	*a-bi-ia* EN-*ia*	my father, my lord,
3	*qí-bi-ma*	speak.
4	*um-ma* ^{m}*Ta-gu*$_{5}$*-uḫ-li-na*	Message of Taguhlina:
5	LÚ *ša-ki-<in>* KUR URU *Ú-ga-ri-it*	The Governor of the Land of Ugarit,
6	⸢DUMU⸣-*ka* ⸢ÌR⸣-*ka*	your son, your servant.
7	⸢*a*⸣*-na* GÌR.MEŠ ⸢EN⸣-*ia a-bi-ia am-qut*	At the feet of my lord, my father, I fall.

8	*a-*⸢*na*⸣ *muḫ-ḫi a-bi-*⸢*ia*⸣ EN-*ia*	To my father, my lord,
9	*lu-ú šul-mu* DINGIR.MEŠ *ša* LUGAL ⸢GAL⸣ EN-*ka*	Greetings. May the gods of the Great King, your lord,
10	*ù* DINGIR.MEŠ *ša* KUR URU *Ú-ga-ri-it*	and the gods of the Land of Ugarit
11	*lu-uk-ru-bu-ka*	bless you,
12	*li-iṣ-ṣu-ru-ka*	(and) keep you.

13	*a-bi* GIG.MEŠ-*ia*	My father, (regarding) my wheat,
14	2 *me-at* 50 PA GI[G].MEŠ	the 250 *barrels* of wh[e]at,
15	*ša it-ta-din* ^{m}*Ad-du-ia*	which Adduya gave
16	*ina* ŠU ^{m}*Tu-ur-ši-ma-ti*	into the care of Tur-šimati
17	*i-na* URU ⸢*Ia*⸣-[*p*]*u-ú*	in Ja[f]fa:
18	*ù a-bu-*[*ia a-kán-n*]*a iq-bi*	Then [my] father said [the following]:
	Lower Edge	
19	⸢2⸣ *me-at* 50 PA G[IG.ME]Š	"The 250 *barrels* of w[hea]t
20	[*l*]*i-id-din*	[l]et him (Tur-šimati) give over

Reverse

21	*⸢i⸣-na* ŠU-*ti* ^{m}*Ad-d*[*u-ia/ya*]	into the care of Add[uya.]"
22	*⸢ša-ni-tam⸣ a-bi-*[*ia*]	Moreover, m[y] father,
23	⸢GIG.MEŠ⸣ *ša ti-te-*[*re-eš*]	(regarding) the wheat which you requ[ested],
24	*ù ul-⸢te-bi⸣-*[*l*]*a-a*[*k-ku*]	indeed, I have already had it sen[t to you.]
25	*ù mi-ri-i*[*l-ti*]*-ia*	But my req[uest]
26	*ša i-*[*l*]*i-i*[*k-k*]*a*$^{?}$*-*[(*am*)*-ma a*]*-na muḫ-ḫi a-bi-ia*	which w[e]nt [out$^{?}$ t]o my father
27	*ul ⸢ta⸣-na-an-⸢din*$^{?}$⸣	you have not granted.
28	*i-na-an-na a-b*[*i-a ṣi-b*]*u-tu-ia*	Now fathe[r] my [pur]pose
29	*⸢i-na mi⸣-ri-i*[*l-ti-ia a-na i*]*a-a-ši*	in my req[uest, for m]e
30	× [× × × × × × (× ×)]-×*-ia*	. [. . . . . . . (. .)] . .
31	⸢EN⸣-[*ia l*]*i-id-din*	[let my] lo[rd] give over
32	*i-n*[*a*] ŠU ^{m}*Ad-du-ya*	int[o] the care of Adduya,
33	⸢LÚ⸣ *a-la-kà-a-ia*	my courier.
34	*ù ⸢a⸣-nu-um-ma* KÙ.BABBAR.MEŠ ^{m}*Ad-du-ya*	And now, (in regard to) the silver of Adduya,
35	*i-*[*l*$^{?}$*-q*]*i*$^{?}$ *na-ki-ri*	my enemy t[oo]k$^{?}$ (it).

Upper Edge

36	*ù ⸢a⸣-*[*n*]*a pa-ni a-bi-ia*	So be[fo]re my father
37	*li-iz-zi-iz*	let him (Adduya) present (himself)

Left Edge

38	*ù a-bu-⸢ia⸣ li-ip-ru-us-šu-nu*	and let my father judge them.
39	*a-nu-um-ma a-*[*n*]*a šul-ma-ni a-bi-ia*	Now, as a "gift" f[o]r my father -
40	1 *me-at* SÍG.ZA.GÌN [*ù*] 10 SÍG. SA$_5$: *ta-ba-ri*	100 (shekels) of *blue/purple* wool [and] 10 (shekels) of *red* wool: *tabarru*-wool (red wool)
41	*ul-te-b*[*i-l*]*a-ak-ku*	I have se[n]t to you.

Commentary

Line 4

For the reading of the name with G, see Van Soldt 1991: 350, n. 209.

Line 5

Short writing (perhaps an ellipsis) for *šakin māti māt* (KUR KUR) URU *Ú-ga-ri-it*. See Owen 1981: 11 for the name of Taguhlina's office; and cf. line 10 for KUR URU *Ú-ga-ri-it*.[3] The geographic term KUR URU GN, lit. "Land of the City of GN," refers to city-states, i.e., the city named and the surrounding territory over which it rules.

Line 11

For the strange precative *lu-uk-ru-bu-ka*, see Huehnergard 1989: 162.

Line 13

GIG = *kibtu*, "wheat" (see *CAD* K 340–41), with references from Ugarit in Owen 1981: 12.

Line 14

PA is most likely an abbreviation for *parīsu*, a large unit of capacity used in the measurement of grain which in contemporary texts is equivalent to approximately 50–60 liters.[4] Our translation "barrel" is meant to convey the sense of a large vessel used as a standard unit of measure. Singer 1999: 716 estimates the grain involved here as "about 15 tons."

Line 17

For Jaffa, cf. Gezer 2:10'.

Line 21

For alternate writings of the name, see Aphek 7:15, 32, 34.

Line 30

Owen 1981: 7 proposed to read this line as follows: [*šu(?)-bi(?)-la(?) ù(?)* GIG.ME]Š-*ia* "[dispatch(?) and(?)] my [whea]t."

Line 38

The form *li-ip-ru-us-šu-nu*, as written, is without full assimilation *sš/šš>ss*. For other examples, see Van Soldt 1991: 387. See Hazor 10:20 for the verb with Š at Late Bronze Age Hazor in a similar context.

Line 40

For the most recent assyriological work on the range of colors designated by SÍG. ZA.GÌN and SÍG.ZA.GÌN.SA$_5$ and SÍG.SA$_5$ (blue, purple, and red wool), see Singer 2008: 22–24. For *tabarru*, see *AHw* 1298; CAD T 21.

3. Cf. Izre'el 1991: II 77 for OA 23:2–3: LÚ *šakin* KUR *U-ga-ri-it*.
4. See Singer 1983: 4. For the measure, see *RlA* 7 522–25 (*Maße und Gewichte. Bei den Hethitern*).

APHEK 8: ADMINISTRATIVE FRAGMENT

Basics: Clay tablet; 11 × 8.5 cm
Reg. No.: Aphek 52060/1 (location unknown)
Primary Publication: Owen 1981: 15 (copy and photo, pl. 2, no. 2)
Studies: Goren, Na'aman, Mommsen, and Finkelstein 2006: 164
Date: Late Bronze Age, ca. 1230 BCE
Language: Presumably Akkadian, although only numerals, Sumerograms, and parts of personal names survive
Find Information: Aphek, Locus 5218 (like Aphek 7)

	Edition (from photo)	**Translation**
1'	1/2 PA [. . .	1/2 *barrel* [(of/for . . .
2'	2/3 ⌜PA⌝ [(×)] ᵐ*Ya*-[. . .	2/3 *barrel* [(of/for) Ya-[. . .
3'	1/2 BANEŠ [(×) ᵐ*In*-[. . .	1/2 *keg* [(of/for) In-[. . .

Commentary

For the unit of capacity PA = *parīsu*, see above, note to Aphek 7:14. For the unit BANEŠ = *ṣimdu* = approximately 25 liters, see *RlA* 7 522–25.

Ashdod

1. Inscribed Cylinder Seal
2–4. Fragments of Neo-Assyrian Stelae

ASHDOD 1: INSCRIBED CYLINDER SEAL

Basics: Jasper; height: 3.2 cm; diameter 1.5 cm (collated)
Reg. No.: IAA 1963-2501/1[1]
Primary Publication: Shaffer 1971: 198–99 (photo, pl. 97; copy, p. 198)
Studies: NEAEHL: 95 (photo)[2]
Date: Found in Iron Age II level. The artistic and epigraphic criteria suggest an earlier date, in the middle of the second millennium.[3]
Language: Akkadian, written in Sumerograms
Find Information: Area G, Locus 4007, Strata 4–5 (see Shaffer 1971: 198)

	Edition	Translation
1	[*Ì-l*]*í-ab-num*	[Il]i-abnum
2	[DUMU *B*]*i-il-lu-lum*	[the son of B]illulum
3	[ÌR] ^{d}*I-šum*	[the servant] of Išum

Commentary

Line 2

Cf. the PN *Bi-lu-lu-um* at Old Babylonian Khafajeh (Harris 1955: 61, no. 7:8, copy, p. 72) and Neo-Assyrian *Bilīlutu* (*PNAE* I 344). As noted by Shaffer, however, a reading [*P*]*í-il-lu-lum* is also possible.

1. This is the official number. The last digit on the object in June 2004 was mistakenly recorded as 3.
2. In the photo caption, read Old Babylonian for Early Babylonian. Another photograph is published in Dothan 1972:3.
3. Shaffer 1971: 198: "it is possible in the opinion of the excavators that it is an intrusion from MB II and LB I levels beneath."

ASHDOD 2–4: FRAGMENTS OF NEO-ASSYRIAN STELAE

These three fragments come from at least two separate originals. Ashdod 2–3, both from Area A, are written in the same script with lines of identical height, but with different indentations at the left edge. Thus, they could be from two different stelae or from two different parts of the same stela. Ashdod 4, from Area G, is written in a different hand altogether. As the three fragments have hitherto been treated as a single unit, we offer a unified bibliography below.

Ashdod 2 and 3 are too fragmentary to even attempt a translation.[4] Ashdod 4 is restored in part on the basis of parallel passages in the inscriptions of Sargon II. See now Fuchs 1994: 62:12–14; 76:7–8; 260:14–19; Frame 1999: 36:16–17. Tadmor 1971: 196 gave a tentative translation with bibliographical references to early editions of the inscriptions of Sargon II.

Ashdod 2
Basics: Black basalt; 10 × 13.8 cm; copy, p. 209
Reg. No.: IAA 63-962 (present location: Israel Museum)

Ashdod 3
Basics: Black basalt; 11.9 × 11.4 cm; copy, p. 209
Reg. No.: IAA 63-931 (present location: Israel Museum)

Ashdod 4
Basics: Black basalt; 22 × 23 × 17 cm; copy, p. 209
Reg. No.: IAA 63-1053 (present location: Israel Museum)

Information common to all three fragments:
Primary Publication: Tadmor 1971: 192–97, photo, pls. 96–97[5]
Studies: Freedman 1963: 138; Dothan 1964: 87; 1972: 11 (photo of Ashdod 4); Tadmor 1966: 95 (photo, fig. 11); Galling 1968: 61 1; Hestrin et al. 1972: 32 (English), 58 (photo in Hebrew edition); Cogan and Tadmor 1988: third plate following p. 228, item (b) (photos); Stern 2001: 14–15 (photo, p. 15); *NEAEHL*: 100 (photo)
Date: Neo-Assyrian period, Sargon II
Language: Akkadian
Find Information: See Tadmor 1971: 192

4. Possible restorations of selected lines are offered in Tadmor 1971: 196–97.

5. Ashdod 2 is Tadmor's fragment I; Ashdod 3 is his fragment III; and Ashdod 4 is his fragment II (Tadmor 1971: 195). For a Hebrew edition of the stela fragments, see Tadmor 1967.

Edition of Ashdod 2

Left Side		*Right Side*	
1'	. . .]-⸢*tim*⸣	1'	LUGA[L . . .
2'	. . .] SIG$_5$	2'	SAL.[. . .
3'	. . .] *KI RU*	3'	*šá* × [. . .
4'	. . . DAGA]L-*tim*	4'	*š*[*a* . . .

Edition of Ashdod 3

Left Side		*Right Side*	
1'	. . .] ×-*ú*	1'	× [. . .
2'	. . . *lí*[*p-ti*	2'	DINGIR [. . .
3'	. . . *í*]*š-tap-par*	3'	*AŠ* × [. . .
4'	. . . *ta*]-*mar-KU*	4'	*a-n*[*a* . . .
5'	. . .] × ⸢DU⸣	5'	*š*[*a* . . .

Edition of Ashdod 4

1 . . . . .] × ^{md}*Ḫum-ba-ni-*[*ga-aš* . . .
2 . . . KUR *Kar-a*]*l-lu* KUR *Šur-d*[*a* . . .
3 . . . . .KUR *M*]*a-da-a-a* K[UR . . .
4 . . . .^{d}*A*]*š-šur ú-*[*šaḫ-rib* . . .
5 . . . .] × [. . .

Translation of Ashdod 4

1 . . . .] . Humbani[gaš . . .
2 . . . . the land of Kara]llu, the land of Šurd[a . . .
3 . . . . the land of the M]edes, the l[and . . .
4 . . . . A]ssur, I [laid waste . . .
5 . . . .] . [. . .

Ashqelon

1. Lexical Fragment

ASHQELON 1: LEXICAL FRAGMENT

Basics: Clay tablet; 5.2 × 4.7 cm
Reg. No.: Ash 97-50.49.L485
Primary Publications: Huehnergard and Van Soldt 1999 (photo and copy, p. 185); Huehnergard and Van Soldt 2008: 327–32 (photo and copy, p. 328)
Studies: Von Dassow 2004: 669
Date: Late Bronze Age II, ca. thirteenth century BCE
Language: When complete, most likely Sumerian, Akkadian, and West-Semitic entries
Find Information: Pottery bucket no. 178, reg. 49535; see Huehnergard and Van Soldt 1999: 184, n. 1

This fragment preserves a piece of the obverse of a western parallel to Urra = *ḫubullu* I that includes local West-Semitic equivalents. The obverse of Hazor 6 also belongs to the Urra tradition.

Edition

Col. i'		*Col. ii'*	
1'	. . . . *ia-ar-ḫ*]*u*	1'	× [. . .
2'	. . . . *ia-ar*]-*ḫi*	2'	UGU [. . .
3'	. . . . -*t*]*i ia-*⸢*ar*⸣-*ḫi*	3'	UGU × [. . .
4'	. . . . -*t*]*i ia-ar-ḫi*	4'	UGU × [. . .
5'	. . . *ma-a*]*l-sà-*⸢*mu*⸣-*ti*	5'	UGU × [. . .
6'	. . . . .*i*]*a-ar-ḫi*	6'	UGU × [. . .
7'	. . . . .*š*]*a-nu-ti*	7'	UGU × [. . .
8'	. . . . . .] ×	8'	⸢UGU⸣ × [. . .

Commentary

A reconstruction of col. i' is offered in Huehnergard and Van Soldt 1999: 191 on the basis of parallel sections from Urra I, and the Ugarit and Emar parallels to Urra; see Huehnergard and Van Soldt 1999: 189–92. For col. ii', see the UGU section, Urra I 267–74 (*MSL* 5 28–29); Huehnergard and Van Soldt 1999: 187.

Col. i', line 3'

The word *ia-ar-hi* written over two lines of text, with the second line smaller and indented.

Line 7'

. . . *š*]*a-nu-ti*, corresponding to Urra I 234 *ša-na-at* (*MSL* 5 26). For the form of NU, cf. Hazor 13:1.

Beer Sheva

1. Votive Cylinder

BEER SHEVA 1: VOTIVE CYLINDER

Basics: Chalcedony; height 3.8 cm; diameter: 1.5 cm (collated)
Reg. No.: IAA 1999-2335 (present location: Israel Antiquities Authority storerooms)
Primary Publication: Rainey 1973 (photo, pl. 26; copy, p. 66)
Studies: Beck 1973; Lipiński 1976: 74; Collon 1987: 133–34, no. 564 (photo 133); Tadmor and Tadmor 1995: 353–54; Stern 2001: 332; Ornan 2003: 72 (copy); Na'aman 2007: 112; *NEAEHL*: 172 (photo)
Date: Inscription: first millennium BCE; Seal: possibly late second millennium BCE with later, first-millennium inscription added; see Ornan 2003: 72; and earlier, Beck 1973: 59[1]
Find Information: See Aharoni 1973: 16

This seal is inscribed in the positive, like the Neo-Assyrian votive cylinder seal Samaria 3, the Neo-Assyrian cylinder seal Wingate 1, and the earlier cylinder letter Beth Shean 2 from the Amarna period.

	Edition	**Translation**
1	*a-na* ^{d}A.^{d}IM EN.GAL	For Apladda, the Great Lord,
2	*be*$^{!}$*-lí-šú* ^{m}*Re-mut*-DINGIR.MEŠ	his lord, Remut-ilani
3	DUMU ^{md}IM-*id-r*[*i*]	the son of Adda-idri
4	DÙ-*ma* BA-*iš*	made (it) and dedicated (it).

Commentary

Line 1

Apladda is a late subsidiary (H)adad deity. The pronunciation of the DN when written with logograms is uncertain, but a syllabic writing ^{m}*Ap-la-da-na-ta-nu* for

1. Collon 1987: 134 assigned a Late Bronze Age date to the object.

Apil-(H)adad-natan, "The Son of (H)adad has Given," as well as a Greek writing ΑΦΛΑΔ, suggest a pronunciation *(H)apladdu/a/i*.[2] For the name Apla-Addu, see now Zawadzki 2009–10, esp. p. 212.

2. For the deity, see Rainey 1973: 61–63, with discussion of the pronunciation of the name on p. 62; Lipiński 1976: 53–74; and *DDD* 719.

Ben Shemen

1. Neo-Assyrian Stela Fragment

BEN SHEMEN 1: NEO-ASSYRIAN STELA FRAGMENT

This fragment was found in the Ben Shemen forest some forty years ago and finally edited in Cogan 2008. Cogan notes that this fragment was found in the same general area of the Sharon Plain as the Qaqun fragment, and is inscribed with similar small cuneiform signs. He therefore suggests that the present fragment might have been part of the same Esarhaddon stela as the still unpublished Qaqun 1 (see p. 115). The Ben Shemen fragment would have fit into the stela after the Qaqun fragment. The text in the Ben Shemen fragment may be compared to the Zenjirli stela, rev. 46–50.

Basics: Limestone (presumed to be part of a stela)
Reg. No.: Israel Museum 71.74.221
Primary Publication: Cogan 2008 (photo, p. 69)
Studies: Tadmor 1973: 72; Ornan 1997: I, 267, n. 1025; Na'aman and Zadok 2000: 181; Leichty 2011: 291–92, no. 1007
Date: Neo-Assyrian period, Esarhaddon
Language: Akkadian

	Edition	**Translation**
1	. . .] × [. . .	. . .] . [. . .
2	. . . *ultu* KU]R *mu-*[*ṣur assuḫma* . . .	. . . from the lan]d of Egy[pt I uprooted
3	. . . *ina*] *muḫ*[?]-[*ḫi māt Muṣur* . . .	. . . o]ve[r Egypt . . .
4	. . .] LÚ.N[AM.MEŠ . . .	. . . gov[ernors . . .
5	. . . *ana eš-šú*]-*ti* [*apqid*	. . . I appointed ane]w [. . .
6	. . . AN.]ŠÁR *u* DI[NGIR.MEŠ . . .	. . . As]hur and the great] g[ods . . .
7	. . . *ukīn dà*]-*ri*-[*šam* . . .	. . . I set for]ev[er . . .

Beth Mirsim

1. Cylinder Seal

BETH MIRSIM 1: CYLINDER SEAL

Basics: Hematite; length: 1.95 cm; diameter: 1.0 cm; photos, p. 226
Reg. Nos.: IAA 32.2718, Rockefeller Museum 890
Studies: Albright 1932: 9–10 (photo, p. 8); 1935: 215, no. 69, 217, no. 73; 1938: 45–46 (pl. 30, nos. 1, 3); Rowe 1936: 237–38 (photo, pl. 26, S. 11); Parker 1949: 11, no. 20 (photo, pl. 3, no. 20); Collon 1987: 52–53, no. 203 (photo)
Date: Middle Bronze Age IIB, ca. seventeenth century BCE
Language: Decorative cuneiform signs
Find Information: Albright 1938: p. 45, pl. 19a (provenance marked by ×)

This seal, which preserves a short inscription in Egyptian hieroglyphs, bears what appear to be six stylized cuneiform signs that have been taken to be decorative elements. It is, however, possible that they were meant to represent a personal name or names. In addition to this piece, Mesopotamian culture is represented at the site by gaming pieces from what is commonly known as the "Royal Game of Ur."[1]

1. Rockefeller Museum display no. 792b. No. 792a is a game board of the "Royal Game of Ur" on a brick from Beth Shemesh. For photo, see *NEAEHL*: 178.

Beth Shean

1. Inscribed Cylinder Seal
2. Cylinder Letter of Tagi to Lab'aya

BETH SHEAN 1: INSCRIBED CYLINDER SEAL

Basics: Lapis lazuli; height: 2.0 cm; diameter: 1.0 cm; photos, p. 226 (cylinder and impression)
Reg. No.: Rockefeller Museum J.1014
Primary Publication: Rowe 1930: 23 (photo, pl. 34, no. 3)
Studies: Nougayrol 1939: 52 (copy, pl. 7 RB. 1); Parker 1949: 6, no. 1 (photo, pl. 1, no. 1); Galling 1968: 13 A 1; Demsky 1990: 164; James and McGovern 1993: vol. 1, p. 231, no. 1 (photo, vol. 2, pl. 58a);[1] Charpin 2007: 187–88
Date: Old Babylonian period, Middle Bronze Age
Language: Sumerian or, more likely, Akkadian written in Sumerograms
Find Information: See James and McGovern 1993: 231

This Mesopotamian-type cylinder seal bears a three-line inscription flanked by goddesses, dated on stylistic grounds to the Old Babylonian period. The original owner of the seal is named as *Ma-a-nu-um*, "the diviner" (*bārû*). It is not certain how or when the seal reached Beth Shean, but the possibility that the object was brought to the city by a traveling *bārû* cannot be ruled out, since liver models have been recovered from Hazor, Megiddo, and other sites in the cuneiform west (for discussion, see Hazor 2–3, 17).

Edition		**Translation**
1	*Ma-a-nu-um*	Manum
2	MAŠ.ŠU.GÍD.GÍD	the diviner
3	ÌR ^{d}EN.KI	the servant of Ea.

1. Another photograph of the seal is available in Pfeiffer 1966: 511.

Commentary

Line 1

The consensus interprets the name as a hypocoristicon of the sentence name *Mannum* . . . "Who is . . . ?"[2] However, the unusual writing with an apparent long *a*-vowel (perhaps for *mānum* / *mânum*) leaves this interpretation open to question.[3]

Line 2

MAŠ.ŠU.GÍD.GÍD = *bārû*. See *CAD* B 121

Line 3

This is the earliest mention of the god Enki/Ea in the southern Levant, and as written it seems to identify the diviner here with Ea's cult, even though Shamash and Adad are normally the patrons of Mesopotamian divination.

BETH SHEAN 2: CYLINDER LETTER OF TAGI TO LAB'AYA

Basics: Clay cylinder; height: 2.4 cm; diameter: 4.0 cm; copy, p. 209; photos, p. 226
Reg. No.: Israel Museum 1997-3310
Primary Publication: Horowitz 1996a (photo and copy, p. 211)
Studies: Horowitz 1994 (photo, p. 85); Horowitz 1997a (photo, p. 97); Rainey 1998: 239–42; Van der Toorn 2000: 99, 106; Hess 2003: 42, Goren et al. 2004: 259; Von Dassow 2004: 667, 672
Date: Amarna period; Late Bronze Age; fourteenth century BCE
Language: Akkadian
Find Information: See Horowitz 1996a: 208

	Edition	**Translation**
1	*a-na La-ab-a-*⸢*ya*⸣	To Lab'aya,
2	*be-li-ia*	my lord,
3	*qí-bí-ma*	speak.
4	⸢*um-ma*⸣ *Ta-gi*	Message of Tagi:
5	*a-na* LUGAL EN-	To the King (Pharaoh) my
6	*li-ia*	lord;
7	*iš-te-me ša-*	I have listened carefully to
8	*pár-ka a-na*	your dispatch
9	⸢*ia*⸣*-ši* × ×	to me . .
10–12	*traces*	*traces*

2. For such names, cf. *CAD* M_1 214–15.
3. Cf. Kienast 1978: II, 24, no. 22: 17: *Ma-a-nu-um* DUMU *Nu-úr-*[× - ×] (Old Babylonian Kisurra).

Commentary

This unique piece preserves the only known example of a cuneiform letter on what appears to be a cylinder seal. In Horowitz 1996a, the author hypothesized that the unusual form was used to disguise the letter as a small clay cylinder seal in order to conceal sensitive information regarding anti-Egyptian activities by the sender and addressee—the two well-known Amarna period Canaanite rulers Tagi and Labʾaya. In this case, the brevity of the letter suggests that it was designed to serve as a surety for a more detailed oral communication to be delivered by the messenger. Alternative views are given in Rainey 1998 and Goren et al. 2004: 259, where the authors, Y. Goren, I. Finkelstein, and N. Naʾaman, offer a petrographic analysis of the cylinder. They suggest that the clay of the cylinder belongs to a well-known group distributed in the Judea-Samaria anticline and is not of the same type as Tagi's El-Amarna letters. Based on this finding, Naʾaman argues that the Tagi of the Beth Shean cylinder is not the Tagi of the Amarna letters, but instead a local official at Shechem. This conclusion seems to be premature:

1. It remains to be proven that all cuneiform tablets were written on local clay. Given the relatively short distance from the Samaria Hills to the Carmel region, how can we be sure that clay for the specific use of cuneiform writing could not be exported from one region to the other?
2. Given Tagi's and Labʾaya's fluid political situation and their troubles with Pharaoh, it is impossible for us to know the whereabouts of the two at the time when Beth Shean 2 was executed. For example, Tagi may have come to Shechem to consult with Labʾaya, but Labʾaya may already have left. Thus, Tagi could have written to Labʾaya on local Shechem clay.
3. As suggested by Finkelstein contra Naʾaman, the cylinder may be only a copy of Tagi's original message (see Goren et al. above).

Any successful interpretation of Beth Shean 2 must explain why the letter was written in the unique physical form of a clay cylinder. If it is merely a letter to Labʾaya from an official from Shechem named Tagi, as suggested by Naʾaman, why the unusual shape?

Lines 7–8

Inf. of *šapāru*, hence the translation "dispatch," which is both a verb and a noun. For the parallels from Amarna, see Horowitz 1996a: 212.

Beth Shemesh

BETH SHEMESH 1: ALPHABETIC CUNEIFORM ABECEDARY

For an edition with bibliography and discussion, see Part III, pp. 161–64.

Gezer

1. Envelope Fragment
2. Letter Fragment
3. Neo-Assyrian Administrative Document: Slave Sale
4. Neo-Assyrian Administrative Document: Land Sale

5$^{?}$. Tablet with Drawings and Erased Signs

During W. Horowitz and T. Oshima's visit to the Arkeoloji Müzeleri in Istanbul, Gezer 3–4 were not available for study. The box that should have contained Gezer 3 (= Fi. 12 = Div. 216) was empty, as the tablet itself was on display at the time of an earthquake in Turkey and then removed for safekeeping. The box for Gezer 4 was occupied by a different tablet which had been erroneously stored as Fi. 13 = Div. 217 for quite some time, as is evident by the fact that A. Shaffer's study materials from the Arkeoloji Müzeleri included a rough sketch of this same tablet. As there is no other notice of the existence of this tablet, we suppose that this tablet is a long-standing intrusion into the Fi. collection which had been switched with our Gezer 4 (the true Fi. 13 = Div. 217) a long time ago. Hence, our Gezer 4 is now missing. Thus, we are quite dubious about the identification of the current Fi. 13 = Div. 217 as a tablet from Gezer. Nevertheless, we have numbered it Gezer 5$^{?}$, since we cannot state definitely that it is not from Gezer.

GEZER 1: ENVELOPE FRAGMENT

Basics: Clay; 3 × 2 × 0.4 cm; photos, p. 227
Reg. No.: Israel Museum 1967-433
Primary Publication: Shaffer 1970 (photo, pl. 24; copy, p. 113)
Studies: Anbar and Na'aman 1986: 7–8, 10–11; Demsky 1990: 162;[1] Na'aman 1994: 176; Zadok 1996: 104; Van der Toorn 2000: 98; Finkelstein 2002: 280; Horowitz and Oshima 2005: 37; Cohen 2008: 85
Date: Old Babylonian period; Middle Bronze Age

1. Demsky incorrectly describes the text as "lexical."

Language: Akkadian
Find Information: See Shaffer 1970: 111

Gezer 1 was recovered in a fourteenth-century archaeological context, but Shaffer 1970: 111 dates the tablet to the seventeenth century on the basis of the ductus.[2] The presence of the Hurrian name Ehlummanti in the text demonstrates that the Hurrians had arrived in Canaan by the time this text was written.[3] The tablet bears similarities in subject and script with Hebron 1.

Edition

Outer Surface of Envelope

Obverse

1' . . . . UDU?.MÁ]Š? *ir-ḫu-um-ma* [. . .
2' . . . .]-˹*ú*˺-*na* [. . .
3' . . . . -*t*]*i-il-la* DUMU *Rab-ba-n*[*a* . . .
4' . . . . *Eḫ-lu*]*m-ma-an-ti* DUMU *Ab-d*[*i*?- . . .
5' . . . . *E*]*ḫ-lum-ma-an-ti* [. . .
6' . . .] *IM* [. . .
7' . . .] × KI [. . .
8' . . *Eḫ-lum-ma-a*]*n-ti* LÚ.UGULA.SIPA [. . .

Reverse (written over the edge onto the obverse)

1' . . .] ×
2' . . . -*ḫ*]*i*?-*iš*

Translation

Obverse

1' . . . . the floc]k? (which) he/they shepherded and [. . .
2' . . . .] . . [. . .
3' . . . . .-t]illa, son of Rabban[a . . .
4' . . . . Ehlum]manti the son of Abd[i?- . . .
5' . . . . . E]hlummanti [. . .
6' . . . . . .] . [. . .
7' . . . . . .] . -city? [. . .
8' . . . . . Ehlumma]nti the overseer of the shepherds [. . .

2. For a comparative sign list, see Shaffer 1970: 113.

3. See Na'aman 1994: 176 for Hurrians and other northern elements in Canaan by the end of the Middle Bronze Age. The partially preserved name . . . -*tilla* on outer surface line 3' is probably also Hurrian.

Reverse
Too fragmentary for translation

	Edition	Translation
	Impression from Tablet on Inner Surface of Envelope	
	Side 1	
1'	. . .] × [. . .	. . .] . [. . .
2'	. . .] *a-na* LUGAL [. . .	. . .] to the king [. . .
3'	. . . *l*]*e-e* [. . .	. . .] . . [. . .
	Side 2 (written over the edge onto Side 1	
1'	. . .] ⸢*e*⸣-*p*[*u-uš* / *šu* . . .	. . .] d[id$^{?}$ . . .

Commentary

Outer Surface, line 1'

For our proposed reading UDU$^{?}$.MÁ]Š$^{?}$ see Hebron 1, *passim*, with discussion. For the verb, cf. Hebron 1:8: . . . *ir-te-ḫu a-na* PN, ". . . shepherded for PN." The root is רעה (cognate to Akkadian *reʾû*) with West-Semitic ע rendered by Ḫ, as is common. For the subject of animals in second-millennium Gezer, see also Gezer 2:12' below.

Line 3'

For *Rabban*[*a*], see Anbar and Naʾaman 1986: 8, 10.

Line 6'

IM may be the end of a theophoric PN with the name of the storm god or a noun in the genitive with mimmation.

Line 7'

Could the trace before the determinative be for IR/ER and thus be the end of a writing of the name of Gezer, e.g., URU *Ga-ze-er*^{ki}?[4]

GEZER 2: LETTER FRAGMENT

Basics: Clay tablet; 5.9 × 2.9 × 1.7 cm; copy, p. 209
Reg. No.: Fi. 17, EŞ 2829 (present location: Arkeoloji Müzeleri, Istanbul)
Primary Publication: Dhorme 1909; Dhorme and Harper 1912 (photo: frontispiece, fig. 4; p. 30, fig. 5); Macalister 1909: pl. III following p. 96 (photo); Driver 1944: pl. 44, no. 2 (photo)

4. This may be more in keeping with some Egyptian renderings of the name, for which see Aḥituv 1984: 101–2, rather than Gazri as in the Amarna Letters (see Knudtzon 1915: 1573). We thank Dr. J. Ford for his aid with the Egyptian materials.

Studies: Albright 1924: 106, n. 14; 1943; Malamat 1961: 228–31; Galling 1968: 13 A 2; Edzard 1985: 252; Zadok 1996: 111; Van der Toorn 2000: 99; Hess 2003: 45–46; *NEAEHL*: 502; Cogan 2007: 247; Cohen 2008: 85
Language: Akkadian
Find Information: Surface find, see Macalister 1909: 96; Dhorme and Harper 1912: 30

The original editors of Gezer 2 took the script of the tablet to be Neo-Babylonian, but more recent studies, from Albright 1924 onwards, date the tablet to the first part of the Late Bronze Age, the time of the Amarna letters and Taanach tablets. Our own inspection of the tablet finds that most of the forms are consistent with those at Amarna and Taanach, but that others seem closer to those in use in Middle Babylonian Mesopotamia.[5] Most noticeably, the A signs are not of the distinctive Late Bronze western type, so it is possible that Gezer 2 dates from the very latest phases of the Middle Bronze Age / Old Babylonian period, i.e., before the distinctive Amarna-type sign forms became standard in Canaan. Alternatively, it may be that the tablet is indeed from the Late Bronze Age, but is written in a mixed hand.

	Edition	**Translation**
1'	. . . . . . *Z*]*I*? × [. . .	. . . . .] . . [. . .
2'	. . .] *aš-šum mi-ni-im* [. . .	. . . .] for what reason [. . .
3'	. . . *a-n*]*a ma-aḫ-ri-ia* [. . .	. . . . b]efore me [. . .
4'	. . . . *l*]*a mi-ni-tam-ma* ⸢*ši*⸣*-ib-*× [. . .	. . . with]out number . . . [. . .
5'	. . .]- ×*-ka* ⸢*el*⸣ *GI RU* [. . .	. . .] your . [. .] *on* . . [. . .
6'	. . .] × *lìb-ba-ka i-na* URU [. . .	. . .] . your heart, in the city (of) [. . .
7'	. . . *lì*]*b-bi-ka li-iq-r*[*i-ib* . . .	. . .] your [h]eart let appro[ach . . .
8'	. . . *a/i-n*]*a* URU *Ki-id-di-im* × [. . .	. . . t]o/i]n the city of Kiddim . [. . .
9'	. . .]*-am* ᵐ*Ba-ṣi*!*-ir-d*[*a-* . . .	. . .] . Baṣird[a- . . .
10'	. . . UR]U *Ia-ap-*[*p*]*u-ú* × [. . .	. . . the cit]y of Jaffa . [. . .
11'	. . . *l*]*i-* ⸢*ša*⸣*-ki-in* [. . .	. . . le]t him place? [. . .
12'	. . . U]DU GU$_4$.ḪI.A [. . .	. . . . sh]eep and cattle [. . .
13'	. . .] ÌR *pa-ni* [. . .	. . . . .] the *aforementioned* slave [. . .
14'	. . .] × [. . .	*trace*

5. This explains the earlier proposed Neo-Babylonian dating. The language of the letter fragment also shows features typical of Old and Middle Babylonian. For example, *CAD* give attestations for *aššum mīnim* (Gezer 2:2) in Old Babylonian and Middle Babylonian (including Boghazköi and Amarna), but not so far in Neo-Babylonian letters or administrative documents (see *CAD* A_{II} 470, M_{II} 95).

Commentary

Line 8′

This city is not known from any other cuneiform source and therefore cannot be identified. Dhorme and Harper 1912: 31 identified it as biblical Gittaim. Albright suggested that the city was most likely "Gittham of Eusebius, between Antipatris and Jamnia which must be Gitta between Beth Dagon and Lydda . . ." (Albright 1943: 29, n. 11). Malamat 1961: 230 and *NEAEHL*: 502 suggest Tell Ras Abu Hamid.

Line 10′

For Jaffa, cf. Aphek 7:17: URU ⸢*Ia*⸣-[*p*]*u-ú*.

GEZER 3: NEO-ASSYRIAN ADMINISTRATIVE DOCUMENT: SLAVE SALE[6]

Basics: Clay tablet; 2 1/4″ × 2 1/4″ × 3/4″ (Macalister 1904: 208)
Reg. No.: Fi. 12, EŞ 2815$^{?}$,[7] Div. 216 (present location: Arkeoloji Müzeleri, Istanbul)
Primary Publication: Pinches 1904 (photo following p. 230, figs. 1–2, typeset cuneiform renderings of the text, pp. 230–31); Johns *apud* Macalister 1912: 23–27 (photo frontispiece, figs. 1–2, 23–24, typeset cuneiform renderings of the text[8])
Studies: Conder 1904: 1905; Johns 1904a; 1904b; Sayce 1904; Galling 1935: 81–86; 1968: 61, 2a; Zadok 1977–78: 47; 1985: 567–70; Becking 1981–82: 80–86 (photo, p. 89); 1992: 114–17; Radner 1997: 17; Na'aman and Zadok 2000: 176, 182; Van der Toorn 2000: 99; Stern 2001: 16; Finkelstein 2002: 286; Hallo 2002: 263–64; *NEAEHL*: 505; Horowitz and Oshima 2004: 36; Cogan 2013a: 24–26
Date: Neo-Assyrian period; 651 BCE (reign of Assurbanipal); Neo-Assyrian script. The text is dated in rev. 5'–6' to the year after the eponym year of Assur-dūru-uṣur (652); the year after is 651. See Millard 1994: 83; *PNAE* 180
Language: Akkadian
Find Information: See Macalister 1904: 207–8

Edition

Obverse

1 NA$_4$.KIŠIB ^{md}ŠÚ.SU ⸢A⸣ [. . .
2 NA$_4$.KIŠIB ^{m}AD.SU A [. . .
3 PAP 2 LÚ.MEŠ EN É.MEŠ A.ŠÀ.[MEŠ . . .
4 É ^{m}*Lu*-PAP.MEŠ *a-di gi*-⸢*i*⸣-[*mir-ti-šu*]

Four uninscribed stamp impressions

6. The tablet was not available for study by W. Horowitz and T. Oshima in April 2004.
7. The question mark appears in the tablet's identification materials at the museum.
8. No actual copy of the tablet has ever been published.

---

5 LÚ.GURUŠ.MEŠ ^{m}*Ṭu-ri-*^{d}*A-a* 2 SAL.MEŠ-*šú* DUMU-*šú*
6 3 ⸢LÚ.MEŠ$^{?}$⸣ [×] × × × × [× ×] × .MEŠ
7 2 GIŠ$^{?}$ [× × × × × × × ×] ×.GA
8 [× × × × × × × × × × × ×] ×-*a-a*
9 [× × × × × × × × × × × × × ^{m}A]D$^{?}$-*ia-qar*
10 *traces*

Reverse

1' ⸢*kas*$^{?}$*-pu*$^{?}$⸣ [. . .
2' *ú-ta-ra* × × × × [. . .
3' *la i-laq-qe ṣi-bit be-e*[*n-n*]*u*
4' *a-na* 1 ME *u_4-me sa-ar-tú a-na kal u_4-me*
5' ^{iti}SIG$_4$ UD.17.KAM *lim-mu ša* EGIR
6' ^{m}AŠ+ŠUR.BÀD.PAP ^{lú}EN.NAM URU *Bar-ḫal-zi*

7' IGI ^{m}*Zag-gi-i* IGI $^{\mathrm{m<<m>>iti}}$AB-*a-a*
8' IGI ^{m}EN.A.AŠ IGI ^{md}ŠÚ.PAP-*ir* UR[U . . (.)]
9' IGI ^{m}*Ḫur-ú-a-ṣi* ^{lú}*ḫa-za-nu-m*[*a*]
10' IGI ^{m}*Bur-ra-pi-iʾ* ^{lú}DAM.[GÀR]
11' IGI ^{m}NUMUN.DU DUMU ^{miti}Ab-⸢*a*⸣-[*a*]
12' IGI ^{m}DÙG-*ta*-DIN IGI ^{m}*Si-iʾ*-[. . .]
13' IGI ^{m}*Man-nu-ki*-LÍMMU-*il* IGI ⸢^{m}⸣[. . .]
14' IGI ^{m}NUMUN-*ú-tú*

Translation

Obverse

1 Seal of Marduk-eriba son of [. . .
2 Seal of Abu-eriba son of [. . .
3 Total, two men, owners of estates (and) field[s . . .
4 the estate of Lu-ahhe in [its] enti[rety]

Four stamp seal impressions: 2 × 2 stamp seals

---

5 The young-men (and) Ṭuri-Aya, his 2 wives (and) his son,
6 3 men$^{?}$. [.] . . . . [. .] . .
7–10 *Too fragmentary for translation*

Reverse

1' the silver$^{?}$ [(*amount missing*) . . .
2' he will return. [If he makes a claim without a lawsuit]
3' he will not take (it). (Guaranteed against) an attack of epi[lep]sy
4' for 100 days (and the slave being) stolen property in perpetuity.

5' The 17th of the month of Sivan, the (year) after (the year of) the eponym
6' Assur-duru-uṣur, the governor of Barhalzi.

7' Witness: Zaggi; witness: Kanunaya;
8' Witness: Bel-apla-iddina; witness: Marduk-naṣir of the cit[y$^{?}$ . . (.)]
9' Witness: Huruaṣi, the mayor;
10' Witness: Burrapi' the mer[chant;]
11' Witness: Zera-ukin son of Kanunay[a];
12' Witness: Ṭabta-uballiṭ; witness Si'-[. . .]
13' Witness: Mannu-ki-Arba'il; witness: [. . .]
14' Witness: Zerutu

Commentary

The most complete discussion of the personal names in Gezer 3–4 is found in Becking 1981–82. For later discussion, see Becking 1992, Zadok 1977–78, and Na'aman and Zadok 2000 (cited in the bibliography above), Hallo 2002, and the relevant entries in *PNAE.*

Obverse, line 8

Perhaps the end of a PN . . . ^{d}*A-a.*

Line 9

Perhaps the name *Abi-iaqar,* for which see *PNAE* 10–11.

Reverse, lines 2'–4'

These lines preserve a legal formula protecting the buyer. See Becking 1981–82: 83; 1992: 116; Postgate 1976: 17–20; *CAD* B 206 *bennu* A c); *CAD* S 188 *sartu* 3. Line 2, when complete, should read: *utarra ina lā dēnīšu idabbubma* (Postgate 1976: 18).

Line 6'

Governor: *bēl pīhāti.*

Line 7'

Our rendering of the name reflects the Assyrian, rather than the Babylonian, month name, *Ṭebētaja*; see *CAD* K 395–96; Cohen 1993: 335.

Line 9'

For this Egyptian name, see Na'aman and Zadok 2000: 176.

Line 10'

Hallo 2002: 264 reads the name *Qar-rāpi',* following Radner 1999: 108, contra previous studies and Elat 1998: 53.

Line 12′

Instead of our translation, Zadok 1985: 568 adopts the more cautious reading HI(?)-*ta-din*.

GEZER 4: NEO-ASSYRIAN ADMINISTRATIVE DOCUMENT: LAND SALE

Basics: Clay tablet; 1 1/2″ × 2″ × 2/3″ (Macalister 1905: 185) (location unknown)

Primary Publication: Johns 1905: 206–10 (photo, p. 206, obverse only; typeset cuneiform rendering, p. 207); Johns *apud* Macalister 1912: 27–29 (photo, frontispiece, fig. 3 obverse only; typeset cuneiform rendering, pp. 27–28)[9]

Studies: Sayce 1905; Galling 1935: 81–86; 1968: 61 2b; Becking 1981–82: 86–88; 1992: 117–18; Zadok 1985: 567–70; Radner 1997: 17; Na'aman and Zadok 2000: 176, 182; Van der Toorn 2000: 99; Stern 2001: 16; Finkelstein 2002: 286; Hallo 2002: 264–65; *NEAEHL*: 505; Eph'al 2010: 52–53; Weippert 2010: 312–13 (Text 164)

Date: Neo-Assyrian period; 649 BCE (reign of Assurbanipal); Neo-Assyrian script. The text is dated to the eponym year of *Ahu-ilāya*. See Millard 1994: 80; *PNAE* 76

Language: Akkadian

Find Information: See Macalister 1905: 185

	Edition	**Translation**
	Obverse	
1	NA$_4$.KIŠIB ^{m}*Na-tan-ia-u*	Seal of Natanyahu
2	EN A.ŠÀ SUM-*a-ni*	the owner of the field being sold
	Three impressions of the same stamp seal	*Three impressions of the same stamp seal*
3	É [× BÁ]N A.ŠÀ SUḪUR ^{m}*Si-ni-i*	(comprising) an estate [with a . *sū*]*tu* (area) field adjacent to that of Sini
4	[× BÁN A.ŠÀ S]UḪUR ^{m}*Si-ni-i*	[(and a . *sūtu* (area) field adj]acent to that of Sini
	Reverse	
1'	IGI ^{m}× × [(×)]	Witness: . . . [(.)]
2'	IGI ^{m}BU.SIK.SUKKAL.GIŠ	Witness: . . . .
3'	IGI ^{m}NUMUN.DU	Witness: Zera-ukin
4'	IGI ^{m}U+GUR.MAN.PAP	Witness: Nergal-šarra-uṣur
5'	^{iti}ZÍZ UD.4.KAM	The month of Shevat, day 4.

9. Like Gezer 3, no hand copy of the text has ever been published.

Lower Edge

1	*lim-mu* ^{m}PAP.DINGIR-*a-a*	The eponym year of Ahu-ilaya
2	^{lú}*šá-kìn Gar-ga-mis*	The governor of Carchemish

Commentary

Line 1

^{m}*Na-tan-ia-u*, Natanyahu, is a Hebrew name meaning "Yhwh has given."

Line 3–4

SUḪUR is a pseudo-logogram for *ṭēhu* in Middle Assyrian and Neo-Assyrian land and house descriptions (see *CDA* 414).

BÁN = *sūtu*. A measure of surface area equivalent to 450 m^2 in the Neo-Babylonian / Late Babylonian system, based on the more common use of BÁN = *sūtu* as a volume measure based on seed capacity (see *RlA* 7 483, table XII). For this measure of surface area in Neo-Assyrian administrative texts, see *CAD* S 424 *sūtu* A, 3. For a Judean *sūtu*, see Postgate 1976: 67–68, with a reference to the *sūtu* of the Land of Judah (GIŠ.BÁN *šá* KUR *Ia-ú-di*) in Johns 1924: 87, no. 148:2 = SAA 14 77.

GEZER 5$^{?}$: TABLET WITH DRAWINGS AND ERASED SIGNS[10]

Basics: Clay tablet; 10.3 × 6.9 × 1.4 cm; copy, p. 210
Reg. No.: EŞ 2811, Fi. 13, DIV 217 (present location: Arkeoloji Müzeleri, Istanbul)
Primary Publication: Horowitz and Oshima 2004: 36 (copy, p. 39)
Date: uncertain

This rectangular tablet includes what appear to be scribal drawings, doodles, and erasures of actual cuneiform signs. Most prominent is the drawing of an arrow, perhaps even the "Arrow" constellation ^{mul}KAK.SI.SÁ = *šūkudu* (Sirius) on the reverse. A nearly identical drawing of the constellation is preserved on the Neo-Assyrian planisphere K.8538 (= CT 33 10; Koch 1989: 56).[11]

10. For the problem of Gezer 5$^{?}$, see above.

11. Compare also the triangular-type figure placed across from the arrow on Fi. 13, with the triangles that form parts of ^{mul}IKU = *ikû*, "The Field" (Pegasus), in K.8538.

Tel Hadid

1. Neo-Assyrian Administrative Document
2. Neo-Assyrian Administrative Document

The editions of Tel Hadid 1–2 below are based on new copies and collations by P. Zilberg and may be used with confidence. The editions in the first edition of *Cuneiform in Canaan* were based on the edition and photographs provided in Na'aman and Zadok 2000. These older editions must now be viewed as preliminary, but can be used for comparison purposes when reading the photographs. The historical analysis offered in Na'aman and Zadok 2000 remains an important contribution to our understanding of the context of the Neo-Assyrian period administrative documents in the Cuneiform in Canaan corpus.

TEL HADID 1: NEO-ASSYRIAN ADMINISTRATIVE DOCUMENT

Basics: Clay tablet; 8 × 3.75 cm; copy, p. 242
Reg. No.: Tel Hadid G-117/95 (present location: Israel Museum)
Primary Publication: Na'aman and Zadok 2000: 159–69 (photo, pp. 164, 166; copy, pp. 165, 167)
Studies: Stern 2001: 16; Finkelstein 2002: 286; Hallo 2002: 262; Galil 2001; Cogan 2013a: 21–23
Date: Neo-Assyrian, 698 BCE;[1] see Na'aman and Zadok 2000: 159

Na'aman and Zadok restore Tel Hadid 1 as a land sale on the basis of a restoration *ár*$^{?}$-*šú*$^{?}$ in line 8 (Na'aman and Zadok 2000: 162).

Edition	**Translation**
Obverse	
1 ⸢*ṣu-pur*⸣ [^{m}× × . . .	The fingernail of [PN . . .

1. The *limmu* of *Šulmu-šarri*, left edge 1; see Millard 1994: 122.

2	⌜A⌝ ^{m}[×]-*ši*-×-[. . .	the son of P[N . . .
3	⌜$^{lú?}$⌝×-[. . .	the . [. . .
4	*ṣu-pur* ^{m}[. . .	The fingernail of P[N . . .
5	*ṣu-pur* ^{m}*A*-⌜*tar-su*$^{?}$⌝- [. . .	The fingernail of Attar-. [. . .
6	*ṣu-pur* ^{m}*A*-⌜*a*⌝-*še-eb-š*[*i* . . .	The fingernail of Aya-šebš[i . . .
7	PAP 4 <LÚ>.MEŠ-*e* EN [. . .	Total, 4 men *owner*[*s of the field*$^{?}$ *being sold*]

8	[É × ×] ANŠE × ŠÚ [. . .	[An estate of . .] hectare(s) . . [. . .
9	[. .] A. ŠÀ [. . .	[. .] field [. . .
10	⌜*ú*⌝-[*pi*]*š-ma* ^{md}KU.[EN.PAP]	Marduk-[bela-uṣur] ex[ec]uted (an agreement)
11	TA *pa-an* LÚ.MEŠ-*e* [*annûte*]	with [these] men
12	*ina líb-bi* 1 MA.NA [KÙ.BABBAR]	in exchange for 1 mina of [silver]
13	LUGAL *il-qe kas-p*[*u*]	according to the royal (mina), he has received, the silve[r]
14	*ga-mur ta-di*[*n* A.ŠÁ$^{?}$]	pai[d in full. *The field*]

Lower Edge

15	*šu-a-te zar-p*[*i laqi*]	in question was legal[ly acquired]
16	*tu-a-ru de-n*[*u*]	Any withdrawal, lawsu[it]

Reverse

1	DUG$_4$.DUG$_4$ *la*-⌜*áš*⌝-[*šu*]	or litigation can no longer occ[ur.]
2	*man-nu ša ina ur-ki* [*ina matēma*]	Whoever in the future, [whenever,]
3	*lu-u* LÚ.MEŠ-*e an*-[*nu-te*]	be it th[ese] me[n,]
4	*lu-u* DUMU.MEŠ-*šú-nu l*[*u-u mammanušunu*]	or their son[s], o[r anyone else related to them,]
5	*ša de-ni* DUG$_4$.[DUG$_4$]	(should any of them) a lawsuit or litig[ation]
6	TA ^{md}KU.EN.[PAP]	against Markuk-bela-[uṣur]
7	*ù* DUMU.MEŠ-*šú* [*mammanušu*]	or his sons, [or anyone else related to him,]
8	*ub-ta-u*-⌜*ni*⌝	seek to bring;
9	*kas-pi a-na* 10-MEŠ-[*te ana bēlīšu itarra*]	[he shall return] tenfold the silver [to its owner].
10	*a-na de-ni-šú* [*idabbubma lā ilaqqe*]	[He may offer a declaration] in regard to his lawsuit, [but he will not succeed in his claim]

11	IGI ^{m}*Za-za-ku* L[Ú × ×]	Witness: Zazakku the . [. . .]
12	IGI ^{md}UTU.NUM[UN- . . .]	Witness: Šamaš-ze[ra?- . . .]

13	IGI ^{md}UTU.PAP. [. . .	Witness: Šamaš-aha-[. . .]
14	IGI ^{m}*Le-še-r*[*u* . . .	Witness: Lešer[u . . .
15	EN LÚ [. . .	the owner of . [. . .
16	[I]GI ^{m}*Na-di-n*[*u* . . .	[Wi]tness Nadin[u- . . .
17	[IGI] $^{m⌜}$*Ṣil*-LUGAL$^{?⌝}$	[Witness] Ṣil$^{?}$-šarri$^{?}$ [. . .

Upper Edge

18	[IGI] $^{⌜m⌝}$× × [×]	[Witness] . . [.]
19	× × × [. . .	. . . [. . .

Left Edge

1	$^{i[t]i}$APIN UD.24.KÁM *lim-me* ^{m}DI-*mu*-MAN	Date: the 24th of Arahsamnu, the eponym year of Šulmu-šarri

Commentary

Line 5

Perhaps Attār-qāmu or Attār-sūrī (PNAE 236).

Line 7

The traces at the beginning of the line might perhaps allow for a reconstruction LÚ.MEŠ. We see more or less what is copied in Na'aman and Zadok 2000: 165, which fits better just the presence of the MEŠ sign.

TEL HADID 2: NEO-ASSYRIAN ADMINISTRATIVE DOCUMENT

Basics: Clay tablet; 4.5 × 3.2 cm; copy, p. 242
Reg. No.: Tel Hadid G-1696 (present location: Israel Museum)
Primary Publication: Na'aman and Zadok 2000: 169–71 (photo, pp. 172–73)
Studies: Finkelstein 2002: 286; Hallo 2002: 263; Galil 2001; Weippert 2010: 314 (Text 166); Cogan 2013a: 23–24 (photo of obv.)
Date: Neo-Assyrian, 664 BCE;[2] see Na'aman and Zadok 2000: 171
Language: Akkadian
Find Information: Na'aman and Zadok 2000: 159

	Edition	**Translation**
	Obverse	
1	1 MA.NA 6 GÍN [KÙ.BABBAR]	1 mina, 6 shekels [of silver]
2	*ša* ^{m}*Ki*-[. . .	belonging to P[N . . .
3	*ina* IGI ^{m}PAP-*ab-be* [. . .	before Ah-abbe (Ahab)

2. The *limmu* of *Šarru-lū-dāri*, rev. 7 (upper edge); see Millard 1994:121.

4	*ku-um ru-bé-e ša* KÙ.BABBAR	In lieu of interest on the silver,
5	^{f}*Ḫa-am-ma-a-a* MUNUS-*šú*	Hammaya, his wife
6	^{f}*Mu-na-ḫi-ma-a* NIN-*su*	(and) Munahima, his sister
7	*a-na šá-par-te kam-mu-sa*	must stay as a pledge.
8	*ina* ^{iti}IZI KÙ.BABBAR SUM-*an*	By the month of Ab he must pay over the silver.

Lower Edge

9	*šum-ma la id-din*	If he has not paid,
10	KÙ.BABBAR *a-na* 3-*su-šú*	the silver, by one third

Reverse

1	*i-rab-bi*	will accrue interest.
2	IGI ^{m}*Si-li-mu*	Witness: Silimu
3	IGI ^{m}GISSU.EN	Witness: Ṣil-Bel
4	I[GI ^{m}*Šá*]*-áš-ma-a-a*	Wi[tness: Ša]šmaya
5	$^{\ulcorner\text{lú}\urcorner}$*mu-ṣur-a-a*	the Egyptian
6	IGI ^{m}*Pa-di-i*	Witness: Padi

Upper Edge

7	^{iti}GU$_4$ UD.16.KAM	Date: The 16th of Iyar
8	*lim-mu* MAN-*lu-dà-ri*	the eponym year of Šarru-lu-dari

Hazor

1. Inscribed Vessel
2. Liver Model Fragment A
3. Liver Model Fragment B
4. Handle of Jug with Two Seal Impressions
5. Court Record
6. School Tablet with Excerpt from Urra = *ḫubullu*
7. Middle Bronze Age Administrative Document
8. Middle Bronze Age Letter Fragment
9. Prism Fragment: Combined Multiplication Table
10. Late Bronze Age Letter
11. Late Bronze Age Administrative Document
12. Middle Bronze Age Letter
13. Fragment of Stone Bowl (*agannu*)
14. Small Administrative Docket
15. Letter Fragment
16. Small Administrative Docket
17. Liver Model
18. Fragments from a Law Collection

The relatively large number and diverse genres of cuneiform finds from Hazor reflect the city's position as the southwesternmost city in the international system of city-states of the Middle Bronze Age, which ranged from Iran to the Mediterranean and included sites such as Qatna, Mari, and Hammurabi's Babylon. Hazor is mentioned numerous times in Mari materials,[1] and is the only city in Canaan to be named in Mesopotamian omens and geographical lists (Horowitz 2000: 27). In the Late Bronze Age, Hazor's importance diminished somewhat, but the city remained one of the most important cities in northern Canaan, and an important scribal center.

The Hazor excavations have yielded three new texts since our 2006 edition, here listed as Hazor 16–18. Hazor 15 was already known by the time of the volume's publication, but had been unearthed too close to the time of publication to allow for an edition to be included. This edition now appears below. In addition, there have been a number of summary articles about the Hazor excavations and Hazor texts, including Horowitz and Oshima 2010b and Horowitz 2012. Further discussion of the Hazor tablets in Hebrew, with photographs and Hebrew editions of selected texts from the Middle Bronze Age, is available in Hebrew in Ben-Tor 2016: 62–71.[2]

1. For a summary, see Bonechi 1992; note the mention of Mari and Ekallatum in the Middle Bronze Age letter fragment Hazor 12:20', 22', 23'. Such documentation for the Mari-Hazor trade at the Hazor end renders the argument in Astour 1991 that Hazor of the Mari texts is never Hazor in the Galilee untenable.

2. A photograph of Hazor 16 is available on Ben-Tor 2016: 107. The English version of this book is expected soon.

HAZOR 1: INSCRIBED VESSEL

Basics: Clay; vessel's dimensions: 43 × 32 cm; inscription's dimensions: 2.5 × 22.5 cm; copy, p. 210
Reg. Nos.: IAA 1967-1187, C 339/1 (present location: Israel Antiquities Authority)
Primary Publication: Artzi and Malamat *apud* Yadin et al. 1960: 115–17 (copy, p. 117; photo and copy, pl. 180)[3]
Studies: Yadin 1957: 122; Albright 1960: 38; Malamat 1960: 18; Galling 1968: 13 A 3a; Yadin 1972: 31 (photo, pl. 10a); Yadin 1975: 40 (photo and copy); Greenfield and Shaffer 1983: 115, n. to l. 28; Edzard 1985: 251; Malamat 1989: 55; *NEAEHL*: 595
Date: Old Babylonian period, Middle Bronze Age
Language: Akkadian PN
Find Information: See Artzi and Malamat *apud* Yadin et al. 1960: 115

The vessel is crudely incised with what is most likely the PN *Išme-Addu* below the forked lightning symbol of Addu, the Canaanite storm god. The forked-lightning symbol was cut deeply into the surface of the vessel while it was still wet. In contrast, the cuneiform signs of the PN are formed from shallow lines that appear to have been etched into the vessel's surface after it had already hardened, rather than traditional cuneiform strokes inscribed with a head and tail. The IM, for example, is scratched into the surface so poorly that it is nearly unrecognizable even though it includes parts of most of the elements of the sign.

Edition		**Translation**
1	^{m}*I*[*š*]-*me*-^{d}IM$^{!}$	Išme-Addu (Addu-Has-Heard)

Commentary

The reading of the PN *Išme-Addu* was first proposed by W. Albright in Yadin 1957: 122.

HAZOR 2–3: LIVER MODEL FRAGMENTS

Hazor 2 Basics: Liver model fragment A; 8 × 5.8 × 0.6 cm;[4] copy, p. 210; photos, p. 227
Hazor 2 Reg. No.: Israel Museum 1967-1188
Hazor 3 Basics: Liver model fragment B; 7 × 4.5 × 1.6 cm; copy, p. 211; photos, p. 228
Hazor 3 Reg. No.: Israel Museum 1967-1189
Primary Publication: Landsberger and Tadmor 1964 (copy, pp. 206–7, figs. 1–2)

3. Hebrew version: Yadin et al. 1959: 108–9 (copy, p. 109; copy and photo, pl. 80).
4. The distance from the surface of the reverse to the highest protruding feature on the obverse is approximately 2.0 cm.

Studies: Yadin et al. 1961a: pl. 315, no. 1 (photo); Galling 1968: A 13 3b; Yadin 1972: 82–83 (photo, pl. 10a); Anbar and Na'aman 1986: 10; Malamat 1989: 55–56 (photo, pl. VIIIb); Demsky 1990: 164; Arnaud 1998: 32; Dalley 1998: 59 (copy); Rainey 1999: 155*; Goren 2000: 36–37; Van der Toorn 2000: 98, 105; Goren et al. 2004: 229; *NEAEHL*: 598 (photo); Horowitz, Oshima, and Winitzer 2010: 136; Maul 2013: (Hazor 2 only) 222 (photo), 340; Cohen 2008: 85

Date: Old Babylonian period; late Middle Bronze Age

Language: Akkadian

Find Information: See Landsberger and Tadmor 1964: 217[5]

The two fragments of liver models Hazor 2–3 were discovered together and have been studied together as a pair. Both preserve apodoses of omens without written protases, but it is clear that the apodoses relate to features present on the models. Such liver models could have been used for educational purposes, either in the general training of scribes or, more specifically, in the training of diviners (*bārû*). In this context, note Beth Shean 1, the cylinder seal that belonged to *Ma-a-nu-um*, "the diviner." The date of the two fragments is uncertain. Consistent use of mimmation with nouns, as well as the verbal system, point to an Old Babylonian / Middle Bronze Age date, but some of the sign forms seem closer to those of the Middle Babylonian / Late Bronze Age.[6] Therefore, we concur with the proposal by Tadmor and Landsberger 1964: 214 that the tablets should be dated "to the latest OB period," i.e., to a time later than the period of the Mari-Hazor contacts, but before the time of the Taanach tablets and the Amarna archives. It seems to us that the two fragments are written in different hands and therefore do not belong to a common original.[7] Three noninscribed fragments of liver models from Hazor have also been recovered (see Landsberger and Tadmor 1964: 208, no. 16). More recently a third fragment of an inscribed liver model was recovered at Hazor. This fragment is presented below as Hazor 17.

Edition of Hazor 2		**Translation**
a)	LUGAL-*um* LUGAL *ú-ka-na-aš*	A king will subjugate a king.
b)	LÚ.KÚR *a-na ma-ti-ia i-t*[*e-bi*]	An enemy will ri[se] against my land
c)	× × AN *ḫa-di/ṭi-tum* KI-*tum*	Joyful/sinful . . . of a god on earth.
d)	*ta-ia-a-r*[*a*]*-at* ⸢DINGIR⸣ *a-na* LÚ	A god's forgive[n]ess for a man.
e)	LÚ.Ì[R] *be-el-šu i-ba-ar*	A slav[e] will rebel against his master.

5. With a note by Y. Yadin, also with a bibliography of preliminary study of the two fragments before the 1964 edition.

6. Note in particular the A sign of Hazor 2 b; and the KI sign in Hazor 2 c.

7. For attempts to reconstruct the two fragments as part of a common original, see Landsberger and Tadmor 1964: 208–9.

Edition of Hazor 3		Translation	
f)			
1	EŠ$_{4}$.TÁR *ma-tam*	1–2	Ištar will devour the land.
2	*i-ka-al*		
3	^{d}NÉ.ERI$_{11}$.GAL	3–4	Nergal will give out a name.
4	*šu-ma-am id*$^{!}$*-dan*$^{!}$		
g)			
1	URU DINGIR.MEŠ-*ša i-tu-ru-ni*		The city, its gods will return there.

Commentary

Hazor 2b

An apodosis with reference to the first person would be most unusual, but note a parallel use of the first person in Hazor 17 b–c.[8]

Hazor 2c

Fem. adjective, either *hadītum* from *hadû*, "to be joyful," or *haṭītum* from *haṭû*, "to sin, commit a crime."

Hazor 2d

Cf. the use of *târu* in Hazor 3g below.

Hazor 3f

Note the apparent Assyrian form *iddan* rather than Babylonian *inaddin*. This might in fact be the present-future form in the local language (cf. Hazor 3g, below).

Hazor 3g

Note the feminine possessive pronoun with URU, "city," although Akkadian *ālu* is normally grammatically masculine. We presume that the writer here was influenced by a West-Semitic dialect, in which the word for "city" was feminine, as in Hebrew (for this phenomenon, see Rainey 1996: I, 126–29).

HAZOR 4: HANDLE OF JUG WITH TWO SEAL IMPRESSIONS[9]

Basics: Clay jug handle with seal impressions; copy, p. 211; photo, p. 228
Reg. Nos.: IAA 1995-1423, Hazor 1306 (present location: Hazor Museum, Kibbutz Ayelet Hashachar)

8. Horowitz, Oshima, and Winitzer 2010: 136. See also Cohen 2008: 85.
9. We express our thanks to Hussein Alhaib (Hazor Museum) for his help in studying the object.

Primary Publication: Yadin et al. 1961a: pl. 316, 3–4 (3 = seal impression A; 4 = seal impression B);[10] Horowitz and Oshima 2005: photo and copy, p. 14
Studies: Galling 1968: 13 A 3c; Horowitz and Oshima 2008: 99–103 (copy and photo, p. 103)
Date: Uncertain
Language: Akkadian
Find Information: See Yadin et al. 1961a, pl. 316

Two impressions of a single stamp seal—impressions A and B—are preserved on the handle of the jug.

Seal impression A: diameter 2.7 cm
Seal impression B: diameter 2.3 cm

The original seal was round (diameter: 2.7 cm). Seal impression B is slightly distorted in terms of size and shape due to the curvature of the jug handle. The impression consists of four signs, arranged symmetrically in a circle, approximately 90° from one another, with the foot of each sign pointing downwards towards the circle. Three of the signs are well preserved, but the fourth is almost entirely missing. At present, it cannot be determined which of the signs is the first in the sequence of four. We propose the following reading:

Edition

KIŠIB *Ṭa-ba*-LUGAL

Commentary

This may be a name of the type *Ṭaba-milku* or *Ṭaba-šarru.*

HAZOR 5: COURT RECORD

Basics: Clay tablet; 4.7 × 5.2 × 2.5 cm; copy, p. 211; photos, p. 228
Reg. No.: Israel Museum 75–240
Primary Publication: Hallo and Tadmor 1977 (photo, pl. 1; copy, p. 3)[11]
Studies: Edzard 1985: 251; Anbar and Na'aman 1986: 8–10; Malamat 1989: 56; Horowitz and Shaffer 1992a: 22, n. 4; Demsky 1990: 163; Na'aman 1994: 176; Zadok 1996: 104; Rainey 1999: 154*; Goren 2000: 36; Rothenbusch 2000: 483–85; Van der Toorn 2000: 98; Hallo 2002: 269–70; Na'aman 2004: 92; Hess 2007: 154
Date: Old Babylonian period; late Middle Bronze Age

10. For Hebrew version, see Yadin et al. 1961b: pl. 316, 3–4.
11. See p. 2, n. 8a for additional readings by A. Shaffer.

Language: Akkadian
Find Information: Found in 1962 by a visitor to Tel Hazor; see Hallo and Tadmor 1977: 2, n. 7

The tablet below records the verdict of a lawsuit regarding an estate and agricultural land at Hazor and agricultural land at another site. The case comes before the king, and the ruling is in the defendant's favor. The tablet closes with a penalty clause and a list of witnesses. The hand and language of the tablet are Old Babylonian, with what appear to be some local modifications: the presence of a peripheral verbal form in line 7, the unexpected use of Ú for the conjunction "and," and inconsistent use of mimmation. There are four explicit examples of mimmation, but at least one example (É-*ti* = *bīti* in line 4) in which mimmation appears to be dropped.

Edition

Obverse

1 ^{m}DUMU-*Ḫa-nu-ta* KI$^{!}$ ^{m}*Ir-pa-*⌜*a*⌝*-du*
2 *ú* ^{m}*Su-um-Ḫa-nu-ta* TUR.ḪA *šal-šu*
3 *di-nam it-ti* ^{mf}*Su-mu-la*-DINGIR-*lum*$^{!}$
4 *ig-ru-ú a-na* É-*ti ú* ^{giš}KIRI$_{6}$
5 *i+na* URU *Ḫa-ṣú-*⌜*ra*⌝ *ú* ^{giš}KIRI$_{6}$ ⌜*i+na*⌝
6 URU *Gi-la-di-ma a-na pa-ni* LUGAL
7 ⌜*i*⌝*-ri-bu* LUGAL *di-na* ^{mf}*Su-mu-la*-DINGIR-*lum*
8 ⌜*i*⌝-[*din*] ⌜*ú*⌝*-ra-am še-ra-am ša di-na-am*
9 [*i-ge-er*]*-ru 2 me-át* KÙ.BABBAR *ip-pá-*⌜*al*⌝
10 [IGI × × DUM]U $^{m!}$*Ya*$^{!}$*-aḫ-zi-ra-d*[*a* × (×)]
11 *traces*

Reverse

1' *traces*
2' ^{m}*A*]*d-du-ZI-*× DUMU$^{?}$ [^{m}]*Ab-di-*⌜*ia*⌝*-du*
3' . . .]-×*-ga*$^{?}$*-ḫa-ba*

Right Edge

1' . . .] LÚ.⌜TUR$^{?}$⌝.[M]EŠ

Translation

Obverse

1 Bin-Hanuta with Irpadu
2 and Sum-Hanuta, three junior attendants,
3 a lawsuit against Sumulailum
4 initiated in regard to a home and a garden
5 in the city of Hazor, and a garden in

6 the city of Gilead$^{?}$. Before the king,
7 they came in. The king (in favor of) the case of Samulailum
8 rend[ered] judgment. Hereafter should anyone (another) lawsuit
9 [initiat]e, he will make a supplementary payment of 200 (shekels) of silver.
10 [Witness:. .the so]n of Yahzirad[a, the$^{?}$.]
11 *traces*

Reverse

1' *traces*
2' . . .] PN the son$^{?}$ of Abdiyadu
3' . . . P]N

Right Edge

1' . . .] *junior attendants*

Commentary

Obverse, line 1

What remains after an erasure is something between Ù and KI, but closer to KI (= *itti*), "with." No conjunction or preposition is necessary to connect the first and second personal names in a chain of three; hence the sign here may indicate a special relationship between PN_1 and PN_2. Note the presence of the conjunction *ú* in the expected place between PN_2 and PN_3 at the beginning of line 2.

Lines 1–2

We take *Ha-nu-ta* in the two names to be for the goddess Anat, following the proposal of Hallo and Tadmor 1977: 4–5, who bring into evidence the writing Beit Anot in Joshua 15:59.[12] We cannot explain the *a*-vowel written at the end of the name, but compare writings with vowels after *t* in the name *A-na-ti* collected in Hess 1993: 34–35. The second name, *Irpa-Addu*, may also occur in the letter fragment Hazor 8:2: ^{m}*Ir-p*[*a* . . .

Line 2

Our examination of the second half of the line yields the reading TUR.HA *šal-šu*, which we take to refer to three (LÚ.)TUR = *ṣuhāru*, "junior attendants," a class of people often attested to in the cuneiform west.[13] Here ḪA would seem to be best explained as a syllabic writing for the plural/collective indicator ḪI.A = ḪÁ, although we admit that we can find no parallels for a plural written TUR.ḪÁ; syllabic writings and TUR.MEŠ are the norm, as may be the case on the right edge of

12. Na'aman 1994: 176 suggests that Hanuta is Hurrian.

13. See Horowitz 2000: 21; Na'aman 2004. Junior in this context often indicates a young age, but can also refer to the relatively low status of the *ṣuhāru*, e.g., junior vs. senior accountant.

our tablet.[14] Emendation, however, may provide a better understanding of the line. See A. Shaffer in Hallo and Tadmor 1977: 6, n. 24: DUMU.SAL.MEŠ-*šu*, "his (Sumhanuta's) daughters"; Anbar and Na'aman 1986: 10: DUMU.MEŠ <DUMU.>SAL-*šu*, "(his) sons and his daughter."[15]

Line 5

Hallo and Tadmor 1977: 9 make note of "the curious form of the construct state *di-na* (for expected *di-in*)."

Line 6

We take *Gi-la-di-ma* to be a place-name + enclitic *ma*. An identification with biblical Gilead is not impossible, despite the objections raised in Hallo and Tadmor 1977: 8 that the name of Gilead should be written with an indication of ע. This presupposes that the guttural would have necessarily been indicated in the Akkadian rendering of the name. This assumes, however, a higher level of scribal competence than seen elsewhere on this tablet. Cf. the inconsistent use of mimmation, the problems in line 2, and the traces of what appear to be extraneous signs on the reverse.

Line 7

For further examples of *erēbu* with theme-vowel *e/i*, rather than *u* in the west, see Rainey 1999: 154*.

Reverse, line 2′

We understand the name to be a phonetic rendering of Abdi-Addu, "the Servant of Addu." Cf. Taanach 7 ii 12: ^{m}ÌR-^{d}I[M . . .

HAZOR 6: SCHOOL TABLET WITH EXCERPT FROM URRA = *ḪUBULLU*

Basics: Clay tablet; 4.8 × 4.2 cm (private collection);[16] copy, p. 212; photos, p. 229
Primary Publication: Tadmor 1977 (photo, pl. 13)
Studies: Galling 1968: 13 A 3d; Edzard 1985: 251; Malamat 1989: 56; Demsky 1990: 162; Van der Toorn 2000: 98, 105–6; Von Dassow 2004: 669, 672
Date: Middle Babylonian period; Late Bronze Age
Language: Sumerian
Find Information: Surface find, see Tadmor 1977: 98, n. 1; Oded Golan: private communication

14. For a rare example of ḪÁ with persons, see LUGAL.ḪÁ in EA 60:14.

15. Another possibility, albeit a more remote one, is that ḪÁ here is a sort of phonetic complement relating to Ḫ/ḪA in *ṣuhāru*, which is meant to indicate this word and not simply TUR/DUMU = *māru*. Cf. the writings TUR.RA and TUR.RI cited for *ṣuhāru* in the dictionaries.

16. We thank Mr. Oded Golan (Tel Aviv) for providing us with access to the tablet.

This tablet was discovered by Oded Golan when, as a lad, he visited Tel Hazor with his family. Golan brought the tablet to Prof. Y. Yadin in Jerusalem, who passed the tablet on to Professor H. Tadmor for publication. Both sides of the fragment are flat and inscribed; hence, it is impossible to determine which side is the obverse and which is the reverse. Side A, which seems to belong to the upper left corner of the original tablet, preserves a few lines of a western parallel to Urra = *ḫubullu* of the type already known from Ugarit and Emar. Hence, we propose a Middle Babylonian / Late Bronze date for our tablet. Side B is nearly illegible, but does not seem to continue the subject matter from side A. This format would seem to identify the text as a school tablet.

	Edition	**Translation**
	Side A, col i	
1	KI.LAM.gu.la	High price
2	KI.LAM.tur.ra	Small price
3	KI.LAM.kalag.g[a]	Strong price
4	KI.LAM.sig$_5$.[ga]	Good price
5	KI.LAM.ḫul.[la]	Bad price
6	˹KI˺.[LAM] × [×]	[. . .] pr[ice]

Side B

1' *Traces from what appears to be the last line*

Commentary

Side A

The present fragment preserves part of a section of Sumerian entries with a piece of vertical ruling preserved to the right of the lines 1'–2'. The surviving lines correspond to entries in canonical Urra II 130–35, as edited in *MSL* 5 61–62, as well as corresponding sections of parallels to Urra from Emar (Sumerian-Akkadian) and Ugarit (Sumerian-Hurrian). The Hazor fragment could be from a Sumerian-only forerunner to Urra on one column, or from a bilingual, or perhaps even trilingual, forerunner written over multiple subcolumns, for which we now have only part of the Sumerian. The shape and thickness of the fragment does not seem to allow for more than three subcolumns.

Parallels to Hazor 6

	Hazor 6	Urra II	Emar[a]	Ugarit[b]
1.	KI.LAM.gu.la	130	110'	ii 18
2.	KI.LAM.tur.ra	131	111'	ii 19
3.	KI.LAM.kala.g[a]	135	115'	ii 23
4.	KI.LAM.sig$_5$.[ga]	132	113'	—
5.	KI.LAM.hul.[la]	—	—	—

[a]Emar 542: 109'–17'.

[b]Thureau-Dangin 1931: 238–39, with photo following p. 244 and copy on pl. 50 following p. 252. For the identification of the second language as Hurrian, see Tadmor 1977: 100.

Lines 1–6

KI.LAM, with the Sumerian reading *ganba*, is equivalent to Akkadian *mahīru*.

Line 5

KI.LAM.hul.la is equivalent to *MSL* V 61, Urra II 133: KI.LAM nu.sig$_5$.ga, *MSL* V 62, Urra II 139: KI.LAM nu.dùg.ga, “not a good price.”

HAZOR 7: MIDDLE BRONZE AGE ADMINISTRATIVE DOCUMENT

Basics: Clay tablet; 4 × 3 × 0.8 cm; copy, p. 212; photos, p. 229
Reg. No.: IAA 1997-3303 (present location: Israel Museum)
Primary Publication: Horowitz and Shaffer 1992a (photo and copy, pp. 24–25);[17] 1992b: 167
Studies: Ben-Tor 1992a; Zadok 1996: 104–5; Rainey 1999: 155*; Goren 2000: 35; Van der Toorn 2000: 98; Charpin 2007: 188; Horowitz 2012: 34 (photo top left).
Date: Old Babylonian period; Middle Bronze Age
Language: Presumably Akkadian when complete, but only personal names, numerals, and Sumerograms are preserved
Find Information: See Ben-Tor 1992a: 19

Hazor 7 preserves the middle portion of an economic document and lists relatively small payments of 1/2 and 1/3 shekel, as well as names of individuals. Thus, an identification as a disbursement tablet of some sort—for example, a payroll list—seems probable.

Edition

Obverse

1' ⸢1/2⸣ G[ÍN KÙ.BABBAR . . .
2' 1/2 GÍN ⸢KÙ.BABBAR⸣ [. . .
3' ⸢1/2⸣ GÍN KÙ.⸢BABBAR⸣ × × [. . .
4' ⸢1/2⸣ [G]ÍN KÙ.BABBAR *I-lu-⸢ka-a-num⸣*
5' ⸢1/2⸣ GÍN KÙ.BABBAR *Iš-me-Èl*
6' 1/2 GÍN KÙ.BABBAR *Ia-aḫ-tuq-*^{d}IM
7' 1/2 ⸢GÍN⸣ KÙ.BABBAR *Ḫi-in-ni-Èl*
8' 1/2 GÍN KÙ.BABBAR *Iš-ni-du*
9' 1/2 GÍN KÙ.BABBAR *Sí-ib-li-du*
10' ⸢1/2⸣ [G]ÍN KÙ.BABBAR *Iš-pu-uṭ-*^{d}IM
11' [1/2 G]ÍN KÙ.BABBAR [*Ḫ*]*a-ab-da-du*

17. A photograph of the reverse is also available in Rabinovich and Silberman 1990: 54.

Lower Edge

1 1/2 GÍN KÙ.BABBAR *A-bi-ra-pí*
2 1/3 GÍN KÙ.BABBAR *Ia-an-ṣur-*^{d}IM

Reverse

1 1/3 GÍN KÙ.BABBAR *In-te-du* LÚ.SIMUG
2 1/3 GÍN KÙ.BABBAR *In-te-du-*^{d}IM$^{!}$
3 1/3 GÍN KÙ.BABBAR *Ib-lu-ṭà-du*
4 1/3 GÍN KÙ.BABBAR *A-bi-*30
5 1/3 GÍN KÙ.BABBAR *Šu-mu-pa-aḫ*
6 1/3 GÍN KÙ.BABBAR *Ib-lu-uṭ-Èl*
7 1/3 GÍN KÙ.BABBAR *Bu-nu-ma-nu*
8 1/3 GÍN KÙ.BABBAR *Ia-da-⸢da⸣*
9 ⸢1/3⸣ [GÍN] ⸢KÙ⸣.[BABBA]R × [. . .

Right Edge

1 . . . IGI.×.G]ÁL ^{m}*Ḫa-ba-du*

Left Edge

Numerals

Translation

Obverse

1' 1/2 shekel silver, PN]
2' 1/2 shekel silver, [PN]
3' 1/2 shekel silver, P[N]
4' 1/2 [sh]ekel silver, Ilu-kayyanum
5' 1/2 shekel silver, Išme-El
6' 1/2 shekel silver, Yahtuq-Addu
7' 1/2 shekel silver, Hinni-El
8' 1/2 shekel silver, Išnidu
9' 1/2 shekel silver, Siblidu
10' 1/2 shekel silver, Išpuṭ-Addu
11' 1/2 shekel silver, [H]abdadu

Lower Edge

1 1/2 shekel silver, Abi-rapi
2 1/3 shekel silver, Yanṣur-Addu

Reverse

1 [1]/3 shekel of silver, Intedu, the smith
2 1/3 shekel of silver, Intedu-Addu

3 1/3 shekel of silver, Ibluṭadu
4 1/3 shekel of silver, Abi-Erah
5 1/3 shekel of silver, Šumupah
6 1/3 shekel of silver, Ibluṭ-El
7 1/3 shekel of silver, Bunumanu
8 1/3 shekel of silver, Yadada
9 1/3 [shekel] of si[lve]r, . [. . .

Right Edge

1 . .] . (a fractional number) Habbadu

Left Edge

Numerals

Commentary

The personal names in Hazor 7 are discussed in detail in Horowitz and Shaffer 1992a: 26–32 with some corrections in 1992b. The name of the storm god ^{d}IM is read Addu here on the basis of the syllabically written names in lines 8'–9', 11', and rev. 3. In lines 5', 7', and rev. 6 we take DINGIR to be for the name of the western god El (*Él*), but readings *ìl*, *ilum*, *ila*, etc. are also possible. Note the peripheral form *išpuṭ* instead of the standard *išpiṭ* in line 10'.

Left Edge

For the numerals on the left edge, see Horowitz and Shaffer 1992a: 32. To the list in n. 32, add Dalley 1991: nos. 62, 163, 228.

HAZOR 8: MIDDLE BRONZE AGE LETTER FRAGMENT

Basics: Clay tablet; 3 × 2.7 × 0.4 cm; copy, p. 213; photo, p. 230
Reg. No.: IAA 1997-3304 (present location: Israel Museum)
Primary Publication: Horowitz and Shaffer 1992b: 165–66 (photo and copy, p. 165)
Studies: Zadok 1996: 104–5; Rainey 1999: 155*; Goren 2000: 35–36; Van der Toorn 2000: 98; Na'aman 2004: 92; Horowitz 2012: 34 (photo at bottom).
Date: Old Babylonian period; Middle Bronze Age
Language: Akkadian
Find Information: See Ben-Tor 1992b: 259–60

	Edition	Translation
1	*a-na Ib-ni-*[. . .	To Ibni-[. . .
2	*um-ma* ^{m}*Ir-p*[*a-* . . .	Message of Irp[a- . . .
3	*aš-šum* SAL.TUR *i-na qa-a*[*t* . . .	Regarding bringing the young woman
4	*ta-re-e-em* × [. . .	in the car[e of . . .

5	DIŠ SAL ^{m}*A-b*[*a-* . . .	one woman, Ab[a- . . .
6	*a-wa-tim ú-pa-*[*ar-ri-ik* . . .	Rai[sed] objections [. . .
7	⸢*um*⸣*-ma* ⸢*ši*⸣*-i-ma a-a-di* × [. . .	Thus she (said): "Until . [. . .
8	*iq-bi-am* [. . .	She said [. . .
9	× × × × ⸢*ŠI*⸣ [. . .	. . . . . [. . .

Commentary

The sign forms are without question good Old Babylonian, and the tablet is beautifully written and executed. Thus, Hazor 8 may in fact be from the royal archives of Hazor, as one is sorely tempted to restore lines 1–2 as follows: *a-na Ib-ni-*[^{d}*Addu* LUGAL *bēlīa*], *um-ma* ^{m}*Ir-p*[*a-*(*a*)*-du* ÌR-*ka*], "To Ibni-[Addu, the king, my lord] Message of Irp[adu, your slave]." Ibni-Addu, king of Hazor, is known from the Mari archives (see, e.g., Bonechi 1992), and ^{m}*Ir-pa-*⸢*a*⸣*-du* is one of the litigants who comes before an unnamed king of Hazor in the lawsuit Hazor 5. Thus, Hazor 5 and Hazor 8 could both be from the time of a King Ibni-Addu of Hazor.

Line 1

Note that *Ibni-*[. . . is written without PN determinative (DIŠ), while the PNs in lines 2 and 5 are written with such a determinative.

HAZOR 9: PRISM FRAGMENT: COMBINED MULTIPLICATION TABLE

Basics: Clay prism fragment; 4.9 × 2.6 × 2.2 cm; copy, p. 213; photos, p. 230
Reg. No.: IAA 1997-3306 (present location: Israel Museum)
Primary Publication: Horowitz 1997b (photo, pp. 192–94; copy, pp. 193–94); a photograph is also available in Rabinovich and Silberman 1998: 54
Studies: Goren 2000: 34–35; Van der Torrn 2000: 98, 106; Horowitz 2012: 34 (photo, top right)
Date: Old Babylonian period; Middle Bronze Age[18]
Language: Sumerian and numerals
Find Information: See Horowitz 1997b: 190, n.1

Hazor 9 preserves but a small portion of the first and last sides of a four-sided prism with a series of multiplication tables of the type now known as "combined multiplication tables."[19] The petrographic analysis of the tablet (Goren 2000: 34–35) indicates that the clay of the tablet is identical to that of EA 228, the letter of Abdi-Tirši of

18. This dating is established on the basis of the form of A in side 1, col. i 2–3 (see Horowitz 1997b: 191–92, n. 10) and the shared formula between Hazor 9 and *ARM* 9 299 (see below).

19. For an introduction to this type of text and general comments on the cuneiform mathematical tradition, see Horowitz 1997b: 190–91.

Hazor (see, earlier, Horowitz 1997b: 197). This suggests that the mathematical prism was prepared locally at Hazor.

	Edition		**Translation**	
	Prism side I col. I		***Base 10 equivalent (restored)***	
1	60-da 2/3 (šanabi)^{bi}-bi		60, 2/3 of it	
2	40.àm		is 40,	
3	šu.ri.a.bi 30 àm		1/2 of it is 30	
4	2	30	2 × 30	(= 60)
5	3	20	3 × 20	″
6	4	15	4 × 15	″
7	5	12	5 × 12	″
8	6	10	6 × 10	″
9	8	7,[30]	8 × 7 1/2	″
10	9	[6,40]	9 × 6 2/3	″
11	10	[6]	10 × 6	″
12	12	[5]	12 × 5	″
13	15	[4]	15 × 4	″
14	⸢16⸣	[3,45]	16 × 3 3/4	″

	Prism side I col. ii		***Base 10 equivalent (restored)***	
1	10 [	8,45]	10 (× 50)	= 500
2	11 [	9,10]	11 (× 50)	= 550
3	12 [	10]	12 (× 50)	= 600
4	1[3	10,50]	13 (× 50)	= 650
5	1[4	11,40]	14 (× 50)	= 700
6	15 [	12,30]	15 (× 50)	= 750
7	1[6	13,20]	16 (× 50)	= 800

	Prism side IV col. i′		***Base 10 equivalent (restored)***	
1	[1]	⸢1⸣,40	1 (× 1 2/3)	= 1 2/3
2	[2	3,2]0	2 (× 1 2/3	= 3 1/3

	Prism side IV col. ii′		***Base 10 equivalent (restored)***	
1	1	1,30	1 (× 1 1/2)	= 1 1/2
2	2	3	2 (× 1 1/2)	= 3
3	3	4.30	3 (× 1 1/2)	= 4 1/2
4	⸢4⸣	6	4 (× 1 1/2)	= 6
5	⸢5⸣	7,30	5 (× 1 1/2)	= 7 1/2
6	⸢6⸣	9	6 (× 1 1/2)	= 9
7	⸢7⸣	10,30	7 (× 1 1/2)	= 10 1/2
8	⸢8⸣	12	8 (× 1 1/2)	= 12
9	⸢9⸣	13,30$^{!}$ (*text 13,20*)	9 (× 1 1/2)	= 13 1/2

10	[10]	15	10 (× 1 1/2)	= 15
11	⸢11⸣	16,30	11 (× 1 1/2)	= 16 1/2
12	[12]	18	12 (× 1 1/2)	= 18
13	[13]	19,30	13 (× 1 1/2)	= 19 1/2
14	[14]	21	14 (× 1 1/2)	= 21
15	[15]	[2]2,30	15 (× 1 1/2)	= 22 1/2
16	[16]	⸢24⸣	16 (× 1 1/2)	= 24

Commentary

Side I, col. i', lines 1–3

This is a version of the standard introduction to reciprocal tables 60-da 2/3.bi 40.àm šu.ri.(a).bi 30.àm (see *RlA* 7: 545, § 5.2b). The extra BI in line 1 above (the first of the two BI signs) is a phonetic complement for the Sumerian reading of the fraction 2/3, *šanabi*, and is a feature shared by this Hazor reciprocal table and its Mari counterpart *ARM* 9 299:[20]

60-da.am 2/3 (šanabi)^{bi}.bi 40.à[m]
60, 2/3 of it is 40

Side IV, col. ii', line 9

Here there is a simple error of arithmetic. 9 × 1 1/2 = 13 1/2, and not 13 1/3 (13,20), as written on the tablet.

HAZOR 10: LATE BRONZE AGE LETTER

Basics: Clay tablet; 4.0 × 4.7 × 0.4 cm; copy, p. 213; photos, p. 231
Reg. No.: IAA 1997-3307, Hazor 16455 (present location: Institute of Archaeology, the Hebrew University of Jerusalem)
Primary Publication: Horowitz 2000: 16–25 (photo and copy, p. 18)
Studies: Goran 2000: 37, 41; Hess 2001; 2003: 40–41; Greenstein 2004; Na'aman 2004: 95–96; Goren et al. 2004: 230; Von Dassow 2004: 671
Date: Late Bronze Age
Language: Akkadian
Find Information: See Horowitz 2000: 16

Edition		**Translation**
Obverse		
1	*a-na* ^{m}*Pu-ra-at-pur-ta*	To Puratpurta
2	*qí-bí-ma*	say.

20. For further discussion of lines 1–3 and scribal contacts between Hazor and Mari, see Horowitz 1997b: 195.

3	*um-ma* ^{m}*Ad-du-ap*-⸢*di*$^{?}$⸣	Message of Addu'apdi$^{?}$:
4	DINGIR.MEŠ *ù* ^{d}UTU *šu-lum-ka*	May the Gods and the Sun (the King) ask after your well-being,
5	*šu-lum* É-*ka* DUMU.MEŠ-*ka*	the well-being of your house, your sons
6	KUR-ti_4-*ka li-iš-a-u*	(and) your land.
7	*at-ta ta-aš-tap-ra*	You have written
8	*a-na ia-ši i-na qa-ti*	to me through the agency
9	^{m}*I-ia-ri-ma*	of Yarima;
10	{*eras.*} *uš*-$šir_9$ DAM.MEŠ-[*š*]*u-nu*	"Send the women
11	*ša* TUR.MEŠ *ù*	of the young men, and

Reverse

12	*mi-im-mi-šu-nu*	their (the young men's) wherewithal."
13	*ù aq-bi*	However, I said:
14	*ut-ta-aš*-$šer_9$-*mi*	"I am sending (them)."
15	*ù a-nu-um-ma*	Now here is
16	^{m}*I-ia-ri-ma ù*	Yarima -
17	{*eras.*} *ša-al-šu ù a-nu-ma*	Ask him! - and here
18	*šu-nu-ma ip-ta-nu*	they are. They moved away,
19	\ *ḫe-te-qú i-pé-ša*	\ *went away from work.*
20	*ù ip-ta-ra*-{*eras.*}-*aš-ni*	The gods have decided between me
21	\ *ša-pa-ṭú-ni*	and them \ *judged me.*
22	DINGIR.MEŠ *iš*-{*eras.*}-*ti-šu-nu*	

Commentary

Obverse, line 3

^{m}*Ad-du-ap*-⸢*di*$^{?}$⸣: Na'aman 2004: 95–96 reads the PN in line 3 *Ad-du-um-mi* and tentatively offers a new translation and interpretation of the tablet wherein Addu-ummi is the ruler in the Beqaʿ region known from EA 170, and Puratpurta the ruler of Hazor. Recollation confirms that the third sign in the name must be AB (*ap*), rather than UM.[21] The second sign, could be taken for MI$^{!}$, but a name *Ad-du*-AB-MI would be meaningless.

Line 19

Greenstein 2004 proposes to take *ḫe-te-qú* as a *Hiphʿil* form, citing the previously attested *ḫi-iḫ-bi-e* from EA 256:7, which corresponds to Hebrew החביא. If correct, this would not change the basic meaning and translation of lines 18–19.

21. UM is similar to AB, but has an additional vertical stroke. See the forms of UM both here and at the beginning of line 3 and in line 15.

Lines 19, 21

The same form of the *Glossenkeil*, a slanted, unbroken DIŠ stroke, is used in the Amarna letter EA 228: 19 from Abdi-Tirši of Hazor.[22]

Line 20

For this sense of *parāsu*, cf. Aphek 7:38 (the Governor's Letter). The subject of this apparently singular verb is the gods (pl.) in line 22. For discussion, see Horowitz 2000: 22–23 and cf. Taanach 2:2–3. See now also now Smith M. 2008: 104–5.

HAZOR 11: LATE BRONZE AGE ADMINISTRATIVE DOCUMENT

Basics: Clay tablet; 3.8 × 5.5 × 0.4 cm; copy, p. 214; photos, p. 231
Reg. No.: IAA 1997-3308 (present location: Institute of Archaeology, the Hebrew University of Jerusalem)
Primary Publication: Horowitz 2000: 16–17, 26–28 (photo and copy, p. 26)
Studies: Goren 2000: 37–38, 41–42; Hess 2001; 2003: 41–42; Goren et al. 2004: 230–31; Charpin 2007: 188; Durand 2006: 89
Date: Late Bronze Age
Language: Akkadian
Find Information: See Horowitz 2000: 16

This three-line document gives a toponym and a PN on each line. The city of Hazor is the second toponym, while the third might be a writing for Nazareth (see Horowitz 2000: 27, n. 44).

Edition

1 *a-na A-ma-ZA-RUM*⸢ki!⸣ m⸢*Da*⸣*-ni-bé-li*
2 *a-na* URU *Ḫa-ṣú-ra* m*Ba-*⸢ʾ⸣*-li-ia*$_5$
3 *a-na* URU *Na-A*[*S*]*-SUR-*[*r*]*a* m*Pu*[*r*]*-ri-i-di*

Translation

1 To/for *Amazarum*?, Dani-beli.
2 To/for the city of Hazor, Baʿaliya.
3 To/for the city of *Nassura*, Purridi.

HAZOR 12: MIDDLE BRONZE AGE LETTER

Basics: Clay tablet; 5.6 × 6.2 × 1.5 cm; copy, p. 214; photos, p. 231

22. See the copy in Bezold and Budge 1892: 98, no. 48, and Na'aman 1996.

Reg. No.: IAA 1997-3305 (present location: Israel Museum)
Primary Publication: Horowitz and Wasserman 2000 (photo and copy, pp. 170–71)
Studies: Goren 2000: 36; Hess 2001: 240; Charpin and Ziegler 2004; Horowitz and Wasserman 2004 (photo, p. 341; copy, p. 343; transliteration and translation on pp. 342, 344); Durand 2006; Charpin 2007: 188
Date: Old Babylonian period; Middle Bronze Age
Language: Akkadian
Find Information: See Horowitz and Wasserman 2000: 169, n. 1

The preserved portion of this letter fragment consists for the most part of an extensive list of textiles, luxury goods, and metal items in great numbers, followed by a command from a superior to underlings, one of whom we take to be the king of Hazor.[23] In the last lines of the tablet the writer indicates that he plans to go to Mari and Ekallatum. Although the immediate circumstances of the letter remain uncertain, Horowitz and Wasserman 2004: 338–40 propose that the letter refers to preparations for the diplomatic marriage of Yasmah-Addu of Mari, son of Samsi-Addu, to a princess of Qatna.

Edition

Obverse

1' *traces*
2' 1 ⸢ŠU⸣.Š[I ^{túg}*u*]*ṭ-ba* [GAL]
3' 1 ŠU.ŠI $^{\text{⸢túg⸣}}$SAL.LA.SAG 2 ŠU.ŠI ^{túg}SAL.⸢LA⸣.[ÚS]
4' 1 ŠU.ŠI ^{túg}*sa-kum* SAG 2 ŠU.ŠI *sa-ku*[*m* ÚS]
5' 1 ŠU.ŠI ^{túg}*za-kum* SAG 2 ŠU.ŠI ^{túg}*za-ku*[*m*] ⸢ÚS⸣
6' 10 ^{túg}⸢GADA.MAḪ⸣ 30 ^{túg}*sa-*⸢*ak*⸣ *bu-*[*r*]*e-e-em*
7' 10 ^{túg}*ki-te-tim* 10 ^{túg}⸢*ki*⸣*-te-tim* {TIM}
8' 20 ^{túg}⸢NÌ.LAM⸣ *bu-re-e*
9' 20 ^{túg}*sa-kum za-kum* 20 ^{túg}*ki-te-et ḫa-li-i*
10' 1 ŠU.ŠI ^{túg}*ḫa-li-im* 2 ŠU.ŠI *ú-tu-up-lu*
11' 3 ŠU.ŠI ^{túg}SI.SÁ.SAG 2 ŠU.ŠI ^{túg}GUZ.ZA
12' 5 ŠU.ŠI ^{túg}SI.SÁ.ÚS 1 *li-im* ^{túg}BAR.KAR

Lower Edge

13' 5 ŠU.ŠI ^{túg}GÚ.UD.A KAL.KAL.SÚ.A
14' 5 ŠU.ŠI ^{túg}GÚ.UD.A DUḪ.ŠI.A
15' 5 ŠU.ŠI ^{túg}GÚ.UD.A BAR.KAR

23. Hazor was known for its textiles in the Amarna period as well. See Hazor 14, EA 22 ii 41, TUG *ḫa-ṣú-ra*, "Hazor (style) garment," and EA 25 iv 40: [TÚG *ḫ*]*a-*[*ṣ*]*ú-*[*r*]*a* (collation: Moran 1992: 83 n. 36).

Reverse

16' 1 *li-im* ^{túg}BAR.SI *ri-ik-sa-am*

17' 5 *li-im* ^{túg}SAGŠU 3 *li-im* ^{giš}IGI.KAK KÙ.<BABBAR>

18' 1 *li-im* ^{giš}IGI.KAK KÙ.GI

19' 2 *li-im* ^{giš}PAN 2 *li-im* ×.ŠU.× ZABAR$_{\times}$(UD.BAR.KA)

20' *ar-ḫi-iš a-na Má-rí*^{ki} *li-ik-šu-da-ni*

21' *ḫi-ṭì-tum mi-im-ma ib-ba-aš-ši-ma*

22' TU.IŠ (for *iš-tu*) URU *Má-rí*^{ki} *qa-ti ik-ta-aš-du*

23' *pa-nu-ia a-na li-ib-bi* É.GAL.ḪÁ

24' *a-na ni-qé-tim ù i-si-na-tim*

25' *e-pé-ši-im ša-ak-nu*

26' ⸢*a-na šu*⸣*-te-er-si-im a-aḫ-ku-nu la ta-na-de-e*

27' [× × × × × × *ḫ*]*a*$^{?}$*-ri-ša-am li-iṣ-ṣú-r*[*u*$^{?}$]

rest broken

Translation

Obverse

1' *traces*

2' 60 [large c]loaks

3' 60 first-class delicate cloths, 120 [second-class] delicate cloths;

4' 60 first-class *sakkum* cloths, 120 [second-class] *sakkum* cloths;

5' 60 first-class *zakûm* cloths, 120 second-class *zakûm* cloths;

6' 10 finest linen garments, 30 *sak burêm* covers;

7' 10 linen cloths, 10 linen cloths^{sic};

8' 20 *lamaḫuššû* robes;

9' 20 refined *sakkum* cloths, 20 *ḫalû* garments;

10' 60 woollen *ḫalû* clothes, 120 scarves;

11' 180 first-class regular articles of clothing, 120 *i'lu* bands;

12' 300 second-class regular articles of clothing, 1,000 felt cloths;

Lower Edge

13' 300 long patchwork shirts;

14' 300 *beaded* shirts

15' 180 felt shirts;

Reverse

16' 1,000 headbands;

17' 5,000 headdresses, 3,000 silver rivets;

18' 1,000 gold rivets;

19' 2,000 bows, 2,000 bronze . . .

20' let them send to me quickly to Mari.

21' Some mishap might happen!
22' After I have arrived at the city of Mari,
23' I intend to go to Ekallatum
24' to perform
25' sacrifices and celebrations.
26' You (pl.) should not be negligent about the preparations!
27' [. . . . . .] they must look out? for the . . .
rest broken

Commentary

Line 2'

For túg*uṭ-ba* see now CAD U/W 349 *uṭba* and CAD T 498–99 *tuttubû.*

Line 14'

For this understanding of DUḪ.ŠI.A (= *duhšû / dušû*), see Dalley 2000.

Lines 20', 22'

For a discussion of the writings of the name of Mari, see Horowitz and Wasserman 2004: 336, and notes to the two lines in Horowitz and Wasserman 2000: 174.

Line 21'

The phrase here is idiomatic. We understand it to mean in effect that nothing can be allowed to go wrong. Hence the demand in the previous line to begin the shipment quickly and the warning in line 26': You (pl.) should not be negligent about the preparations!

HAZOR 13: FRAGMENT OF STONE BOWL (*AGANNU*)

Basics: Stone; 8.4 × 8.1 × 7.25 cm; copy, p. 214; photo, p. 232
Reg. No.: Hazor 2000-71200 (present location: Institute of Archaeology, the Hebrew University of Jerusalem)
Primary Publication: Horowitz and Oshima 2002: 179–83 (photo, p. 179; copy, p. 182)
Date: Late Bronze Age
Language: Akkadian
Find Information: See Horowitz and Oshima 2002: 179–80

The surviving text is from the dedicatory inscription of a stone *agannu*, in which line 1 identifies the object as such.[24] This type of beginning is typical in West-Semitic dedicatory inscriptions (see Horowitz and Oshima 2002: 182, n. 8, with further bibliography).

24. One possible restoration of the line is *a-ga-nu š[a abni. . .* , "Bowl o[f stone . . ." (as in EA 14 iii 65).

Edition		Translation
1	. . .] *a-ga-nu* × [. . .	. . .] the bowl . [. . .
2	. . .] LÚ.PA D[I$^?$.KU$_5^?$ . . .	. . .] the overseer (and) j[udge$^?$ . . .
3	. . .] *ù ú-še-*[*li*$^?$ . . .	. . .] and he dedic[ated$^?$
4	. . .] *ù ki-a-*[*am* . . .	. . .] and thu[s . . .
5	. . . *ina*] ⌜*maḫ*⌝-*ri* [DN$^?$ . . .	. . . in] front of [the god$^?$ . . .

Commentary

Line 2

LÚ.PA = ugula = (*w*)*akl*u, DI.KU$_5$ (restored) = Akkadian *dajānu*, or, more likely in this period in Canaan, *šāpiṭu* (שופט).

HAZOR 14: SMALL ADMINISTRATIVE DOCUMENT

Basics: Clay tablet; 2.5 × 1.9 × 0.2 cm; copy, p. 215; photo, p. 232
Reg. No.: Hazor 2000-61027 (present location: Institute of Archaeology, the Hebrew University of Jerusalem)
Primary Publication: Horowitz and Oshima 2002: 183–84 (photo and copy, p. 184)
Studies: Charpin 2007: 188; Durand 2006; Horowitz and Oshima 2010a
Date: Late Bronze Age
Language: Akkadian
Find Information: See Horowitz and Oshima 2002: 183

Edition		Translation
9	GADA *ba-ab-na-tum*	9 fine-quality linen garments.

Commentary

The reading of the final word in Hazor 14 is now assured by Hazor 16: 1: 7 *ba-ab-na-tum*. For Hazor and textiles, see Hazor 12 above.

HAZOR 15: LETTER FRAGMENT

Basics: Clay Tablet, 7.3 × 5.0 × 2.0 cm (copy, p. 242; photo, p. 246) (present location: Israel Museum)
Reg. No.: none assigned as of Horowitz and Oshima 2007
Primary Publication: Horowitz and Oshima 2007: 34–40 (photo and copy, p. 36)
Date: Most likely Middle Bronze Age, Old Babylonian Period[25]
Language: Akkadian
Find Information: Horowitz and Oshima 2007: 34

25. See Horowitz and Oshima 2007: 35.

A small fragment of what appears to be an administrative tablet from the second millennium was recovered in the 2004 excavations at Hazor. The tablet is inscribed on only the upper portion of the obverse, leaving a vacat on the lower portion of the obverse and the entire reverse. This goes against the conventions of the scribal tradition and led us to argue in the original edition that this tablet was only a draft copy of the final document. The guess offered in Horowitz and Oshima 2007: 39, to understand this text as referring to a situation of a type of antichretic debt, remains just that. Other storylines may be proposed to explain what is inscribed on the current tablet.

Edition

Obverse

1' . . .] × × (×) [. . .
2' . . . . . .]-KU-⌜*ka*⌝ [× × (×)]
3' . . . .] ^{m}DU-[×-×]
4' . . . *i*]*n-ni*-⌜*il*[?]⌝ *še-ra-am* × [× ×]
5' . . .] × [U]R$_5$.RA-*šu-nu* DUMU *ú*-[× ×]
6' . . .] × × ×-*at-tim-ma* É × × ×
7' . . .]-×-*ma id-dan-nam im*-⌜*ka*⌝-×-×
8' . . . *t*]*u-ma-nu ṣa-ab n*[*a*[?]]-⌜*a*[?]-*li*⌝
9' . . . *ip*/*pu-ṭu*]*r-šu-nu-tim*
10' . . .] ⌜*a*⌝-*wa-ta tu*-⌜*ma*⌝-*nu*
11' . .] ⌜*i*[?]⌝-[*n*]*a* ⌜*maḫ*[?]⌝-*ri id-nu-um*

Translation

1' . . .] . . . [. . .
2' . . . . . .] . of yours [. . .
3' . . . .] P[N]
4' . . .] *he will become a bound-tenant*[?] . <Here>after . [. .]
5' . . .] . their [d]ebt, the son will/has [. .]
6' . . .] . . . . . . the house . . .
7' . . .] . and he will give over . . . .
8' . . .] . . you will count as the people of the tenancy[?]
9' . . . releas]ed/releas]e them
10' . . .] (in) this matter you will count
11' . .] before/in front give over!

Commentary

line 10'

Here *a-wa-ta* without mimmation is yet another example of inconsistent use of mimmation in our Middle Bronze corpus. See above, p. 70.

line 11′

The verbal form that ends the document is not good Akkadian. We should expect *idnām* (with ventive *-am*). We suppose that the form that we have is influenced by the local language. See further the note in the primary publication.

HAZOR 16: SMALL ADMINISTRATIVE DOCKET

Basics: Clay tablet, 2.2 × 3.4 × 1.1 cm; photo, p. 242; copy, p. 246
Reg. No.: Hazor 2006 B6-4078, L009
Primary Publication: Horowitz and Oshima 2010a (photo, p. 129; copy, pp. 129–30)
Study: Horowitz 2012: 35 (photo).
Date: Late Bronze Age
Language: Akkadian
Find Information: Horowitz and Oshima 2010a: 129

This small administrative docket is nearly identical to Hazor 14, which was found in the same archeological context.

Edition

1	7 *ba-ab-na-tum*	7 *fine-quality linen garments*
2	1 GADA	1 linen (garment)

Comments

Hazor 16 solves a problem that arose with the publication of Hazor 14, viz. that the editors could not decide in the case of Hazor 14 whether *ma/ba-ab/ap-na-tum* was the personal name of a female who was somehow connected with the nine objects made of linen (GADA), or whether the nine GADA *ma/ba-ab/ap-na-tum* were themselves objects of linen. In Hazor 16 it is clear that the *ma/ba-ab/ap-na-tum* in line 1 and the object GADA in line 2 are two separate and distinct sets of items.[26]

HAZOR 17: LIVER MODEL

Basics: Red clay liver model, 6.3 × 6.8 × 1.4 cm; copy, p. 243; photo, p. 246
Reg. No.: Hazor B49019 L07–025
Primary Publication: Horowitz, Oshima, and Winitzer 2010 (photo, p. 135; copy, p. 134)
Study: Horowitz 2012 35 (photo)

26. For more information, see the primary publication.

Date: Middle Bronze Age
Language: Akkadian
Find Information: Horowitz, Oshima, and Winitzer 2010: 133

Hazor 17 is of the same genre and presumed time as Hazor 2–3. The model preserves at least parts of five entries, with each referring to a nearby feature of the liver on the model. The edition below is taken from the *editio princeps*. See there for discussion and commentary.

Edition

a) . . .] × [. . .
b) *˹i˺+na mu-iṣ-la-li iṭ-ṭa* LÚ.KÚR *a-da-ak*
c) *i+na nu-ba-ti-<<ti>> iṭ-ṭa* LÚ.KÚR *a-da-ak*
d) *ki pi-it bar-ti*
e) LÚ A.ŠÀ *ta-ši-ma-ti-šu i-ka-ša-ad*
f) *ta-as-li-it* LÚ DINGIR-*lum*$_4$ *im-hu-ur*

Translation

a) . . .] . [
b) In the afternoon, it will become dark, the enemy I will kill.
c) In the evening, it will become dark, the enemy I will kill.
d) Like the start (opening) of a rebellion.
e) A man will reach *the realm of wisdom.*
f) A god received the prayer of a man.

Commentary

Note the lack of mimmation in Hazor 17 b-d, but the writing with lum$_4$ in Hazor 17f. For this phenomenon elsewhere in the Middle Bronze corpus from Hazor, see p. 14 in the introduction above. For the use of first person here in the protases, see the commentary to Hazor 2*b* (above, p. 66).

HAZOR 18: FRAGMENTS FROM A LAW COLLECTION

Basics: Hazor 18a: Clay Tablet Fragment, 2.5 × 1.7 × 1.1 cm; copy, p. 243; photo, p. 247
Hazor 18b: Clay Tablet Fragment, 1.0 × 0.8 × 0.4 cm; copy, p. 243; photo, p. 247
Reg No.: Hazor B49019 L07–025
Primary Publication: Horowitz, Oshima, and Vukosavović 2012 (Fragment A: photo, pp. 160, 162, copy p. 161, Fragment B photo and copy, p. 165)
Studies: Horowitz 2012: 35–36 (photo); Shanks 2013: 18 (photo)

Date: Middle Bronze Age
Language: Akkadian
Find Information: Surface find; see Horowitz, Oshima, and Vukosavović 2012: 158

The two fragments Hazor 18a–b were discovered together, are formed from the same clay, and share the same topic and apparently also format. Thus, we take them as being from the same original. Both belong to a law collection of the type best known from *The Laws of Hammurabi*, but other texts of this type from the same general period have been collected in Roth 1998. The original edition makes note of parallels between the laws on the Hazor fragments and these other collections. The first four laws make reference to three parties: a slave, his owner, and a third individual who apparently rents the slave.

The context of the first set of laws is the situation of a man (*awīlum*) hiring a slave (*wardum*) from the owner of the slave (*bēl wardim*), with subsequent damage befalling the slave. This is most clear in LHz A § 4, where the slave is to be returned to his owner.

The next law, which begins with an "If a man . . ." clause, begins a new set of laws.

Edition[27]

Fragment A obv.

LHz A § 1 0' [→[28] *šum-ma* . . .
1' 12 ⸢GÍN⸣ [KÙ.BABBAR *a-na* . . .

LHz A § 2 2' → *šum-ma* ⸢*ap*⸣-[*pu-um* . . .
3' 10 <GÍN KÙ.BABBAR> *a-na be-el* Ì[R . . .]

LHz A § 3 4' → *šum-ma ši-in-nu-*[*um* . . .
5' 3 GÍN KÙ.BABBAR ⸢*a*⸣-*n*[*a be-el* ÌR . . .

rev.

LHz A § 4 1 → *šum-ma le-et* [. . .
2 *ù* ÌR *a-na be-el* Ì[R . . .
LHz A § 5 3 → *šum-ma* LÚ GIŠ.P[I.TUG . . .
4 ⸢*ù*⸣ ÌR *i*[*m*$^{?}$- . . .

---

27. The numbering system for the laws and lines of the fragments of the original edition is maintained here.

28. We use the character → to indicate the incisions on the left edge of the first line of LHz §§ 2–5. We restore → for LHz A § 1 as well.

Fragment B

LHz B § 1 1' . . .]-⸢*ú*?⸣ × [. .
2' . . .] ⸢*a*⸣-*na be*-[*el* ÌR . . .

LHz B § 2 3' . . .] × × [. . .

Translation

Fragment A (LHz §§ 1–5)

Obverse

LHz A § 1 [0'] [If . . .
1' 12 shekels of [silver to . . .

LHz A § 2 2' If (it is) the n[ose . . .
3' 10 <shekels of silver> to the owner of the s[lave . . .

LHz A § 3 4' If (it is) a tooth [. . .
5' 3 shekels of silver t[o the owner of the slave . . .

Reverse

LHz A § 4 1 If the cheek of [the slave *is slapped* . . .
2 and the slave to the owner of the s[lave . . .

LHz A § 5 3 If a man, the e[ar . . .
4 and the slave . [. . .

Fragment B (LHz 6–7)

LHz B § 1 1' . . .] . . [. .
2' . . .] to the own[er of the slave . . .

LHz B § 2 3' . . .] . . [. . .

Commentary

LHz A § 2: We take the U-sign at the start of line 3' as as the numeral 10 and so insert *shekels of silver* on the basis of LHz A §§ 1 and 3. A reading as the conjunction *u* is much less likely, particularly give the use of Ù for the conjunction in Laws §§ 4–5.

Hebron

1. Administrative Document

HEBRON 1: ADMINISTRATIVE DOCUMENT

Basics: Clay tablet; 6.2 × 5.2 × 2.3 cm;[1] copy, p. 215; photos, p. 232
Reg. Nos.: H. 86-1, Israel Museum K. 11092
Primary Publication: Anbar and Na'aman 1986 (photo, pl. 1; copy, p. 4)
Studies: Na'aman 1994: 176; Zadok 1996: 104; Rainey 1999: 155*; Van der Toorn 2000: 98; *NEAEHL*: 608 (photo); Hess 2007: 158–59
Date: Old Babylonian period; late Middle Bronze Age[2]
Language: Akkadian
Find Information: Tel Hebron, Area S; see *NEAEHL*: 607

The document pertains to the transfer of domesticated herd animals and seems to involve the local king, perhaps the king of Hebron. However, the exact nature of the transaction(s) is unclear from the surviving tablet, especially the role of Hili-El, who is mentioned a number of times. The tablet is poorly written and executed. It would appear from the ruling lines that the scribe originally intended to arrange his text in tabular format, but did not follow his own rulings in most cases. Moreover, many of the sign forms seem hurried or careless, and there are a number of erasures. The hand of the scribe bears a certain similarity to that of Gezer 1, which is also an administrative document relating to shepherding.

Edition

Obverse

1 . . . M]ÁŠ.GÍR[!] 1 UDU.MÁŠ *a-na Pá-di-da* 1 UDU[!].MÁŠ 1 UDU.NÍTA. AMAR.BA *Ḫi-li-Èl*

1. Anbar and Na'aman 1986: 3 estimate the width of the original tablet as 9.0 cm.

2. The sign forms are consistent with the Old Babylonian period tablets from Hazor in our corpus, but the loss of mimmation in rev. 4', *mu-ša-di-na-ti*, suggests a date later than the time of the Mari-Hazor contacts. See discussion, pp. 13-14.

2 . . . AMA]R.BA.GÍR! 3 UDU 3 UDU.MÁŠ 2 UDU?.NÍTA.AMAR.BA *Ḫi-li-Èl*

3 . . . M]ÁŠ 23 UDU 15 UDU.MÁŠ 1 UDU.NÍTA.AMAR.BA *Ḫi-li-Èl*
4 . . .] LUGAL

5 . . .] × LUGAL 19 UDU 15 UDU.MÁŠ 1 UDU.NÍTA.AMAR.BA *Ḫi-li-Èl*
6 . . .] MÁŠ {*erasure*}

7 . . .] × LUGAL 9 UDU 11 UDU.MÁŠ 2 UDU.NÍTA.AMAR.BA *Ḫi!-li!-Èl*
8 . . .] × LUGAL *ir-te-ḫu a-na In-ti* 2 UDU.NÍTA *Su-ku-ḫu*

9 . . . LUG]AL 9 UDU 1 UDU.MÁŠ

10 . . .] 3? UDU.MÁŠ 2 UDU.NÍTA.AMAR.BA {*erasure*}
11 . . . *Ḫ*]*i*-[*li*]-⸢*Èl*⸣

Reverse

1' . . .]-⸢*ḫa*⸣-*di* 1 UDU.NÍTA.AMAR.BA

2' . . . *im*]-*ṭú-ú* 1 UDU
3' . . .] 1
4' . . .]- ×-*IK ú mu-ša-di-na-ti*

5' . . . MÁ]Š.GAL!.GÌR! 77 UDU *na-qú*
6' . . . PA]P 46 UDU.MÁŠ

7' . . .] × × × (*partially erased*)

Translation

Obverse

1 . . .] shorn-[g]oat, 1 small-cattle for Padida, 1 small-cattle (and) 1 sheep with lamb, Hili-El

2 . . .] shorn [sheep with l]amb, 3 sheep, 3 small-cattle, 2 sheep with lamb, Hili-El

3 . . . g]oat, 23 sheep, 15 small-cattle, 1 sheep with lamb, Hili-El
4 . . .] the king

---

5 . . .] . the king, 19 sheep, 15 small-cattle, 1 sheep with lamb, Hili-El

6 . . .] goat.

---

7 . . .] . the king, 9 sheep, 11 small-cattle, 2 sheep with lamb, Hili-El

8 . . .] . the king, shepherded for Inti, 2 sheep, Sukuhu

---

9 . . . the ki]ng, 9 sheep, 1 small-cattle

---

10 . . .] 3$^{?}$ small-cattle, 2 sheep with lamb,
11 . . . H]il[i]-El

Reverse

1' . . .] -hadi 1 sheep with lamb

2' . . . were mi]ssing 1 sheep
3' . . .] 1
4' . . .] . . and female tax collectors

5' . . .] mature shorn [goa]ts, 77 sheep for offerings
6' . . . A tota]l of 46 small-cattle

7' . . .] . . .

Commentary

The terminology of Hebron 1 is unusual. We suggest that the second sign in lines 1–2 and rev. 5 is a form of GÍR, the standard Sumerogram for "knife," in the sense of shorn animals, for which cf. Urra XIII:4–5 (*MSL* VIII/1 7):

udu-GÍR.gu.la = *ar-ri*
udu.GÍR.ak.a = *gaz-za*, "shorn sheep" (see *CAD* G 60 *gazzu*)

The sense of the term UDU.MÁŠ in line 1 and *passim* is uncertain. We understand it to be a compound meaning "sheep (and) goats," i.e., "small cattle" = Hebrew צאן. Alternatively, UDU here could be a determinative, i.e., ^{udu}MÁŠ, simply meaning "goat." We understand UDU.NÍTA.AMAR.BA to be unconventional writing for "sheep with lamb," despite the element NÍTA = *zikaru*, "masculine, male" in the term. For evidence for UDU.NÍTA as a writing for the feminine noun *immertu*, "female sheep, ewe," see *CAD* I/J 128–29, discussion sub. *immertu*.

Obverse, line 1

We understand the PN as a phonetic writing for *Padi-Adda*.[3]

Lines 5–8

The traces of the sign at the first of lines 5, 7–8 before LUGAL may be *šá*. If so, translate, ". . . of the king."

Line 8

We take *ir-te-hu* from *re'û*, "to shepherd." Cf. Gezer 1:1': UDU$^{?}$.MÁ]Š *ir-hu-um-ma* [. . . In both forms the cuneiform Ḫ represents West-Semitic ע.

Line 10

The scribe seems to have started to write the PN *Ḫi-li-Èl*, but then changed his mind and instead indented the name on the next line.

Reverse

The end of the ruling survives at the top right-hand corner of the reverse.

Line 1'

. . .]-⌜*ha*⌝-*di* here is most likely part of a broken PN in which the second element is the DN (*Ḫ*)*addu*.

Line 5'

Note the writing for 77 in base 10 notation (7 × 10 + 7), rather than in standard sexagesimal notation (1 × 60 + 17).

Lines 5'–6'

The totals given here are far greater than the sum of animals accounted for in the surviving text. We presume that the missing animals were accounted for in the now broken parts of the tablet.

3. Cf. the analogous names ^{m}*Ad-du-ap-*⌜*di*$^{?}$⌝ in Hazor 10:3 and ^{m}*Ba-ʾ-lu-pá-di* in Shechem 2 rev. 4.

Tel el-Ḥesi

TEL EL-ḤESI 1: THE AMARNA PERIOD LETTER EL-AMARNA 333

Basics: Clay tablet; 5.8 × 5.2 × 1.6 cm; copy, p. 215
Reg. No.: Fi. 11 (present location: Arkeoloji Müzeleri, Istanbul)
Date: The Amarna period; Late Bronze Age
Language: Akkadian
Find Information: Albright 1942b: 32; Bliss 1894: 52–54, with his account of joy at finding the tablet

This letter, found in 1892, was the first cuneiform text to be uncovered in the Land of Israel. It was assigned the El-Amarna number EA 333 and has long been treated as if it were part of the Amarna archive. Thus, a translation with bibliography is available in Moran 1992: 356–57, to which should be added Sayce 1893;[1] A. Sayce in Bliss 1894: 184–87 (copy, pp. 184–85), with further comments by Sayce himself on pp. 52–58; Scheil 1894 (reproduction of tablet on pp. 433–34); Winckler 1896: 340–41, no. 219; Gressman 1909: 127–28; 1926: 370; Galling 1968: 13 A 7; Edzard 1985: 252; Rainey 1996: vol. 4, p. 181, *s.v.* [EA] 333; Van der Toorn 2000: 99; Horowitz and Oshima 2004; and now Rainey-Schniedewind 2015: 1220–21, with some discussion on pp. 1–2, 6. The characters and events mentioned in the letter place it within the context of EA 329–32, sent from Lachish. The edition below utilizes our new copy of the tablet, as well as Hilprecht's 1896 copy and photo.[2] Hilprecht's copy is very accurate even by modern standards, in contrast to the relative inaccuracy of the Taanach copies by Hrozný from the following decade.

1. With a line-by-line transcription of the text in cuneiform on p. 26.

2. Hilprecht 1896, photo, pl. 24, nos. 66–67; copy, pl. 64, no. 147. A comparison of Hilprecht's copy with our own shows that the tablet has not suffered much damage over the past century.

	Edition	Translation
	Obverse	
1	[*a-na* L]Ú.GAL *qí-bí-m*[*a*]	[To the Gre]at Man say.
2	[*um-ma* ^{m}*P*]*a-a-pí*	[Message of P]apu:
3	⸢*a-na*⸣ [G]ÌR+MEŠ-*ka am-*⸢*qú*⸣*-ut*	At your [f]eet I fall.
4	*lu-ú ti-i-de i-nu-ma*	You should know that
5	*tu-ša-ṭú-ma* ^{m}DI.[K]U$_{5}$.^{d}IM	acting disloyally are indeed Šipṭi-Baʿlu
6	*ú* ^{m}*Zi-im-ri-da*	and Zimrida
7	*pu-uḫ-ri-iš ù*	together and so
8	*iq-ta-bi-mi*	Šipṭi-Baʿlu said to Zimrida:
9	^{m}DI.KU$_{5}$.^{d}IM *a-na* ^{m}*Zi-im-ri-da*	
10	⸢*ṣa*⸣*-bi* URU *Ia-ra-mi*	"the forces of the city of Yarami
11	[*š*]*a-par-mi a-na ia-a-ši*	[w]rote to me (saying):
12	[*i*]*d-na-ni-mi*	[G]ive me
	Reverse	
13	[× +] 1 GIŠ.PAN ⸢*ù*⸣ 3 GÍR-*um*	[× +] 1 bows, and 3 daggers,
14	*ù* 3 *nam-*⸢*ṣa*⸣*-ru-ta*	and 3 swords
15	*šum-ma-mi a-na-ku*	If I
16	*uṣ-ṣú-na* UGU KUR	will go forth against the land
17	*ša* LUGAL *ù a-na ia-ši*	of the king, would you with me
18	*en-ni-ip-ša-ta* ⸢*it*⸣*-t*[*i-i*]*a*	act on my side?"
19	*ù a-di-mi ú-ti-ru-m*[*i*]/*n*[*im*]	Further he turned to me (saying):
20	*šu-uṭ mu-ul-ka*	"Be disloyal to the crown!
21	*ša ú-ša-aṭ mil-ka*	The one who is disloyal to the king
22	⸢^{m}⸣*Pa-a-pu ù uš-ši*$^{!}$*-ir-šu*	is Papu. So send him
23	⸢*i-na*⸣ *pa-ni-ia ù*	before me." So
24	[*i-na-an-n*]*a* ^{m}*Ra-bi-Èl ú-wa-ši-i*[*i*]*r*	[no]w I am sending Rabi-El.
25	[*lu*]*-*⸢*ú*⸣ *yu-pal-šu*	He will answer him
	Left Edge	
26	[*i-na*] *a-wa-ti an-ni-ti*	[regarding] this matter.

Commentary

Line 1

This title also occurs in Aphek 7:1.

Lines 5–6

We follow Hess 1993: 143–44 in the reading of the name. For Baʿlu in the name rather than Addu, note the examples given in Hess 1993: 14 in Ugaritic.

Reverse, line 13

Moran 1992: 357, no. 333, n. 5: "traces favour 10+1, with room for another 10." Upon inspection we see the merest trace of what could be a 10, or perhaps another 1. Cf. Hilprecht's copy, which gives the bottom of two vertical strokes at this point. Sayce 1893: 26 (reproduced in Bliss 1894: 125) copied 3 with a question mark, while Scheil 1894: 434 reads 2.

Line 22

It seems that the scribe wrote IGI^{II} and then erased the added two verticals, leaving ŠI.

Tell Jemmeh

1. Clay Cylinder Seal

TELL JEMMEH 1: CLAY CYLINDER SEAL[1]

Basics: Clay; diameter: 9 mm; height: 22 mm
Reg. No.: Smithsonian 1023 (present location: the Smithsonian Institution)
Primary Publication: Horowitz and Ornan 2014
Studies: NEAEHL: 668
Date: Middle Bronze Age
Find Information: Field III, Square J 2, layer 16, locus 1; found August 3, 1982

Cylinder seal inscribed with a row of what appear to AN-signs in Row 3 and a different sign in Row 5, here apparently used as decorative elements. The maker of the Tell Jemmeh seal may have copied the signs from a cuneiform incantation in his possession. W. Hallo, in a letter dated September 1, 1990, to the excavator of the seal, G. van Beek of the Smithsonian Institution, makes reference to the incantation Nies 1920, no. 16, which includes a series of seven AN signs and seven KI signs, perhaps for Sumerian *an.ki* meaning "heaven and earth." Such incantations are edited and discussed in Horowitz 2011: 208–20, 414.

1. The authors gratefully acknowledge the cooperation of Prof. G. van Beek (the Smithsonian Institution).

Jericho

1. Administrative Tablet
2. Inscribed Cylinder Seal
3.[?] Inscribed Cylinder Seal from the Jericho Area

JERICHO 1: ADMINISTRATIVE TABLET

Basics: Clay tablet; 4.0 × 5.0 × 1.9 cm; copy, p. 215; photos, p. 232
Reg. Nos.: IAA 35.2878, Rockefeller Museum 1485 (present location: the Rockefeller Museum)
Primary Publication: Smith 1934 (photo, pl. 43, no. 1; copy, p. 117)
Studies: Albright 1942a: 28; Galling 1968: 13 A 4b; Edzard 1985: 252; Zadok 1996: 111; Van der Toorn 2000: 98
Date: Late Bronze Age
Language: Akkadian
Find Information: See Garstang 1934: 116

The inscription continues onto the reverse, which is otherwise noninscribed. For this physical format, cf. Hazor 11 and Shechem 2.

	Edition	**Translation**
1	*Sa*-[G]I/[Z]I-*IG-ni m*[*a-r*]*u*	PN, older[?] s[o]n of Ta[g]utaka
2	*r*[*a*]-⸢*bu*[?]-*ú*[?]⸣	
3	⸢*ša*⸣ *Ta*-[*g*]*u-ta-ka*	

JERICHO 2: INSCRIBED CYLINDER SEAL

Basics: Hematite; diameter: 10 mm; height: 21 mm
Reg. No.: J. 54.62 (location unknown)
Primary Publication: Porada 1965: 656–58 (photo, pl. 15, no. 2; copy, p. 656, fig. 304, no. 1)

Studies: Galling 1968: 13 A 4a
Date: Second millennium BCE
Language: Akkadian
Find Information: See Porada 1965: 657

	Edition	**Translation**
1	^{d}UTU ^{d}UTU	Shamash, Shamash
2	^{d}*A-a*$^{!d}$*A-a*	Aya, Aya

JERICHO 3$^{?}$: INSCRIBED CYLINDER SEAL FROM THE JERICHO AREA

Basics: Hematite; diameter: 10 mm; height: 22 mm; photos, p. 233 (present location: the Rockefeller Museum)[1]
Primary Publication: Amiet 1955: 409–10 (photo, pl. 5, no. 2)
Studies: Galling 1968: 14 A 9
Date: Second millennium BCE
Language: Akkadian
Find Information: Museum purchase (see below)

The seal was purchased by the Palestine Museum (now Rockefeller Museum) from a seller who claimed that the seal came from the Shuneh region on the eastern bank of the Jordan River. Given this uncertainty, we include the item in our corpus due to the proximity of the reported find site to Jericho.

	Edition	**Translation**
1	^{d}AMAR.UTU-*ni-šu*	Marduk-nišu
2	DUMU ^{d}EN.ZU-*re-me-ni*	the son of Sin-remeni
3	ÌR ^{d}IM	the servant of Adad

Commentary

In addition to cuneiform signs, the seal preserves Egyptian hieroglyphs and non-Mesopotamian motifs (an *ankh* and a monkey). Thus, there can be little doubt that the seal is a western product, rather than a Babylonian import. Nevertheless, given the Babylonian personal names, it is most likely that the DN in line 3 should be realized as Akkadian Adad, rather than as western (H)addu/Baʿal.

1. No registration details available to the authors.

Jerusalem

1. Letter Fragment
2. Letter Fragment

The two tiny fragments Jerualem 1–2, both from the Ophel excavations on the eastern hill of Jerusalem, offer the first direct evidence of the use of cuneiform in Jerusalem. This was previously known only indirectly from the letters of the Amarna-age king of Jerusalem, Abdi-Heba. No direct connection can be made between the two new fragments and the previously known material.

JERUSALEM 1: LETTER FRAGMENT

Basics: Fragment of a clay tablet, 28.254 × 20.522 mm; copy, p. 244; photo, p. 247
Reg. No.: 7327 (present location: the Ophel Archaeological Garden, Jerusalem)
Primary Publication: Horowitz, Mazar, Goren, and Oshima 2010 (photo and copy, p. 7)
Study: Horowitz, Mazar, Goren, and Oshima 2014: 138, Sanders 2016[1]
Date: Late Bronze Age
Language: Akkadian
Find Information: From the Ophel excavations on the eastern hill of Jerusalem (see Horowitz, Mazar, Goren, and Oshima 2010: 4–5)

This fragment is so small that it is not possible to restore even a single complete phrase. The Late Bronze Age date is suggested by the archeological context of the fragment, and is confirmed by the few signs that are available. The identification of the tablet as a letter, rather than administrative document, is based primarily on the fine physical execution of the tablet rather than reconstruction of the tablet's text, although this too is consistent with the identification of Jerusalem 1 as a letter. The petrographic analysis offered in the primary publication indicates that the clay used for the tablet is local to the Jerusalem area.

1. Further discussion of Jerusalem 1 is available in Christopher Rollston's blog, Rollston Epigraphy: Ancient Inscriptions from the Levantine World, "Reflections on the FragmentaryCuneiform Tablet from the Ophel," July 14, 2010, with responses from W. van Soldt and J. Huehnergard.

Edition		Translation
Obverse		
1'	[× (×)]× × [. .	*traces*
2'	*⸢i-ša⸣-am-m*[*u-ú* . . .	they will hea[r . . .
3'	*iš*-TUM *a-na a*[*l*?- . . .	. . . for . [. . .
4'	*i-pé-ša* × [. . .	to do . [. . .
5'	× × [. . .	*traces*
Reverse		
1'	*traces or vacat with scratches*	
2'	ZI BI × [. . .	. . . [. . .
3'	*šu-nu* [. . .	they [. . .
4'	[*n*]*u*-[. . .	. [. . .

JERUSALEM 2: LETTER FRAGMENT

Basics: Fragment of clay tablet, 9.5 × 9 × 5 mm; copy, p. 243; photo, p. 248
Reg. No.: 20006 (present location: Israel Antiquities Authority)
Primary Publication: Horowitz, Mazar, Goren, and Oshima 2014 (photos and copy, p. 130)
Date: Late Bronze Age
Language: Akkadian?
Find Information: Ophel excavations, locus 13–071

The fragment's very small size makes any positive identification of date, genre, and even language nearly impossible. Nevertheless, it seems to be from the same general period and genre as Jerusalem 1. However, in the case of Jerusalem 2, the petrographic analysis indicates that the clay of the fragment comes from Nile sediments indicating Egyptian origin. The original edition suggests a possible Ramesside date for the fragment, i.e., slightly later than the Amarna Letters.

Edition

Obverse

1' . . .] × [. . .
2' . . . U]G-GU[R . . .

Bottom Edge

1 . . . Š]U R[U . . .

Tel Keisan

1. Administrative Fragment

TEL KEISAN 1: ADMINISTRATIVE FRAGMENT

Basics: Clay tablet; 5.0 × 2.5 × 2.5 cm; copy, p. 216
Reg. No.: K8069 (present location: The Hebrew University of Jerusalem)
Primary Publication: Sigrist 1982 (photo, pl. 5 A; copy, p. 33); Zilberg 2015 (copy, p. 91)
Studies: Van der Toorn 2000: 99; Stern 2001: 16
Date: Iron Age; Neo-Assyrian period; ca. 750–650 BCE; Neo-Babylonian script
Language: Akkadian
Find Information: Sigrist 1982: 32; Zilberg 2015: 90

The Tel Keisan administrative fragment appears to be a ration list, in which various individuals receive a single ration of bread. The tablet was recovered in an Iron Age archaeological context dating from ca. 750–650 BCE, i.e., the time of the height of Assyrian power in the west. Yet the sign forms all appear to be written in a Neo-Babylonian hand with a blunted stylus. Thus, we suggest that the tablet was written by a provincial Babylonian scribe, perhaps in the service of the Assyrian administration.[1] The new edition below is based on Zilberg 2015.

Edition		**Translation**
Obverse		
1'	⸢1 NINDA⸣ ^{m}I[GI- . . .]	1 ration for ^{m}*Pā*[*n* . . .]
2'	1 NINDA ^{m}EN.BÀD	1 ration for ^{m}*Bēl-Dūrī*
3'	1 NINDA ^{m}ŠEŠ-*nu*-[*ri* . . .]	1 ration for ^{m}*Aḫu-nū*[*rī*]
4'	1 NINDA ^{m}*Ḫat-a-a-*[*a* . . .]	1 ration for ^{m}*Ḫattā*[*iu*]
5'	1 NINDA ^{m}IGI-^{d}15	1 ration for ^{m}*Pān-Ištar*
6'	1 NINDA ^{m}*Ḫa-ma-din-nu*	1 ration for ^{m}*Ḫamadinnu*

1. For Babylonians in Neo-Assyrian period administrative texts in our corpus, see Na'aman and Zadok 2000 (the editions and discussion of Tel Hadid 1–2).

7'	1 NINDA LÚ.GA[L$^{?}$ . . .]	1 ration for *ra*[*b*$^{?}$- . . .]
8'	1 NINDA ^{md}*na*-[. . .]	1 ration for ^{md}*na*-[. . .]
9'	1 NINDA ^{m}AD[. . .]	1 ration for ^{m}*Abu*-[. . .]
10'	1 NINDA ^{m}*Šad-d*[*in*$^{?}$-*nu*$^{?}$]	1 ration for ^{m}*Šad*[*dinnu*$^{?}$]
11'	1 NINDA ^{m}× [. . .]	1 ration for ^{m}P[N]
12'	1 NINDA [^{m} . . .]	1 ration for [^{m}PN]

Reverse

1'	⸢1 NINDA⸣ ^{m}*b*[*a*$^{?}$ . . .]	1 ration for ^{m}B[A . . .]
2'	1 NINDA $^{m⸢d⸣}$× [. . .]	1 ration) for ^{md}P[N]
3'	⸢1⸣ NINDA ^{m}MAN-*l*[*u*$^{?}$-*da*$^{?}$-*ri*$^{?}$]	1 ration for ^{m}*Šarru-l*[*ū*$^{?}$-*dāri*$^{?}$]
4'	1 NINDA $^{md+⸢}$AG⸣ [. . .]	1 ration for ^{md}*Nabû*-[. . .]
5'	*šá* URU × [. . .]	of the city [. . .]
6'	1 NINDA $^{m⸢}$IM⸣$^{?}$ [. . .]	1 ration for ^{m}P[N . . .]
7'	1 NINDA ^{md}[. . .]	1 ration for ^{md}[PN . . .]
8'	1 NINDA $^{m⸢}$KUR⸣-[. . .]	1 ration for ^{m}P[N]
9'	1 NINDA ^{m}[. . .]	1 ration ^{m}[PN]
10'	⸢1⸣ [NINDA ^{m} . . .]	⸢1⸣ [ration for ^{m}PN]

Khirbet Kusiya

KHIRBET KUSIYA 1: NEO-ASSYRIAN ADMINISTRATIVE FRAGMENT

Basics: Clay tablet; 3.9 × 2.8 × 2.3 cm; copy, p. 216; photos, p. 233
Reg. No.: IAA 1985-349 (present location: Israel Antiquities Authority)
Studies: Jewish Museum 1986: 15 (photos); Ornan 1997: 333; Na'aman and Zadok 2000: 180–81
Date: Neo-Assyrian period
Language: Akkadian
Find Information: Surface find; see Na'aman and Zadok 2000: 180–81

This fragment was exhibited in the mid-1980s as part of an exhibition titled *Among Ancient Empires* (Jewish Museum 1986).[1] The fragment at that time bore a stamp seal impression and thus can positively be identified as belonging to the administrative genre.[2] Given that the only word that can be read with certainty is "his fields" in line 4', the subject matter of the document is uncertain. However, one might guess that what we have here is a record of a transaction involving fields.

Edition	**Translation**
Obverse	
1' . . .]-*šú*	. . .] of his
2' . . .] × × × *ŠID/MES*	. . .] . . . .
3' . . .]-*ia-nu-ri-ni*	. . . P]N?
4' . . .] × A.ŠÀ.MEŠ-*šú*	. . .] . his fields
5' . . . DA]M-*su Me-na-ni*	. . his [wif]e, Menani
6' . . .]-*ni*	. . .] .

1. See that publication for the attribution of the object to Khirbet Kusiya. The IAA, in its documentation of the object, makes a similar attribution.

2. See photo in Jewish Museum 1986, reproduced on p. 233. The seal impression has subsequently been effaced.

7'	. . .] *AN*	. . .] .
8'	. . .] × *BU*	. . .] . .

Reverse

1'	. . .] × KI	. . .] . .
2'	. . .] ×	. . .] .
3'	. . .]-*ú*-*UZ*	. . .] . .
4'	. . .] GAL	. . .] big
5'	. . . Š]À-*bi* URU	. . . insi]de the city
6'	. . .] ×	. . .] .

Commentary

The present fragment appears to preserve the ends of a number of lines of an administrative text. If so, many of the surviving signs could belong to the final parts of personal names. We offer the following most tentative suggestions.

Line 2'

If the penultimate sign is the remains of DINGIR, read ^{d}MES for Marduk (cf. Megiddo 2:1 and Shephela 1:4').

Line 5'

The last three signs may be for an Elamite name, along the lines of *Menânu* (see *PNAE* 748), or an Akkadian PN *Menânni*, "love me."[3]

3. For *menû* in personal names, see *CAD* M_{II} 19.

Megiddo

1. The Gilgamesh Fragment
2. Inscribed Cylinder Seal
3. Inscribed Cylinder Seal
4. Inscribed Cylinder Seal
5. Inscribed Jar Stopper
6. Administrative Document

MEGIDDO 1: THE GILGAMESH FRAGMENT

Basics: Clay tablet; 10 × 10 × 3 cm; copy, p. 217; photos, p. 233

Reg. No.: Israel Museum 55-2

Primary Publication: Goetze and Levy 1959: photo, pl. 18; copy, p. 122 (Hebrew version; pp. 108–15); Koch-Westenholz and Westenholz 2000: 445 (copy, p. 451); George 2003: 339–47 (copy, pl. 30)

Studies: Soden 1963: 82; Landsberger and Tadmor 1964: 214; Galling 1968: 13 A 5c; Landsberger 1968: 128–35; Magnusson 1977: 23; Tigay 1982: 123–29, 285–86; Edzard 1985: 251; Demsky 1990: 164–65; Bottéro 1992: 272–74; Pettinato 1992: 280–81; Hecker 1994: 670; Tournay and Shaffer 1994: 174–77; George 1999: 138–39; Rainey 1999: 154*; Van der Toorn 2000: 98, 105; *NEAEHL*: 1011 (photo); Von Dassow 2004: 667, 672; Goren, Mommsen, Finkelstein, and Na'aman 2009 (photo, p. 765)

Date: Middle Babylonian period, Late Bronze Age

Language: Akkadian

Find Information: Surface find. D. Ussishkin reported in an oral communication that the tablet was found in a field 30 meters to the north of the tel and not as reported in Goetze and Levy 1959: 121.

The present fragment preserves 38 lines from the left side of the middle portion of what appears to be a single column tablet from a western version of the Middle Babylonian period Akkadian Gilgamesh Epic. The edition below follows that of A. George in his comprehensive new edition of the Gilgamesh narratives (2003: 339–47), which is based on the new copy produced by T. Oshima for the present volume. Another recent copy, by A. Westenholz, is available in Koch-Westenholz and Westenholz 2000: 451. The restorations in the translation are from George 2003.

D. Ussishkin presents a new overview of the archaeological and historical context of the tablet in his Hebrew and forthcoming English monographs on Megiddo.

Edition

Obverse

1' [× ×] × [. . .
2' [×] × *⸢IZ⸣ Z[I / R[I* . . .
3' *[i$^{?}$-q]a$^{?}$-ab-bi* × [. . .
4' *[ú$^{?}$]-na-ak-ki-i[s$^{?}$* . . .
5' *[a]t$^{?}$-ta i-nu-ma* [. . .
6' *[š]a-du-ša ù ni-[* . . .
7' [^{giš}TI]R ^{giš}EREN.MEŠ *aš-bu* [. . .
8' *[ni]-ni-ir-ra i-na ri-[* . . .
9' [×]- × *-ši an-ni-tum* × [. . .
10' *[dam]-qa-at ù mi-[* . . .
11' *[aq-ra]t dam-qa-at ù* × [. . .
12' [×] × *pa-aš-qat i-na šu-ut-[ti-ia* . . .
13' *[la]-⸢nam⸣ ku-re-e ra-bi* [. . .
14' *[pa-nu]-šu ša-ak-nu ri-[it-ti-* . . .
15' *[ṣ]ú-up-ru ša e-r[i-i* . . .
16' [×] × *-šu ka-la N[I$^{?}$* . . .
17' *[ša e-r]i$^{?}$-⸢i$^{?}$⸣ ri-it-t[a-šu* . . .
18' [× × × × × ×] × [. . .

Reverse

1' *di-im-ma-[tu$^{?}$* . . .
2' *a-na ib-ri-⸢ia⸣* [× × × × ×] × [. . .
3' *a-ḫu-uz* ^{m}PAN.MAŠ [× × (×)] × *ZI* × [. . .
4' *ú-ul i-šu-ma šu-* × -[× *ú]-ul i-Z[I / R]I* . . .
5' *tu-uš-te-er-pí-da-an-ni AM RU N[A* . . .
6' *šu-mi-ia me-e ⸢el-lu$^{!}$⸣-ti li-iq-[qu-ú* . . .
7' *ib-ri ⸢ša⸣ ú-še-⸢zi⸣-ba-an-ni i-n[a$^{?}$* . . .
8' *ša-na-am* u_4*-ma i-na ma-ia-l[i* . . .
9' *ù* 4 u_4*-ma i-na ma-ia-⸢li⸣* UGU × [. . .
10' *mu-ur-⸢ṣú⸣ ik-ta-bi-⸢it* UGU⸣*-š[u* . . .
11' ^{m}*En-ki-du i-na ma-[i]a-li na-[di* . . .
12' *il-sí-⸢ma* ^{m}⸣PAN.MAŠ *ú-še-[* . . .
13' *i-na ri-i[g-m]i-šu id-* × [. . .
14' *ki-ma* TU$^{⸢mušen}$ *ú⸣-dá-am-m[i-im$^{?}$* . . .
15' *e-ṣa-IT i-na mu-š[i$^{?}$* . . .
16' *a-ša-re-ed* × [. . .
17' *a-na ib-ri-š[u* . . .

18' *lu-ba-ak-ki* [. . .
19' ⸢*a-na-ku*⸣ *a-na i-*[. . .
20' [× × ×] ⸢*BU*?⸣ [. . .

Translation

Obverse

1'–2' *traces only*
3' [*was*] speaking . [. . .
4' [*I*] cut dow[n . . .
5' [*Y*]*ou,* when [. . .
6' Its [M]ountains and w[e *destroyed Humbaba who in*]
7' [The] Cedar [Fore]st dwelt, [*we seized the Bull of Heaven and*]
8' [we] slew (it). In . [. . .
9' [.] . . this . [. . . . . . . *your dream*]
10' [was fav]orable and . [. . .
11' [it was precio]us, it was favorable and . [. . .
12' [.] . was difficult. In [my] dre[am . . . *there was a man*]
13' he was short of [sta]ture, he was large of [. . . *like the (roaring) Anzu-bird*]
14' was the set of his [face], the pa[ws *of a lion were his hands*]
15' [The t]alons of an ea[gle *were his claws* . . .
16' his [.] . all . [. . .
17' [Of an *eag*]*le* was [his] han[d . . .
18' [. . . .] . [. . .

Reverse

1' Moani[ng . . .
2' for my friend [. . . . .] . [. . .
3' Take hold, O Gilgamesh, [. . (.)] . . . [. . .
4' He had no . . [.] he did [n]ot . . [. . .
5' You enabled me to roam . . . [. . .
6' My name, may [they] pou[r] pure water [. . .
7' My friend who rescued me fro[m . . . . *Enkidu lay sick for one day and*]
8' a second day. In the be[d . . . . *a third*]
9' and fourth day. In the bed on . [. . .
10' The sickness grew too much for hi[m . . .
11' Enkidu was cast [down] on the bed [. . .
12' He called forth, Gilgamesh, he [. . .
13' At his c[r]y he . [. . .
14' Like a dove he sobb[ed . . .
15' was too little. In the *nig*[*ht* . . .
16' the foremost of [. . . . . . . *he was mourning*]
17' for hi[s] friend [. . .

18' I will (make?) mourn [. . .
19' I myself for . [. . .
20' [. . . .] . [. . .

Commentary

Reverse, line 3'

For this version of Gilgamesh's name, cf. the writing of dGIŠ.PAN.MAŠ, which occurs in Hittite Gilgamesh and in a Gilgamesh omen from Boghazköi; see George 2003: 80, 84 and cf. Horowitz 2016: 45.

MEGIDDO 2: INSCRIBED CYLINDER SEAL

Basics: Lapis lazuli; height: 2.8 cm; diameter: 1.0 cm; photos, p. 234 (cylinder and impression)

Reg. No.: I. 3488, Rockefeller Museum 897

Primary Publication: Guy and Engberg 1938: 184, page facing pl. 90, no. 8 (copy), pl. 90 no. 8 (photo)

Studies: Parker 1949: 6, no. 3 (photo, pl. 1, no. 3); Galling 1968: 13 A 5a; Limet 1971: 70–71, no. 4.11; Collon 1987: 60–61, no. 246 (photo); Oshima 2003: 27; *NEAEHL*: 1010 (photo); Cohen: 2008 85

Date: Middle Babylonian period, Late Bronze Age

Language: Sumerian

Find Information: Megiddo Tomb 217, Chamber A, see Guy and Engberg 1938: 31

	Edition	Translation
1	dMes umun bùlug	May Marduk the great lord,
2	dingir šà.lá.sù	the merciful god,
3	arḫuš rém tuk[u].a	hav[e] mercy and love.

Commentary

This Megiddo seal inscription shares formulae with contemporary seals from Kassite-period Babylonia (see, e.g., those edited by Lambert in Matthews 1990: 88–97).

Line 3

We take rém to be a pseudo-Sumerogram. Cf. the Akkadian equivalent of the line *re-me ra-a-me*, “mercy and love,” e.g., Matthews 1990: 89, no. 69:3, note also Megiddo 4.

MEGIDDO 3: INSCRIBED CYLINDER SEAL

Basics: Jasper; height: 33 mm, diameter: 14 mm; location uncertain[1]
Primary Publications: Schumacher 1908a: 142–43 (photo); 1908b: pl. 46a (copy); Nougayrol 1939: 2–3, no. III (TM. 2), copy pl. 12
Studies: Watzinger 1929: 86, no. 7; Galling 1968: 61 4
Date: Uncertain
Language: Akkadian written in Sumerograms
Find Information: Stratum 6 Room R, see Schumacher 1908a: 143

	Edition	Translation
1	[*I*]*z*$^{?}$-*kùr*-^{d}IM	Izkur$^{?}$-Addu
2	DUB.SAR	the scribe
3	DUMU [× × ×]	the son of [. . .]

Commentary
Line 1
For the reading of the PN, see Nougayrol 1939: 2.

MEGIDDO 4: INSCRIBED CYLINDER SEAL

Basics: Faience; height: 3.5 cm; diameter: 1.3 cm; photos, p. 234 (cylinder and impression)
Reg. No.: IAA 39.515 (present location: Rockefeller Museum)
Primary Publication: Loud 1948: pl. 160, no. 6 (photo and copy)
Date: Middle Babylonian period, Late Bronze Age
Language: Akkadian
Find Information: Loud 1948: page before pl. 160

The quality of the engraving is so poor that Loud reports that I. Gelb believed the seal to be a forgery, despite the fact that the piece was found *in situ*. The words of W. G. Lambert (Matthews 1990: 67) come to mind here: "In addition many [seals] seem to have been engraved by illiterate craftsmen."

	Edition	Translation
1	^{d}ŠÀ.ZU	Marduk,
2	[*b*]*è*-*lí*-*ì*	my lord,
3	ARḪUŠ TUKU.ḪA$^{?}$	have mercy.

1. The seal may be held in the Rockefeller Museum but was not in the main collection.

Commentary

Line 2

The signs are [N]I-NI-NI.

Line 3

The HA? at the end of line 3 might represent the Sumerian precative.

MEGIDDO 5: INSCRIBED JAR STOPPER

Basics: Clay; height: 3.5 cm; diameter at base: 1.9 cm; copy, p. 217; photos, p. 234
Reg. No.: I.3552 (present location: Rockefeller Museum)
Primary Publication: Lamon and Shipton 1939: pl. 72, no. 18 (photo), page facing pl. 73, no. 18 (copy)
Studies: Albright 1942a: 28, n. 4; Galling 1968: 13 A 5b; Zadok 1996: 111; Hess 2003: 36
Date: Late Bronze Age
Language: Presumably Akkadian, but includes only PN + measurement unit written in Sumerian
Find Information: Unprovenanced find from "Schumacher's works [trenches and dumps] at Megiddo"; see Lamon and Shipton 1939: p. xviii

The inside of this clay jar stopper bears a two-line cuneiform inscription. Line 1 has a cuneiform rendering of an Egyptian PN. Line 2 seems to preserve a unit of capacity written in Sumerian. An Egyptian hieroglyph is found on the object's top.

	Edition	**Translation**
1	m*Al-tu-un-šu*	PN
2	BANEŠ	*Keg*

Commentary

Line 1

This is a new reading of the name, based on our copy. For the form of AL, cf. Shechem 2:3.

Line 2

For this unit of capacity, which equals approximately 25 liters, see Aphek 8.

MEGIDDO 6: ADMINISTRATIVE DOCUMENT

Basics: Fragment of a cuneiform tablet; 25 × 23 × 10 mm
Primary Publication: Cogan 2013b (photos, pp. 132–33; copy, pp. 132–33)

Date: Late Bronze Age
Find Information: Picked up from the surface in Area BB on the eastern side of the Tel.

Cogan points out in the primary publication that his fragment of a cuneiform tablet was picked up by a visitor to Tel Megiddo. It is currently in private hands, but its holder gave permission for its publication. Although quite small in size, it is nevertheless identifiable by its script and contents as typical of texts that have been retrieved from Late Bronze contexts in Israel.

	Edition	**Translation**
	Obverse	
1	[×]-*tim* UDU.ḪI.A [. . .	[.] . sheep [. . .
2	×-*tim* 10 UDU.ḪI.A ⸢*a*⸣-[*na*$^{?}$ . . .	. . 10 sheep t[o$^{?}$ . . .
3	⸢10⸣ UDU.ḪI.A *a-na Te-*×[. . .	10 sheep to Te-[. . .
4	10 UDU.ḪI.A *a-na Pi-e-*[. . .	10 sheep to Pe-[. . .
5	10 UDU.ḪI.A *a-na Zi-e-*[. . .	10 sheep to Ze-[. . .
6	10 UDU.ḪI.A *a-na Ut*$^{?}$-[. . .	10 sheep to Ut-[. . .
7	[10] ⸢ UDU⸣ .Ḫ[I.A . . .	10 she[ep to . . .
	Top Edge	
1'	[*a*]-*na* ×[	[t]o [
2'	[ ]*a-na* ×[	[ ]to [
	Left Edge	
1	*ba/ma-am-*[. . .	. . [. . .
2	10 UDU.[(ḪI.A) . . .	10 sheep [. . .

Commentary

Cogan (2013b) concluded that Megiddo 5 might record some sort of standard payment for something, or else be related some type of celebratory act, since 10 sheep are given to each person in each line where the number of sheep is preserved.

Lines 3–6

The personal name marker DIŠ is conspicuous by its absence. Cf. Hebron 1 in this volume.

Mikhmoret

1. Persian Period Administrative Text

MIKHMORET 1: PERSIAN PERIOD ADMINISTRATIVE TEXT

Basics: Clay tablet; 2.7 × 3.8 × 2.3 cm
Reg. No.: Tel Mikhmoret M130 (present location: unknown)
Primary Publication: Paley, Spar, and Stieglitz (in press)
Studies: Van der Toorn 2000: 99; Stern 2001: 361, 404; *NEAEHL*: 1044–45 (photo, p. 1045)
Date: Persian period; Cambyses Year 5 (525 BCE)
Language: Akkadian
Find Information: Area S, see *NEAEHL*: 1044–45

Mikhmoret 1 is a fragment from a slave sale that is written in Babylonian script using standard Neo-Babylonian formulae for this type of document. The edition below is from the new Paley, Spar, and Stieglitz edition soon to be published in *Israel Exploration Journal*. See this edition and Zilberg in press for discussion of the historical background of the piece. Note the Judean unit of measure the *pym* in obv. 3.

Edition

Obverse

1 [^{m} × × ×] ⸢A⸣-*šú šá* ^{md}EN-⸢ŠEŠ⸣-[× ×]
2 [*ina ḫūd* ŠÀ-*b*]*i-šú* ^{f}*qal-lat-su* [× ×]
3 [ŠÁ]M.BI 20 ⸢*pi*⸣-*im* [. . .]
4 [*a*]-*na* 15 GÍN K[Ù].BAB[BAR × ×] ×
5 [*a-na* ŠÁM *ḫ*]*a-ri-iṣ a-n*[*a* × × ×]
6 [*i*]*d*-⸢*din*⸣ *pu-ut* ^{m}[*si-ḫu-ú* .]
7 [*pa-qí-ra-nu* . . . .]
(rest of obverse broken)

Reverse

1' [^{m} . . .] × × ⸢A-*šú*⸣ [*šá* . . .

2' [^{m} . . . A- *šú*] *šá* ^{m}⸢*ḫa*$^{?}$ ⸣-*am- mi* [. . . . .]
3' [^{m} . . .] A- *šú šá* ^{m}⸢*Mar*⸣-*duk-a*[*b*$^{?}$- ×]- ⸢*a*⸣
4' [^{m} . . . A- *š*]*ú šá* ^{md}AG-SU DUMU ^{m}*Ina*-SÙ[H$^{?}$-SUR]
5' [^{md}× - ×]-PA A- *šú šá* ^{m}ŠU-*ṣa-bat* ^{lú}A.[BA]
6' [^{lú}UMBISAG ^{m} . . .]- *bi* A- *šú šá* ^{md}AG-ŠEŠ^{meš}-S[U]
7' [× × × ^{ki}] ^{iti}⸢APIN ⸣(?) UD 10.KÁM MU 5.KÁ[M]

Upper Edge
8' [^{m} *Kám– bu- zi*]- *ía* LUGAL ⸢E ⸣^{ki} *u* KUR.KUR^{meš}

Translation

Obverse
1 [PN] son of Bēl-ahhē-[. .]
2 [By his] own [free will], his slave women [PN]
3 [for] the [pric]e of 20 pym of [. . .]
4 [value]d at 15 shekels of [. .] . silver
5 [for the price a]greed t[o PN]
6 [s]old. Guarantee against [challengers and]
7 [claimants . . . .]

Reverse
1' [. . .], son o[f . . . , descendant of . . .]
2' [. . . son] of . . . . . [. . .]
3' [. . .], son of *Marduk* . [.] .
4' [. . . son o]f *Nabû-erība* descendant of *Ina-tē*[*šî-eṭir*]
5' [. . .] . son of *Qāta-ṣabat* the *se*[*pīru*]
6' [the scribe . .] . son of *Nabû-ahhē-idd*[*ina*]
7' [GN] Month of Araḫsamnu (?), day 10, year 5

Lower Edge
8' [Cambys]es King of Babylon and the Lands

Commentary

The reverse begins in the middle of the list of witnesses.

Tel en-Naṣbeh

1. Inscribed Bronze Ringlet

TEL EN-NAṢBEH 1: INSCRIBED BRONZE RINGLET

Basics: Bronze ringlet fragment; thickness: 11.5 mm; 11 mm. wide, curving on an outside diameter of 15.5–16 cm, approximately one-third of a full circle (McCown 1947: 151); photo, p. 233

Reg. No.: None available (present location: the Badé Institute of Biblical Archaeology, Pacific School of Religion, Berkeley, CA)

Primary Publication: Horowitz and Vanderhooft 2002 (photo, p. 319); McCown 1947: 150–53 (photo, pl. 55, no. 80)[1]

Studies: Zorn 1997: 38 (photo), 66; Vanderhooft 1999: 108–9; 2003: 253; *NEAEHL*: 1102; Dalley 2013: 179–80

Date: Neo-Assyrian, Neo-Babylonian, or Late Babylonian

Language: Akkadian

Find Information: The find information for this piece was apparently not documented in the field, perhaps because the cuneiform inscription did not come to light until the object was cleaned in Berkeley; see McCown 1947: 150–51

Edition

. . .]-*a-ia-da* A (*māra*) *ra-man-šú ana* DIN ŠI-*šu* (*balāṭ napištīšu*) R[U . . .

Translation

. . .]-yada, his very own son, for the well-being of his life dedi[cated . . .

1. The original publication of this piece, including summaries of the preliminary readings and interpretations by W. F. Albright, G. Cameron, and A. Sachs, has been superseded by the new understanding of the text in Horowitz and Vanderhooft 2002.

Qaqun

1. Esarhaddon Stela Fragment

QAQUN 1: ESARHADDON STELA FRAGMENT

Basics: Limestone; 36 × 18 × 23 cm
Reg. No.: IAA 1974-565 (present location: Israel Antiquities Authority)
Studies: Porath et al. 1985: 213–14 (photo, p. 214); Ornan 1997: 289; Na'aman and Zadok 2000: 181; Eph'al 2005: 109; Cogan 2008: 67–69; Leichty 2011: 190–91, no. 102
Date: Neo-Assyrian period, Esarhaddon

The stela fragment is to be published by E. Weissert, who reports that the text describes Esarhaddon's campaign to the Sinai Desert. Eph'al 2005: 109 and Cogan 2008: 67–69 provide an overview of the contents and historical context of the object. Cogan 2008: 68 suggests that Qaqun 1 may belong to the same original as our Ben Shemen 1 (see above, p. 44).

Samaria

1. Inscribed Bulla with Royal Asssyrian Seal Impression
2. Judicial Document
3. Votive Cylinder in the Form of a Cylinder Seal
4. Fragment of Neo-Assyrian Stela
5. Inscribed Coin (*Drachma*)
6. Inscribed Coin (*Obol*)
7. Inscribed Coin (*Obol*)

SAMARIA 1: INSCRIBED BULLA WITH ROYAL ASSYRIAN SEAL IMPRESSION

Basics: Clay
Reg. No.: Samaria 2925 (location unknown)[1]
Primary Publication: Reisner et al. 1924: vol. 1, 247, no. 2 (copy and photo, vol. 2, pl. 56a); Becking 1992: 112, no. 1
Studies: Alt 1941: 103; Sachs 1953: 170, no. 40 (photo, pl. 19, no. 3); Galling 1968: 61 5b; Postgate 1974: 22, no. 7.2.21; Van der Toorn 2000: 99; Stern 2001: 16; Cogan 2013a: 19–20 (photo)
Date: Neo-Assyrian period
Language: Akkadian
Find Information: None given in the sources cited above.

Edition	**Translation**
a-na ^{md}*A*[*š+šur*-×-(×)-*i*]*n*	To A[ssur- . . . -i]n

Commentary

Previously, Alt 1941: 103 and Becking 1992: 112 restored ^{md}*A*[*ššur*-iddi]*n*.[2] Other restorations are, of course, possible.

1. This item was not part of the Fi. collection in Istanbul in 2004, and is reported not to be at Harvard University.
2. For the name, see *PNAE* 187–88.

SAMARIA 2: JUDICIAL DOCUMENT

Basics: Clay tablet fragment; width: 4.85 cm;[3] copy, p. 217

Reg. Nos.: Fi. 16, Samaria 1825, DIV 218 (present location: Arkeoloji Müzeleri, Istanbul)

Primary Publications: Reisner 1924: vol. 1, 247, no. 1 (copy and photo, vol. 2, pl. 56b); Becking 1992: 112–13, no. 2; Radner 1995; Jas 1996: 80–81; Donbaz 1998 (copy, p. 25)

Studies: Langdon 1936; Alt 1941; Galling 1968: 16 5c; Postgate 1976: 59–60; Zadok 1977–78: 52; Donbaz 1988: 6, n. 13; Zadok 1991: 31; Radner 1997: 18; Na'aman and Zadok 2000: 176–77; Van der Toorn 2000: 99; Stern 2001: 15–16 (photo, p. 15); Hallo 2002: 270–71; Horowitz and Oshima 2004: 37; *NEAEHL*: 1306; Weippert 2010: 314 (Text 167), Cogan 2013a: 20–21

Date: Neo-Assyrian period

Language: Akkadian

Find Information: See Reisner 1924: vol. 1, 247; Jas 1996: 81, Hallo 2002: 270

Reisner 1924: 247 read the beginning of a Hebrew name אב . . . on the seal impression. For the latest copy of the full tablet, see Donbaz 1998.

	Edition	**Translation**
1	[*š*]*um-ma ina* ŠÀ-*bi* UD.10.KÁM	[I]f on the 10th day
2	*ša* ^{iti}NE ^{m}U+GUR-*šal-lim*	of Ab Nergal-šallim
3	DU$_{11}$.GA ^{m}*A-a*-PAP.MEŠ	so orders, Aya-ahhe
4	*a-na* LÚ.GAL.URU.MEŠ	to the great man of the cities
5	[*it-t*]*a-din* GUD ⸢6⸣ × ×	[will p]ay an ox and 6 . .

Commentary

The document was collated by the authors in Istanbul. Earlier editors have proposed various readings for the end of line 5.

SAMARIA 3: VOTIVE CYLINDER IN THE FORM OF A CYLINDER SEAL

Basics: Steatite; height: 3.8 cm; diameter: 1.7 cm; copy, p. 217

Reg. No.: I. 10645, Sebastia Excavations 1931 (present location: Israel Museum)

Primary Publication: Gurney, in Crowfoot et al. 1957: 87, no. 18 (photo, pl. 15, no. 18a–b); Becking 1992: 113–14, no. 3

3. The fragment is from the bottom edge of the original and is rounded. Hallo 2002: 270 gives the measurements of the fragment as 2 × 4.9 × 1.9 cm.

Studies: Parker 1949: 7, no. 5 (photo, pl. 1, no. 5); Galling 1968: 61 5d; Na'aman and Zadok 2000: 177, 180; Van der Toorn 2000: 99; Stern 2001: 322; *NEAEHL*: 1306
Date: Neo-Assyrian period
Language: Akkadian
Find Information: Sebastia excavations 1931, B c III, above wall of "tower," no. 179 (Israel Museum: written communication)

The inscription on the cylinder is written in positive script, so that the impression is in the negative. This, in addition to the inscription's request that the seal bless gods on behalf of the seal's owner, demonstrates that the cylinder had a votive function. Cf. Beer Sheva 1.

	Edition	**Translation**
1	^{na4}KIŠ[IB]	The se[al]
2	*šá* ^{md}PA-*za-qi*[*p*]-*e*[*n*$^{?}$-*ši*]	of Nabu-zaqi[p]-e[nši$^{?}$]
3	LÚ [× ×]	the [. .]
4	ÌR *šá* ^{md}⌜AMAR⌝.U[TU × ×]	the servant of Mardu[k- . .]
5	LÚ.GÌR.N[ÍTA]	the commis[sioner.]
6	^{d}[PA]	The gods [Nabu]
7	^{d}*Taš-me-t*[*um*]	(and) Tašmetu[m]
8	^{d}AMAR.UT[U]	(and) Mardu[k]
9	^{d}*Zar-pa-ni-tum*	and Zarpanitum -
10	*a-na* EN ^{na4}KIŠIB	for the sake of the seal's owner
11	*lik-ru-ub*	May it (the seal) bless (these gods).

Commentary

Line 2

For this name, see *PNAE* 905.

Line 6

Scribal convention requires that the last sign of a line be written at the end of the line. Hence, it appears that the scribe began to write the PA for Nabu's name next to the determinative, but then, realizing his error, erased this first PA, and then wrote the sign in its proper place at the now missing right margin. Nabu is the husband of Tašmetum and the son of Marduk and Zarpanitum.

Line 11

The verb in line 11 is as written singular; hence, the subject should be the seal itself. Another possibility is to take the form as a Neo-Assyrian inverse writing for *likrubū* and so translate, "May the gods bless (him)."

SAMARIA 4: FRAGMENT OF NEO-ASSYRIAN STELA

Basics: Stone stela fragment; 24 × 10.5 × 11.5 cm; inscription occupies area of 16 × 7.9 cm; copy, p. 218
Reg. No.: IAA 33.3725 (present location: Rockefeller Museum)
Primary Publication: Gadd, in Crowfoot 1957: 35 (photo and copy, pl. 4, nos. 2–3)
Studies: Galling 1968: 61 5 a; Hestrin et al. 1972: 32, 57 (photo); Cogan and Tadmor 1988: photo, pl. following p. 228 (a.); Becking 1992: 114, no. 4; Stern 2001: 15 (photo); *NEAEHL*: 1306 (photo)
Date: Neo-Assyrian period
Language: Akkadian
Find Information: See Crowfoot 1957: 35

	Edition	**Translation**
1'	. . .] × × [. . .	. . .] . . [
2'	. . .] ⌜*u_4*⌝-*me U*[*Z*$^?$ . . .	. . .] day/storm I$^?$ [. . .
3'	. . .] *u_4-me áš*-×-[. . .	. . .] days/storm I$^?$. [. . .
4'	. . . *i*]*b-ba-nu u* × [. . .	. . . w]ere built and . [. . .
5'	. . .] BURU$_5$.ḪÁ × [. . .	. . .] locusts . [. . .
6'	. . .] *áš-me-ṭu* × [. . .	. . .] dust storm . [. . .
7'	. . .] *ma-si-n*[*a*$^?$ . . .	. . .] *thei*[*r*$^?$] *land* [. . .
8'	. . .] × × [. . .	. . .] . . [. . .

Commentary

Due to the fragmentary nature of the object only a few words can be identified: "days/storm," "locusts," "dust storm," and what appears to be a N-stem verbal form from *banû* in line 4'.

Lines 5' and 6'

The word *erbû*, "locusts," occurs a few times in Neo-Assyrian royal inscriptions (see *CAD* E 257, Sargon II, Sennacherib, Assurbanipal). Line 6', *ašmēṭu,* also written as above, is given as a synonym of *ašamšūtu*, "dust storm," in Malku II (see *CAD* A_{II} 450, *AHw* 82).[4] References to locusts and a storm on a stela from Samaria suggest an episode during Sargon II's 721 BCE campaign in the west, leading to his conquest of the city—perhaps the description of a battle, or some sort of difficulty encountered by Sargon II during the campaign. Such an episode, however, is not yet attested elsewhere in Sargon II inscriptions.

4. If the trace of the last sign in line 6' is of A, perhaps even restore *a*[*šamšūtu*].

SAMARIA 5–7: COINS[5]

A number of coins bearing cuneiform signs have been recovered at Samaria. These can be classified into two types: a *drachma* (which we designate as Samaria 5) and *obols* (which we designate as Samaria 6–7). Two examples of Samaria 5 were published by Meshorer and Qedar 1991: no. 58/1–58/2. Later what would appear to be no. 58/1 alone was republished as Meshorer and Qedar 1999: no. 128. Samaria 5 preserves what appears to be the sign ŠÚ in the upper right-hand corner of its obverse. Dalley, who published drawings of two unidentified examples of the coin in Dalley 1998: 64, understood ŠÚ to give "the first syllable of the city name in cuneiform." Lemaire and Joannès 1994: 85 suggested a reading of MAŠ for 1/2, interpreting this to represent the value of the coin (i.e., 1/2 unit).

To date, only one example of Samaria 6 and two of Samaria 7 have been published. Samaria 6 is the *obol* of Samaria 5. The published example of Samaria 6 (Meshorer and Qedar 1999: no. 129) contains what appear to be three cuneiform signs: a DIŠ in the upper left portion of the coin and two cuneiform signs on its lower obverse—what appears to be a ŠÁ to the right and what appears to be a KUR to the left. The DIŠ could represent the value "1 unit," while KUR ŠÁ for the land of Samarina or the like (cf. Lemaire and Joannès 1994: 84–85). The published examples of Samaria 7 (Meshorer and Qedar 1999: nos. 157, 157.01) are two versions of a single *obol* but of different size and weight. Each has what look may be two DIŠ signs or MIN inscribed on the upper right-hand side of the obverse. Horowitz 2018 reads this sign as a late Babylonian ŠÁ, and takes the ŠÚ and ŠÁ signs for the name of Samaria (Hebrew *Šomron*), suggesting that the presence of these cuneiform signs on late period coins are iconic markings of the continued existence of the community established by the Assyrians at Samaria in the eighth century. Earlier opinion suggested that the signs on the coins may have only had a decorative purpose (Lemaire and Joannès 1994: 86).[6]

SAMARIA 5: *DRACHMA*

Basics of Samaria 5/1: Diameter: 14.5 mm; weight: 3.67 grams (present location: Israel Antiquities Authority)
Basics of Samaria 5/2: Diameter: 14.5 mm; weight: 3.60 grams[7] (private collection)
Reg. No.: None given

5. The authors acknowledge the contributions of Ms. Jennifer Kaufman, and Gil Davis of Macquarie University.

6. Cf. Beth Mirsim 1 for an example of the possible use of cuneiform signs as decorative elements, this time on a Late Bronze cylinder seal. Mildenberg 1996: 131 suggests that the coins may not have been minted at Samaria.

7. The discrepancy in weight between the two examples could be accounted for by a missing sliver.

Primary Publication: Meshorer and Qedar 1991: 55, no. 58 I/2 (drawings, photo, pl. 9); 1999: 107, no. 128 (only Samaria 5/1; drawing, photo, pl. 19)
Studies: Lemaire and Joannès 1994; Dalley 1998: 64;[8] Van der Toorn 2000: 99; Horowitz *in press*
Date: Late Persian period; fourth century BCE

SAMARIA 6: *OBOL*

Basics: Diameter: 9 mm; weight: 0.83 grams (private collection)
Primary Publication: Meshorer and Qedar 1999: 107, no. 129 (drawing, photo, pl. 19)
Studies: Gerson 2001: 113 S-11 (photo), 118; Meshorer, Bijovsky, and Fischer-Bossert 2013: 221, no. 250 (photo pl. 181); Horowitz *in press.*
Date: Late Persian period, fourth century BCE

SAMARIA 7: *OBOL*

Basics of Samaria 7/1: Diameter: 9 mm; weight: 0.56 grams (private collection)
Basics of Samaria 7/2: Diameter: 1.0 mm; weight: 0.62 grams (private collection)
Primary Publication: Meshorer and Qedar 1999: 112 no. 157 (Samaria 7/1), 157.01 (Samaria 7/2) (drawing, p. 112; photo, pl. 23)
Study: Gerson 2001: 114 S-29 (photo), 118; Horowitz *in press*
Date: Late Persian period, fourth century BCE

8. S. Dalley gives drawings of four sides of coins, two of which have the ŠÚ sign on the upper right-hand corner of the obverse as in our Samaria 5, but offers no information which would allow us to positively identify her examples with those in Meshorer and Qedar's publications.

Sepphoris (Ṣippori)[1]

1. Fragment of Inscribed Achaemenid Persian Royal Vase
2–4. Tablet Fragments A–C

SEPPHORIS 1: FRAGMENT OF INSCRIBED ACHAEMENID PERSIAN ROYAL VASE

Basics: Stone vessel fragment; 5.5 × 4.9 × 1.6 cm; photo, p. 234
Reg. No.: Kelsey 90109 (present location: the Kelsey Museum of Archaeology, University of Michigan)
Primary Publication: Stolper 1980: 176 (copy); 1996: 166–67 (photo, p. 166)
Studies: Meyers and Meyers 2009: 139*–40* (photo, p. 139*)
Date: Persian period, Artaxerxes
Language: Parts of Akkadian and Elamite versions survive; the vessel most likely originally bore the name of the king in Old Persian and Egyptian as well (see Stolper 1996: 166)
Find Information: No specific information available. The vessel fragment is listed in the field log, and so must have been present at Sepphoris at the time of the excavations, although no excavation label for the object currently exists

	Edition	**Translation**
1	^{m}*Ir-tak-i*[*k-šá-iš-šá* 3.20]	Arta[xerxes, the King] (Elamite)
2	$^{⸢\text{m}⸣}$*Ar-ta-a*[*k-šá-as-su* LUGAL]	Arta[xerxes, the King] (Akkadian)

SEPPHORIS 2–4: TABLET FRAGMENTS A–C

In 1997, G. Beckman published three inscribed clay tablet fragments (present location: the Kelsey Museum of Archaeology, University of Michigan), reconstructed from

1. The authors wish to thank Professor Gary Beckman (University of Michigan) and Ms. Robin Meador-Woodruff (the Kelsey Museum of Archaeology) for their cooperation in the study of the Sepphoris materials.

material held in common from the 1931 Waterman excavations at Sepphoris (Beckman 1997). This publication included copies of the three fragments, identified as Kelsey 89908 A, B, and C, as well as some suggested readings. Beckman 1997:82 suggested different dates for each of the three fragments, although none is large enough to provide a representative repertoire of signs for dating purposes. It seems to us unlikely that the three fragments could date from different periods. All three were reconstructed from materials held together at the museum, suggesting that the group came from a common archaeological context. Further, the earliest period excavated by Waterman was the Iron Age (*NEAEHL*: 1324–25). The appearance of a Neo-Babylonian date formula in Sepphoris 3 confirms that the tablet should be dated to the Neo-Babylonian or the Achaemenid period.

Sepphoris 2: Fragment A; *Dimensions*: 59 × 9 × 4 mm (collated)
Sepphoris 3: Fragment B: *Dimensions*: 9 × 17 × 8 mm
Sepphoris 4: Fragment C: *Dimensions*: 12 × 28 × 5 mm (collated)

Edition of Sepphoris 2

1'	. . .] × *Ḫ*[*U* . . .	
2'	. . .] *u AB* [. . .	
3'	. . .] × 2 × [. . .	*Too fragmentary for translation*
4'	. . .] × *UB* [. . .	
5'	. . .] × [. . .	
6'	. . .] × [. . .	
7'	*Vacant*	
8'	. . .] × × [. . .	
9'	. . . *L*]*Ú* [. . . . . . *ME* / *ME*[*Š*$^{?}$] 3 [. . .	
10'	. . .] *GA* [. . . . . .] ⸢*ŠU*⸣ × [. . .	

Edition of Sepphoris 3

1'	. . .] DIN$^{?}$-*su-i*[*q-bi* . . .	. . .] Ballassu-i[qbi . . .
2'	. . . ITU × UD] 8 KAM MU [. . .]	. . . Month X, Day] 8, Year [. . .
3'	. . . LUGAL] ⸢E⸣.KI [*u* KUR.KUR.	. . . King of] Babylon [and the lands

Edition of Sepphoris 4
Side A

1'	. . . *B*]*I UŠ*$^{!}$ *A*/*ZA* 2 × [. . .	
2'	. . .] *ra*$^{!}$-*m*[*u D*]*A-sa* [. . .	*Too fragmentary for translation*
3'	. . .] × *KI* × × [. . .	

Side B

1'	. . .] *KA* × [. . .

Commentary

Beckman 1997 attempted to date Sepphoris 4 to the Old Babylonian period. This is based, for the most part, on his reading of the term MU.ÚS.SA, "the coming year," on Side A:2', since this term falls out of use during the Kassite period (see Brinkman 1971). Our proposal to read the line differently releases us from the obligation to consider such an early date for Sepphoris 4. The last two signs may represent a partial GI.

Shechem

1. Letter
2. Administrative Tablet with List of Witnesses
3. Missing Fragment

Shechem 1–2 were both recovered in the 1926 excavations at Tel Balata, but were not found together.

SHECHEM 1: LETTER

Basics: Clay tablet; 4.8 × 3.2 × 1.7 cm; photos, p. 235
Reg. No.: IAA 32.2892 (Balata Excavations 1378; present location: Rockefeller Museum)
Primary Publications: Böhl 1926: 325–27, no. 2 (photo, pl. 44; copy, pl. 46); 1974 (copy, p. 23);[1] Albright 1942a: 30–31; Shaffer 1988 (copy, p. 164); Demsky 1990: 165–70; Na'aman 2004: 93–94
Studies: Landsberger 1954: 59, n. 121; Albright 1955: 22–23; Pritchard 1969: 490; Campbell 1965: 211–13; Galling 1968: 13 A 6b; Edzard 1985: 251; Anbar and Na'aman 1986: 10–11; Na'aman 1994: 176; Zadok 1996: 106; Rainey 1999: 154*–55*; Van der Toorn 2000: 98; Von Dassow 2004: 669, 671; Charpin 2007: 188; Hess 2007: 158
Date: Old Babylonian period, late Middle Bronze Age[2]
Language: Akkadian
Find Information: See Böhl 1926: 321–22; 1974: 24

This edition is based on the copy of A. Shaffer, with collations by the authors as noted.

1. Same copy in both articles, as well as in Albright 1956: 102.
2. See discussion above, pp. 13–14. The sign forms, most notable the A signs, are consistent with the Old Babylonian / Middle Bronze Age repertoire, and mimmation occurs in line 8 (*mi-nu-ú-um*). On the other hand, the use of *inūma* as a subordinating conjunction in line 9 is typical of the Amarna letters and their contemporaries (see Rainey 1996: III, 74–89).

Edition / Translation

Obverse

	Edition	Translation
1	*⸢a⸣+na Pí-ra-aš-še* /-× [× (×)-*i*]*a*	To *Pirašše* . [(.)], *m*[*y lord*$^{?}$]
2	*qí-bí-ma*	say,
3	*um-ma Ma-ni-ti-ìl*/^{d}[(×) ÌR-*k*]*a*	Message of Maniti-Il/DN (.) yo]ur [servant]
4	*iš-tu* MU.3.KAM *a+n*[*a a-ka-a*]*n-na*	Three years ago, t[o her]e
5	[*t*]*u-ša-bi-la-an-ni-*[*ma*]	[y]ou had me sent!
6	*⸢ú⸣-ul* ŠE *ú-ul* Ì *ù-l*[*u* SÍG/TÚG]	Neither grain, nor oil, no[r clothing]
7	*ša tu-ša-ab-ba-lu-*[*ni*]	is what you keep sending [me]!
8	*mi-nu-ú-um ḫi-ṭì*	What is my crime
9	*i-nu-ma ú-ul ta-pa-ṭ*[*e*]*-r*[*a-an-ni*]	that you will not rel[ease me?]
10	*ṣú-ḫa-ru-ú ša it-ti-⸢ia⸣*	The junior attendants who are with me
11	*il-ta-na-ba-ṭù*	keep on suffering.
12	*a-bu-šu-nu ú um-ma-š*[*u-nu*]	Their fathers and t[heir] mothers,

Reverse

	Edition	Translation
1	*ka-la-*[*šu-nu . . . . . -k*]*a-a*	all of [them are/have . . . y]ou!
2	*⸢a-na⸣-ku* × [. . .]	I . [. . .]
3	*⸢ar-tu-ub⸣* [. . .]	I have continued [. . .]
4	*i+na-an-na* [. . .]	Now [. . .]
5	*mi-im-ma a-*[*ka-lam* . . .]	Whatever *f*[*ood* . . .]
6	*šu-bi-la*[*m* . . .]	have delivere[d . . .]
7	*a+na mu-uḫ-ḫi-i*[*a* . . .]	to m[e . . .]
8	*ù li-ša-ḫi-⸢za-an-ni⸣*	and / so let him instruct me.

Commentary

A number of divergent understandings of the letter's general content have been offered. Following Shaffer 1988, we understand the subject matter to be the complaint of a professional in charge of junior apprentices (*ṣuḫāru*)[3] that deliveries of grain, oil, and clothing had not been sent to him.[4] Na'aman 2004: 94 offers a new twist, proposing that the letter was written by Maniti- . . . himself, who, being both a *ṣuhhāru* and probably a scribe, was able to write a complaint about his situation in his own hand. Others have taken the subject of the letter to be that of complaints regarding youngsters in a scribal school (see below).

3. For this category of personnel, see Na'aman 2004; and above, note to Hazor 5:2.

4. For these as basic commodities, see *CAD* L 237 *lubūšu* 3. a), with writings both SÍG.BA and TÚG.BA for clothing allowances.

Line 1

The trace after *Pí-ra-aš-še* could continue the personal name, e.g., *Pí-ra-aš-še-n*[*a*] (see Shaffer 1988: 164), or could start the title "my lord," written E[N-*i*]*a*, or syllabically.

Line 3

The PN may be restored as *Ma-ni-ti-ìl* or *Ma-ni-ti-*^{d}[IM/EN] or the like; perhaps as a sandhi writing of a name of the type *Mannu itti* DN.

Line 4

Three years, being two regular years of 12 lunar months and a leap year of 13 months, was a standard length of time for contracts in the ancient Near East. Hence, as a rule of thumb, three-year contracts were for 37 lunar months, whereas annual contracts could have been for either 12 months or 13 months, or perhaps for 360 days.[5]

Line 6

Perhaps read: *ú-l*[*a*].

Line 11

Collation, as well as a close inspection of MA (ll. 2–3, 9, 12) and BA (l. 7), reveal that the verbal form should be read with BA. Our reading and interpretation follow that of the extensive discussion of the line in Shaffer 1988: 166–68. Here Shaffer takes *il-ta-na-ba-ṭù* as a Gtn form from a verb *labāṭu/lubbuṭu*, with a meaning "to suffer."[6] Previous scholars have read BA = *pá*, taking the form to be a Gtn of *lapātu*, "to touch," with various specific meanings of the verb,[7] while others have read MA, taking it from *lamādu*, "to study."[8]

SHECHEM 2: ADMINISTRATIVE TABLET WITH LIST OF WITNESSES

Basics: Clay tablet; 2.6 × 3.7 × 3.2 cm; copy, p. 218; photos, p. 235
Reg. No.: IAA 32.2891 (Balata Excavations 1350; present location: Rockefeller Museum)
Primary Publication: Böhl 1926: 321–25, no. 1 (photo, pl. 44; copy, pl. 45)

5. See Shaffer 1988: 165, comment on l. 4; Horowitz 1996b: 38–39.

6. Shaffer notes other examples of this verb listed in *CAD* L 92 *sub lapātu* 4. k). Na'aman 2004: 93–94 also takes the verb to be *labāṭu* with this same meaning.

7. See Landsberger 1954: 59, n. 121, which prompted a response in Albright 1955: 22–23: "The letter deals with non-payment of school dues, not with immoral behaviour." Böhl 1974; Rainey 1999.

8. This was first proposed by Albright 1942a: 31a. See also Albright 1955; Demsky 1990, in the context of scribal schools.

Studies: Albright 1942a: 28–30; Landsberger 1954: 59, n. 123; Campbell 1965: 208–11; Galling 1968: 13 A 6a; Edzard 1985: 251; Na'aman 1994: 177; Zadok 1996: 106; Rothenbusch 2000: 483; Van der Toorn 2000: 98; Hess 2003: 47–48; Cohen 2008: 85
Date: Late Bronze Age
Language: Akkadian
Find Information: See Böhl 1926: 321–22; 1974: 24

Shechem 2 preserves the bottom half of an administrative tablet in which only part of a list of witnesses survives. The scribe continues his lines around the right-hand edge of the tablet on to the reverse, as is the case in the contemporary texts Hazor 11 and Jericho 1, and in the alphabetic text Taanach 15.

Edition		**Translation**
Obverse		
1'	⸢*ši-bu*⸣ [m]*Ka-n*[*a*]-*pé*-⸢*el*⸣	Witness: PN
2'	*ši-bu* m*Ḫa-ba-du* DUMU *Na-ṣí-ib-ti*	Witness: Habbadu son of Naṣibti
3'	*ši-bu* m*Su-ar-mu-ḫu* DUMU *Pá-al-ṣí-i*	Witness: Su'armuhu son of Palṣi
4'	[*š*]*i-bu* m*Ia-id*-[*da*]-⸢*du*⸣	[Wi]tness: Ya'id[da]du
Reverse		
1	[*ši-bu* m× -(×)]-×-[×]	[Witness: P]N
2	[*ši*]-*b*]*u* ⸢m⸣×-×-*bi*	[Witne]ss: PN
3	⸢*ši*⸣-*bu* m*Ia-an-ti-na-du*	Witness: Yantinadu
4	*ši-bu* <m>*Ba-*ʾ*-lu-pá-di*	Witness: Baʿlu-padi
5	[*ši-bu* m×] × × [. . .]	[Witness: P]N

Commentary

Line 1'

See Hess 2003: 48 for different writings of this same name, *Ka-na-pa-ìl* at Mari and *Ka-na-pí-li* at Ugarit.

Line 2'

The name is certainly not from the Akkadian root CAD N_{II} 33 *naṣābu* A, "to suck, to lick." We believe that this name comes from the West-Semitic root $nṣb_1$ "to erect," which is probably the same root that CAD gives as *naṣābu* B, "to settle(?)." See *Dictionary of Northwest Semitic Inscriptions* (DNWSI) 749ff. Cf. the PN in Taanach 14:13: [m*N*]*a-ṣa-ab-*⸢*ba*⸣.

Line 3′

Su'armuhu: Compare Amarna ^{m}*Šu-wa-ar-da-ta*/^{m}*Šu-ar-da-tum* (see Hess 1993: 151) with a discussion of Šu(w)ar = Indo-Iranian **suvar*. *Pá-al-ṣí-i*: the same name occurs in alphabetic cuneiform on the Tabor knife (see below).

SHECHEM 3: MISSING FRAGMENT

L. E. Toombs reports in Campbell et al. 1971: 16 the discovery of what appeared to him to be a fragment from the right-hand edge of a letter.[9] The whereabouts of the fragment are presently unknown.

9. The find is also mentioned by Demsky 1990: 163.

Shephela

1. Fragment of Stone Lamaštu Plaque

SHEPHELA 1: FRAGMENT OF STONE LAMAŠTU PLAQUE

Basics: Stone: 7.4 × 8.8 cm (present location: private collection)
Primary Publication: Cogan 1995 (photo, p. 156; copy, p. 157)
Studies: Van der Toorn 2000: 99–100; Stern 2001: 16–17 (copy, p. 17); Jajan 2009: 108
Date: Neo-Assyrian period
Language: Akkadian
Find Information: On southern bank of Naḫal Guvrin, ca. 3 km northwest of Kibbutz Beth Guvrin; see Cogan 1995: 155

The current fragment belongs to the bottom left-hand corner of a Lamaštu plaque with a short incantation on its obverse and a carving of a Lamaštu scene on its reverse. As noted by Cogan 1995: 158, the surviving portion of the current plaque does not correspond to any of the known formulations. New readings and discussion are available in Jajan 2009. A new edition by Jacqueline Vayntrub is in preparation. The edition and translation below follow Cogan.

	Edition	**Translation**
1'	. . .] × [. . .	. . .] . [. . .
2'	. . .] *si-si*[*k*$^{?}$-*ti*$^{?}$]	. . .] *he*[*m* of a garment]
3'	. . .] $^{\ulcorner d \urcorner}$*En-líl* × [×]	. . .] Enlil . [.]
4'	. . .]-*nu u* ^{d}MES	. . .] . and Marduk
5'	. . .]-×-*ši KID A DI* ×	. . .] . . . . .
6'	. . .]-× *A* ÉN	. . .] . . Incantation.

Commentary

Lines 3′–4′

We would expect further names of deities between the names of Enlil and Marduk. For line 4′, a restoration of [. . . ^{d}*A*]-*nu* is possible.

Line 5′

Jajan 1994 reads the last signs *ú-a-di-an-*[*ni*$^{?}$].

Taanach

1. Letter of Ehli-Tešub to Talwašur
2. Letter of Ahiami to Talwašur
3. Administrative Tablet with List of People Called for Service
4. Administrative Tablet with Personal Names

4a. Administrative Fragment with Personal Names[1]

5. Letter of Amenhatpa to Talwašur
6. Letter of Amenhatpa to Talwašur
7. Administrative Tablet with List of Personal Names
8. Letter Fragment

8a. Letter Fragment

9. Letter Fragment
10. Letter Fragment
11. Letter Fragment
12. Fragment of Administrative Tablet with List of Personal Names
13. Inscribed Cylinder Seal
14. Administrative Tablet with List of Personal Names
15. Alphabetic Cuneiform Text

Taanach has yielded 17 cuneiform finds, the second largest number from any one site in our corpus (after Hazor). The original group of 14 tablets and fragments, as well as a fifteenth item, an inscribed cylinder seal, were excavated by E. Sellin in 1903–4 and deposited in Istanbul. The remaining two items, an administrative document and an alphabetic tablet, were excavated in the 1960s. The 17 finds include nine letters or letter fragments, six administrative documents or fragments, a seal, and an alphabetic text. The Taanach tablets in standard cuneiform most probably date from the late fifteenth century.[2]

Between the time of the closing of the first edition of *Cuneiform in Canaaan* in 2005 and the date of the present book a set of three articles on the Taanach tablets appeared in the volume marking the hundredth anniversary of the original Taanach publications (Kreuzer 2006). These appear below in the bibliography as Horowitz and Oshima 2006, Horowitz, Kreuzer, and Oshima 2006, and Pruzsinszky 2006. The first provides an overview of the Taanach tablets; the second gives new German translations of the texts with some short notes; and the third provides a new study of the personal names. The volume also offers a reprint of the original editions of the

1. We have used the numbers 4a and 8a, following the traditional system established by Hrozný (see below).
2. For the dating of the Taanach texts, see Rainey 1999: 153*–56*.

Taanach tablets by Hrozný on pp. 245–54 and 307–15. Cochavi-Rainey 2005: 305 and Berlejung 2006: 230–31 also provide a short review of the Taanach texts. The survey immediately below by W. Horowitz and T. Oshima reflects the state of scholarship as of 2005 with some brief updates.

THE HISTORY OF STUDY AND PUBLICATION

The main group of 14 tablets and fragments from Sellin's excavations was first published by F. Hrozný in the Taanach excavation reports (Hrozný 1904; 1905). In these studies Hrozný published editions, copies, and photographs, and established the traditional numbering system for the Taanach texts, including the convention of identifying two small fragments as Taanach 4a and 8a.[3] For the subsequent 100 years, no new copies or photographs of these pieces were published, although the four nearly complete letters, Taanach 1–2 and 5–6, were studied and edited numerous times. The first study to offer substantial changes and improvements over the original publication was that of A. Glock (1983), who used collations carried out by himself and E. Gordon in 1966.[4] These collations, which were recorded in Glock's notebooks, serve as a second witness to the text of the letters, although Glock himself did not prepare new copies or full editions of the texts. A third witness for the letters is Rainey's 1999 edition of Taanach 1–2 and 5–6. Here Rainey offers further improvements, based on the readings of both Glock and Gordon, as well as Rainey's own 1971 collations.[5] Glock and Gordon also collated the letter fragments Taanach 8–8a, 9–10, and 11, but did not publish their findings. Finally, the family of our late colleague, Professor Aaron Shaffer, has allowed us to use his unpublished notes on the Fi. collection, which include preliminary editions, photographs, and a number of provisional copies of tablets.[6]

The administrative tablets and fragments from Sellin's excavations are Taanach 3, 4a, 7, and 12. These, like the letters, were published in full with editions, copies, and photographs in Hrozný 1904 and 1905, yet attracted far less attention than the letters. In fact, no new editions of the administrative tablets or fragments were ever published, although a number of scholars studied the personal names at Taanach,

3. As previously mentioned, we too follow this system, in order to avoid creating two conflicting sets of numbers. This is why the highest-numbered text in Taanach is 15, even though 17 items were found there.

4. We would like to thank Anson F. Rainey for granting his permission to work with Glock's notebooks, and Shlomo Izre'el for facilitating this study.

5. Passages from the letters are also quoted in Rainey 1996; see index in vol. 4, pp. 187–88.

6. We thank Mrs. Ethel Shaffer for making these materials available to us. Mrs. Shaffer informed us that Aaron visited the museum in Istanbul a number of times; therefore, we cannot be sure when the copies and photographs were made. However, it is certain that Shaffer's photos are later than those published by Hrozný since they show evidence of deterioration since Hrozný's time. We put into evidence below the photographs and a provisional copy of Taanach 2, which was brought up to publication standard by T. Oshima, and a copy of Taanach 8. We would like to thank Nathan Wassesrman for bringing the materials to our attention.

including those in the administrative group. These included Halévy 1904 and later Gustavs 1927 and 1928. More recently, the names were included in a broader study of second-millennium personal names from Canaan conducted by Zadok (1996), who makes use of the unpublished collations of the administrative lists of Glock and Gordon[7] and gives a comprehensive bibliography. For the second edition we can add the important work on the Taanach personal names Pruzsinszky 2006. A short study of the Taanach personal names is found in Hess 2003: 37–40.[8]

In April 2004, W. Horowitz and T. Oshima traveled to Istanbul to study the tablets belonging to the Fi. (Filistin) collection of the Arkeoloji Müzeleri. At that time, they were able to examine and prepare new copies for most of the Taanach texts.[9] Unfortunately, Taanach 2 and 5 were not available for study at this time, as they were not in the archives, but were held in a separate location among the museum's display objects for safekeeping during renovation work.[10] Two additional Taanach tablets—the fragments Taanach 4a and Taanach 12—were not part of the Fi. collection, and their present location is unknown. We presume that both fragments were already missing from the Arkeoloji Müzeleri in 1966 at the time of Glock and Gordon's visit, since their notebooks offer no comments or collations for these fragments.[11] Thus, the two fragments must have been lost or misplaced sometime between 1905 and 1966. Horowitz and Oshima were also unable to see the cylinder seal Taanach 13 during their visit to Istanbul.

The editions of the Taanach tablets in the Fi. collection—Taanach 1, 3–4, 6–11—are based on the copies prepared during the Horowitz-Oshima visit to Istanbul. The editions of Taanach 2 and 5 are based on the photographs in Hrozný 1904 and 1905, as well as on the later work of Glock, Gordon, Rainey, and Shaffer.[12] The editions of the now missing fragments Taanach 4a and 12 are based on Hrozný's work.

This methodology is not without its own set of problems even in the case of those tablets in the Fi. collection that Horowitz and Oshima were able to see in Istanbul. A comparison of Hrozný's editions from 1904 and 1905 and the work in Istanbul a century later shows a number of discrepancies. In some cases, Hrozný's copies proved to be unreliable and have been corrected over the years by the collations of Glock and Gordon, by Rainey's collations, and more recently by our own.

7. See Zadok 1996: 106. Some of the collations are also given in Glock 1971, who includes a sign list comparing the sign forms on Taanach 14 with those on Taanach tablets in the Fi. collection, as well as Megiddo 1 (the Gilgamesh fragment) and Amarna letters from Megiddo (pp. 24–25).

8. Many of the names also appear in more general studies of personal names, such as Tallqvist 1914 and Hess 1993, as well as D. Sivan's study of Northwest Semitic (1984).

9. We gratefully acknowledge the kind help and gracious courtesy extended to us by Prof. V. Donbaz during our stay in Istanbul. A summary of our activities at the museum is to be found in Horowitz and Oshima 2005.

10. Notes in the storage boxes in which these two tablets rested in the archives confirmed the tablets' museum numbers.

11. Aaron Shaffer's notes do not include any reference to the two tablets either.

12. For uncertain signs and signs on the edges we follow Rainey 1999.

Moreover, the tablets have suffered somewhat over the years. In particular, a significant portion of the reverse of Taanach 3 has broken away. In other places, Hrozný saw signs that are not now visible. In the case of signs that Hrozný saw but that are no longer present on the original tablets, it is reasonable to assume that at least some of the signs have simply rubbed off over time. Hence, we typically give Hrozný the benefit of the doubt and restore what he saw in brackets. In the case of disagreement between Hrozný and ourselves, we follow our own eyes.

TAANACH 1: LETTER OF EHLI-TEŠUB TO TALWAŠUR

Basics: Clay tablet; 5.6 × 5.5 × 1.5 cm; copy, p. 219; photos, p. 236
Reg. Nos.: Fi. 1, EŞ 2788 (present location: Arkeoloji Müzeleri, Istanbul)
Primary Publications: Hrozný 1904: 113–14 (photo, pl. 10; copy, p. 121); Maisler 1937: 56–58; Albright 1944: 16–20; Rainey 1999: 156*–57
Studies: Peiser 1903: 321–22; Holma 1914; Ebeling, in Gressman 1926: 371;[13] Landsberger 1954: 59; Galling 1968: 14; Albright, in Pritchard 1969: 490; Rainey 1977: *passim*; Glock 1983: 59–60; Görg 1988; Schneider 1992: 236; Na'aman 1994: 177; Rainey 1996: IV, 187 (index); Zadok 1996: 106, 110; Na'aman 2004: 94–95; Berlejung 2006: 331–32; Horowitz, Kreuzer, and Oshima 2006: 87–88; Cochavi-Rainey 2007: 307; Rainey-Schniedewind 2015: 1502
Language: Akkadian
Date: Late Bronze Age, fifteenth century BCE
Find Information: See Glock 1983: 58–59

	Edition	**Translation**
	Obverse	
1	*⸢a-na⸣* ^{m}*Tal-wa-šur*	To Talwašur
2	*qí-bí-ma*	say.
3	*um-ma* ^{m}*Eḫ-li-*^{d}IM	Message of Ehli-Tešub:
4	*bu-lu-uṭ dam-qí-⸢iš⸣*	Live well.
5	DINGIR.⸢MEŠ⸣ *li-iš-a-lu*	May the gods ask after
6	*⸢šu⸣-lim-ka šu-lum*	your health, the health
7	É-*ka* DUMU.MEŠ-*ka*	of your house (and) your sons.
8	*at-ta ta-aš-pu-⸢ra⸣*	You wrote
9	*a-na ia-ši aš-šum* 50$^{!}$ KÙ.BABBAR.⸢ḪÁ⸣	to me concerning the 50 (shekels) of silver.
10	*ù a-nu-ma a-na-⸢din⸣-[n]a*	So now I am giving over
11	50 KÙ.BABBAR.ḪÁ *ki la ⸢e⸣-[p]u-šu*	50 (shekels) of silver. How could I not do so?

13. For an earlier translation, see Ungnad in Gressman 1909: 128–29.

12	*ša-ni-tam ⸢a-na mi⸣-n[im]*	Moreover, wh[y]
13	*la*$^{!}$*-a*$^{!}$ *tu-wa-š[a-ru-ni]*	are you not sending

Reverse

14	*šu-lum-ka a-na i[a-ši]*	(news) of your health to m[e.]
15	*ù a-wa-tam m[i]-i[m-ma]*	So wha[tever] word
16	*ša ti-iš-mé*	that you heard
17	*iš-tu aš-ra-nu-um*	from there,
18	*šu-up-ra-am it-<ti>-i[a]*	write to me.
19	*ša-ni-tam ù šum-ma*	Moreover, if
20	*i-ba-ši ú-ba-an*	there is even a finger
21	^{giš}*za-ar-ni-nu*	of *zarninu*-wood
22	*ù mu-ur-ru*	or myrrh
23	*ù id-na-am*	then give (them) to me.
24	*ù a-wa-tam te-ra-ni*	So send back word to me
25	*aš-šum* SAL.TUR ^{f}*Ka-×-×*	concerning the young woman/ junior servant of Ka . .
26	*⸢ša⸣ i-na* URU *Ru-bu-⸢ti⸣*[^{ki}]	who is in Rubuti
27	*[a]-⸢na⸣ ša-al-mi-ša*	[as t]o her well-being,

Left Edge

28	*ù šum-ma i-ra-bi*	and when she grows up,
29	*[l]i-id-di[n]-ši a-na* KÙ.BABBAR *ip-⸢ṭe*$_4$*⸣-ri*	[l]et him giv[e] her for ransom money,
30	*ù lu-ú a-[n]a be-lim*	or f[o]r a husband.

Commentary

Line 1

This Hurrian name appears four times in the Taanach letters (Taanach 1:1; 2:1; 5:1; 6:1); always with the same writing, ^{m}RI.PI.SUR. Rainey 1999: 157* *passim* reads ^{m}*Tal-wi-šar* on the basis of Egyptian (*Twlw3śr* =*Tu-l-wá-śá-r*).[14] However, we cannot concur. The last sign is clearly SUR/ŠUR, rather than ŠAR, a common sign with reading *šar/šir*$_9$*/šer*$_9$ in Amarna and the west, but never *sur/šur*.[15] Thus, the cuneiform version of the name may best be rendered Talwašur, although we admit that the name might have been pronounced different in ancient Taanach—Talwašor or perhaps even Tolwašor. See also now Pruzsinsky 2006: 106–7.

Line 3

For the reading of the name with the Hurrian DN, see Rainey 1999: 157*.

14. For the Taanach name in the context of Egyptian personal names, see also Schneider 1992: 236.
15. See, e.g., Izre'el 1991: II, 121.

Lines 5–7

This Canaanite blessing is nearly identical to that of Hazor 10:4–6 (see Horowitz 2000: 20).

Line 12

The scribe writes NI in *ša-ni-tam* without vertical strokes, both here and in line 19, with *ni-tam* forming a sort of ligature. Thus also, e.g., Taanach 2:13, 19, 21; 6:6, 12, 18. Elsewhere, the NI sign at Taanach is as expected.

Line 13

The first two signs in the line, *la*$^{!}$-*a*$^{!}$, are badly distorted by a RI sign, which intrudes from line 29, written on the left edge.

Line 18

This use of *itti*, with the meaning of "to, towards," is noted in Rainey 1996: III, 37–38, which quotes our passage.

Line 21

The meaning of the word is still uncertain. Na'aman 1994: 177 suggests that it is a Hurrian term.

Line 26

The identification of this town, which is also mentioned twice in the Amarna letters, is still unknown.[16]

TAANACH 2: LETTER OF AHIAMI TO TALWAŠUR

Basics: Clay tablet; copy, p. 219; photos, p. 236

Reg. No.: Fi. 2, EŞ 2789 (present location: Arkeoloji Müzeleri, Istanbul)

Primary Publication: Hrozný 1904: 115–17 (photo, pl. 10; copy, p. 121); Maisler 1937: 54–56; Albright 1944: 20–23; Rainey 1999: 157*–59*

Studies: Peiser 1903; Ebeling, in Gressman 1926: 371; Sachs 1937–39: 372–73; Landsberger 1954: 59; Moran 1963: 174; Galling 1968: 14; Rainey 1977: 63–64 and *passim*; Glock 1983: 60–61; Na'aman 1988; Rainey 1996: IV, 188 (index); Zadok 1996: 106–7, 110; Von Dassow 2004: 670–71; Cochavi-Rainey 2005: 307; Berlejung 2006: 232; Horowitz, Kreuzer, and Oshima 2006: 88–89; Charpin 2007: 188; Cohen 2008: 85; Smith M. 2008: 56.

Language: Akkadian

16. See Moran 1992: 391, with a much longer and earlier discussion in Albright 1944: 19.

Date: Late Bronze Age, fifteenth century BCE
Find Information: See Glock 1983: 58–59

	Edition	**Translation**
	Obverse	
1	*a-na* ^{m}*Tal-wa-šur [q]í-bí*	To Talwašur [s]ay:
2	*um-ma* ^{m}ŠEŠ-*ia-mi* EN DINGIR.MEŠ-*nu*	Message of Ahiami: May the Lord God
3	ZI-*ka lí-iṣ-ṣur* ŠEŠ *at-ta*	guard your life. You are a brother
4	*ù na-ra-mu i-na aš-ri šu-wa-at*	and a beloved friend in that place.
5	*ù i-na* ŠÀ-*bi-ka i-nu-ma*	Now, it is in your mind that
6	*ar-ba-ku i-na* É *ra-qí*	I have entered into an "empty house"
7	*ù id-na-an-ni ú-ba-an*	so give me a finger (give me an inch)
8	2 ^{giš}*ma-ga-ri-ma ù* GIŠ.PAN	(in regard to) two chariot wheels and a bow
9	*ù* 2 ^{túg}*up-pa-aš-ia-ni-ma ù*	and 2 *uppašannu*, so
10	*šum-ma ga-am-ra-at* GIŠ.PAN	if the bow is finished
11	*i-pé-ša-am ù uš-ši-ra-aš-ši*	being made, then send it to me
12	*i-na* ŠU ^{m}*Pu-ur-da-ya*	through the agency of Purdaya
13	*ša-ni-tam pí-qí-id a-na* URU.DIDLI.ḪÁ-*ka*	Furthermore, command your towns
14	*ù lu-ú ti-pu-šu ip-ša-šu\-nu*	that they should do their work.
	Reverse	
15	UGU SAG.DU-*ia ma-am-ma-an*	On my head is everything
16	*ša it-tab-šu a-na* URU.KI.DIDLI.ḪÁ	which took place in regard to the cities.
17	⸢*i*⸣-*na-an-na a-mur-ni i-nu-ma*	Now, see that
18	*i-pu-šu* DÙG.GA *it-ti-ka*	I am doing you a favor.
19	*ša-ni-tam šum-ma* GI.GAG$^{!}$.Ú.TAG.GA URUDU.ḪÁ	Furthermore, if copper arrows
20	*i-ba-aš-šu ù lu-ú tu-da-nu-na*	are around, then have them given over.
21	*ša-ni-tam li-ru-ba-am* ^{m}DINGIR-*ra-pí-i*	Furthermore, let Ilu-rapi enter
22	*a-na* URU *Ra-ḫa-bi ù lu-ú*	into Rehov$^{?}$ and I will certainly
23	*i-wa-ši-ra* LÚ-*ia a-na maḫ-ri-ka*	send my man to you
24	*ù lu-ú i-pu-šu ḫa-at-nu-tam*	and I will certainly arrange a marriage.

Commentary

The edition was prepared from Hrozný 1904, Rainey 1999, and Shaffer's photographs and provisional copy.

Lines 2–3

Baʿalu ilānu. For the translation "The Lord God," despite the apparent plural, note the use of the singular verbal form *liṣṣur*, and cf., in our corpus, Hazor 10:20–22, for what appears to be plural DINGIR.MEŠ as the subject of singular *ip-ta-ra-*{erasure}*-aš-ni.*[17]

Lines 8–10

As noted by Na'aman 1988: 180, the goods being requested are all from the realm of chariot warfare and are therefore representative of the upper-class status of Ahiami. For the item in line 9, see now CAD U/W 182 *uppasannu* (an object made of wool or leather).

Lines 13–14

The fem. pl. for towns is used here. See Hazor 3 g with note (above, p. 68).

Lines 15–16

Meaning: "I am responsible for everything that took place in regard to the cities."

Line 19

A list of various writings for arrows is given in Sachs 1937–39: 372–73.

Line 22

For a discussion of this place-name, see Rainey 1999: 158*–59*.

TAANACH 3: ADMINISTRATIVE TABLET WITH LIST OF PEOPLE CALLED FOR SERVICE

Basics: Clay tablet; 10 × 9 × 3.2 cm; copy, p. 219; photos, p. 237
Reg. No.: Fi. 3, EŞ 2790 (present location: Arkeoloji Müzeleri, Istanbul)
Primary Publication: Hrozný 1904: 117–19 (photo, pl. 11; copy, p. 122); Maisler 1937: 59–60
Studies: Landsberger 1954: 59; Galling 1968: 14; Heltzer 1981: 81; Zadok 1996: 107; Horowitz and Oshima 2004: 34; Horowitz, Kreuzer, and Oshima 2006: 89–90
Language: Akkadian

17. For a discussion of this phenomenon, see Horowitz 2000: 22–23; Rainey 1996: I, 147. Cf. *YHWH ʾelōhîm* in the Bible and analogous forms in Ugaritic, Phoenician, and Palmyrene Aramaic. See also M. S. Smith 2010: 55–56, n. 83, and Na'aman 2005: 249–50.

Date: Late Bronze Age, fifteenth century BCE
Find Information: See Glock 1983: 58–59

The context of Taanach 3 is the mobilization of personnel for some purpose. The verb in line 6' and probably in rev. 16' as well (*dekû*)[18] has a number of meanings appropriate to this context, including "to levy taxes," "to call up corvée workers," "to mobilize soldiers," and "to summon officials."[19] Each PN appears to have had a number associated with it, but the function of these numbers, as well as that of the surviving text as a whole, is not certain.

Note that the bottom left corner of the reverse (at rev. 8' ff.) broke away sometime between Hrozný's edition and the photograph made available to A. Shaffer. In this portion of our edition, we leave the readings from Hrozný's copy in brackets.

	Edition	**Translation**
	Obverse	
1'	[^{m}×-×-×-×] 1	[PN] 1
2'	[^{m}×-×-×-×] 1	[PN] 1
3'	[^{m}×-×-×]-× 1$^{?}$ (*text AŠ*)	[P]N 1$^{?}$
4'	[^{m}×-×-*d*]*a-da* 1	[P]N 1
5'	[^{m}×-×-*d*]*a-bi-di* 1 10	[P]N 1. (Total of) 10
6'	[*š*]*a id-ku-ú*	[w]hom they called up.
7'	[^{m}]⸢*E*⸣-*li-tu* 1	Elitu 1
8'	^{m}DUMU-*Ḫu-bi-ri* 1	Bin-Hubiri 1
9'	^{m}[DUM]U-*Ra-ba-ya* 1	[Bi]n-Rabaya 1
10'	[^{m}×] × × [× ×]	[P]N [. .]
	Reverse	
1'	[^{m}× . . .	[PN]
2'	^{m}*Mi-ta-*[*ti* . . .	Mita[ti . . .]
3'	^{m}DUMU-*E-ze-e-*[× ×]	Bin-Eze[. .]
4'	^{m}*Ze-ra-ya* LÚ.SU 1	Zeraya, the Sutean$^{?}$ 1
5'	^{m}*Ta-a-gu* 1	Tagu 1
6'	^{m}DUMU-⸢*Ba*⸣-*wa-za-en-zi* 1	Bin?-Bawazaʾenzi 1
7'	^{m}⸢*Uz*⸣-*di-a-ša* 3	Uzdiaša 3
8'	[^{m}*Ka-m*]*a-ru* 1	[Kam]aru 1
9'	[^{m}*Ya-ṣ*]*ur-rù-zi-ir-ta-wa* 2	[Yaṣ]urruzirtawa 2
10'	[^{m}*P*]*u-ra-gu-uš* 2	Puraguš 2
11'	[^{m}*A-i*]*a-*⸢*ri*⸣ 3	[Ay]ari 3
12'	[^{m}*Ia-d*]*i-in-nu* 1	[Yad]innu 1
13'	[^{m}*Ya-mi*]*-ba-an-da-*LUGAL 1	[Yami]banda-. 1
14'	[^{m}×-*d*]*a-ya* LÚ.AŠGAB 1	[P]N, the leatherworker 1

18. Hrozný's copy reads [*i*]*d-ku-ú*. We can now only confirm [*id-k*]*u*$^{?}$-⸢*ú*⸣.
19. Landsberger 1954: 59, n. 123, followed by Zadok 1996, reads line 6' as the PN [*N*]*a-it-ku-ú*.

15'	[^{m}×]-×-*lu* 1 20	[P]N 1, (total of) 20
16'	[*ša id-k*]*u*$^{?}$-⌜*ú*⌝	[whom they called u]p$^{?}$

Lower Edge

. . .] × *U ŠU*$^{?}$	. . .] . . .

Left Edge
Col. i
traces

Col. ii

1	[^{m}×]-×-^{d}IM [. . .	[.] . -*Storm God* [. . .
2	[^{m}]⌜*A*⌝-*bi*-[. . .	Abi[. . .
3	[^{m}]*Ad-da*-×-[. . .	Adda-. [. .]
4	^{m}*Pu-ri-i*[*š*- . . .	Puri[š . . .
5	^{m}×-*mi*-[. . .	P[N]
6	$^{m⌜}$DUMU-*A*⌝-×-×	Bin-A[. . .

Commentary

Note the relatively high percentage of PNs of the form *Bīn*- . . . (20–25 percent of the names preserving the opening elements) in this and the other administrative texts from Taanach.

Reverse, line 1'

The traces from this line on Hrozný's copy are no longer visible.

Line 3'

Hess 1993: 59 takes this to be a form of Amarna *Bin-a-zi-mi*. The initial e-vowel in the Taanach name seems to indicate the original consonant *ʿayin* from the root ʿZY; see Sivan 1984: 205.

Line 4'

Heltzer 1981: 81 suggests that LÚ.SU here is for the Suteans, but does not give another example of this writing in his book. We cannot find another example of LÚ.SU = Sutean either, and so cannot be certain that Heltzer is correct.

Line 9'

No line of Taanach 3 has more than one name. Hence, we take this name to consist of two elements, the first being the verbal form *yaṣṣuru* from **yanṣuru*.[20] We cannot identify the second element Zirtawa, but cf. ⌜^{m}⌝*Zi-ir-wa-ša* in Taanach 7 ii 4.

20. Cf. *Ia-an-ṣur-*^{d}*Addu*, "Addu has protected," in Hazor 7, lower edge 2.

Line 10'

This could be another name beginning with the element Pur/Pura-, for which see Horowitz 2000: 23–24.

Line 13'

The element *banda* here derives from Indo-European *bánduḫ* (see Hess 1993: 226; Zadok 1996: 108). For *banda* see also the PN in Taanach 4:13'. The LUGAL in the name, with uncertain reading, would seem to be part of the PN. It seems nearly inconceivable that a royal name would be placed in such an inauspicious position in an administrative document.

Left Edge

There appear to be two columns on the left edge. Most of the surviving signs come from col. ii, but signs or traces are found to the left of col. ii 3' ff.

TAANACH 4: ADMINISTRATIVE TABLET WITH PERSONAL NAMES

Basics: Clay tablet; 8.8 × 9.0 × 2.4 cm; copy, p. 220; photos, p. 237
Reg. No.: Fi. 4 EŞ 2787 (present location: Arkeoloji Müzeleri, Istanbul)
Primary Publication: Hrozný 1904: 119–21 (photo, pl. 11; copy, p. 122); Maisler 1937: 60–62
Studies: Landsberger 1954: 59; Galling 1968: 14; Zadok 1996: 107–8; Horowitz and Oshima 2004: 34; Horowitz, Kreuzer, and Oshima 2006: 90–91; Cohen 2008: 85
Language: Presumably Akkadian, although only PNs, a numeral, and the Sumerogram DUMU, "son," are preserved
Date: Late Bronze Age, fifteenth century BCE
Find Information: See Glock 1983: 58–59

Taanach 4, like Taanach 3, is now in a much poorer state of repair than that indicated in Hrozný's copy of a century ago.

Edition / Translation

Obverse

	Edition	Translation
1'	⸢^{m}⸣[× ×]× [(×)]×	[P]N
2'	^{m}[×]-×-*tu-na*	[P]N
3'	^{m}*I-lu-lu* DUMU *Su-bi-ir-ri*	Ilulu son of Subirri
	———	———
4'	^{m}DUMU-*Za-nu-*⸢*qí*⸣*-ma*	Bin-Zanuqima
5'	[^{m}×]-*el-zu*$^{?}$*-na* DUMU *Na-ba-ṭi*	[P]N son of Nabaṭi
	———	———
6'	[^{m}AN]-*ya-mu-*⸢*na*⸣	[.]-yamuna

7'	[^{m}×-×]-×-*nim*	[P]N
8'	^{m}×-×-*rù*	PN
9'	^{m}[×]-×-^{d}IM ^{m}*E-lu-ra-am*$^{!}$*-ma*	. . -*Storm God*, Eluramma
10'	^{m}[×]-*ru-a-da*	[P]N
11'	^{m}⸢*Na*⸣-[*g*]*u-na-zu*	PN
12'	[^{m}*R*]*A*$^{?}$*-BE-šu* DUMU *A-gi-*[*i*]*a*	[P]N son of Agiya
13'	[^{m}] ×-*ba-an-du* DUMU *B*[*A*$^{?}$*-D*]*A*$^{?}$*-na* 10	[P]N son of PN 10
14'	[^{m}×]-⸢*da-ši*⸣*-ak* [. . .] ×	[P]N

Reverse

1'–2'	*traces*	
3'	[^{m}×]-×-*a-nu* DUMU *Mi-i*[*s-ki*]	[P]N son of Mi[ski]
4'	[^{m}*Ḫ*]*a-ri-ZU-*[(×)]	[P]N
5'	[^{m}]*Qa-ti-nu-*×	[P]N
6'	^{m}*Dup-da-ya* DUMU *Za-gu-*[. . .	Dupdaya son of P[N]
7'	^{m}ÌR-*ša-ru-na* DUMU *Zi-*⸢*ib*⸣-[. . .	Abdi-šaruna son of P[N]
8'	^{m}*Ta-aš-ru-mu*	Tašrumu
9'	[× ×] × [× × ×] ×-*ia*	[. .] . [. . .] . .

Commentary

Line 6'

As copied, the name might possible be a hypochoristicon of the DN *Yamm*, but many other readings are possible, including [^{m}×]-*an-ya-mu-na*. See Zadok 1996: 108, and Gröndahl 1967: 144: *Ia-mu-na*; and cf. Taanach 3:13': [^{m}*Ya-mi*]-*ba-an-da*.

Line 9'

The name also occurs in Taanach 7, 12, and 14; see Index of Personal Names.

Line 14'

The final sign here is possibly a sign from over the edge of the reverse.

TAANACH 4A: ADMINISTRATIVE FRAGMENT WITH PERSONAL NAMES

Basics: Clay tablet (now missing)

Primary Publication: Hrozný 1904: 119–20 (copy. p. 122); Maisler 1937: 60

Studies: Galling 1968: 14; Zadok 1996: 108; Horowitz, Kreuzer, and Oshima 2006: 91.
Language: Presumably Akkadian, although only parts of PNs are preserved
Date: Late Bronze Age, fifteenth century BCE
Find Information: See Glock 1983: 58–59

The small fragment is not part of the current Fi. collection of the Arkeoloji Müzeleri, and its whereabouts are unknown. A photograph of this fragment was not included in Hrozný's editions.

Edition		Translation
1'	[ᵐ×]-*PI*-× [. . .	[P]N
2'	ᵐ*Y*[*a*ˀ]/*B*[*a*ˀ]-*an-d*[*a*ˀ- . . .	P[N]
3'	ᵐ*Na-ši-m*[*a*- . . .	P[N]
4'	[ᵐ]×-*ZI*-[. . .	[P]N

TAANACH 5: LETTER OF AMENHATPA TO TALWAŠUR

Basics: Clay tablet; photos, p. 238[21]
Reg. No.: Fi. 5, EŞ 2798 (present location: Arkeoloji Müzeleri, Istanbul)
Primary Publication: Hrozný 1905: 36–37 (photo, pl. 1, pl. 3): Maisler 1937: 51–52; Albright 1944: 23–24; Rainey 1999: 169*
Studies: Hrozný 1906; Feigin 1934: 226–27; Landsberger 1954: 59; Galling 1968: 14; Rainey 1977: 64 and *passim*; Malamat 1961: 218–27; Glock 1983: 61; Zadok 1996: 106; Horowitz and Oshima 2004: 34; Cochavi-Rainey 2005: 306; Berlejung 2006: 233–34; Horowitz, Kreuzer, and Oshima 2006: 91–92
Language: Akkadian
Date: Late Bronze Age, fifteenth century BCE
Find Information: See Glock 1983: 58–59; Sellin 1905: 34–35

Taanach 5–6 are both from Amenhatpa to Talwašur and are apparently from Megiddo. In Taanach 5:13–15, there is a request that items be sent to Megiddo; the ductus of both letters resembles that of the Amarna letters from Megiddo (Rainey 1996: II, 31); and the repeated use of the Northwest Semitic enclitic *-mi* in Taanach 5–6 (seven times—Taanach 5:4, 6; Taanach 6:6, 8, 10, 13, 19—but not once in Taanach 1–2 is a tendency shared with the Megiddo Amarna letters (see Izre'el 1998a: 42).

Edition		Translation
Obverse		
1	*a-na Tal-wa-šur*	To Talwašur
2	*um-ma A-ma-an-ḫa-at-pa*	Message of Amanhatpa:
3	ᵈIM ZI-*ta-ka li-iṣ-ṣur*	May the Storm God guard your life.

21. A. Shaffer's files did not include a completed copy of Taanach 5.

4	*uš-še-ra-am-mi* ˹ŠEŠ˺.MEŠ-*ka*	Send me your brothers
5	*qa-du* GIŠ.GIGIR.MEŠ-*šu*-[*nu*]	together with the[ir] chariots,
6	*ù uš-še-ra-am-*˹*mi*˺	and send me
7	ANŠE.KUR.RA GUN-*ka*	the horse(s), your tribute;
8	*ù* IGI.DU$_8$.ḪÁ	and an audience gift;
9	*ù ka-li*	and all
10	˹LÚ.MEŠ *a*˺-*si*$_{17}$-*ri*	the captives

Reverse

11	*ša i-ba-aš-*˹*šu-ú*˺	who are presently
12	*it-ti-ka*	with you.
13	*uš-še-ra-šu-*˹*nu*˺	Send them
14	*u*$_4$*-mi ma-ḫa-ri*	tomorrow
15	*a-na* URU *Ma-gi-id-\da*	to Megiddo.

Commentary

Line 3

The DN was most likely realized as Baʿal at this time and place; see Horowitz 1996a: 216, n. 18, with evidence from Pella.

Line 10

We follow Albright 1944: 24 n. 79 and Rainey 1999: 160* in understanding the word to be *asīru*, "prisoner of war, captive foreigner used as a worker," with the unusual reading SI$_{17}$ for ŠI.[22] For the word with LÚ in similar contexts at Amarna, Alalakh, and Ugarit, see *CAD* A$_{II}$ 332.

TAANACH 6: LETTER OF AMENHATPA TO TALWAŠUR

Basics: Clay tablet; 5.8 × 5.0 × 2.0 cm; copy, p. 220; photos, p. 238

Reg. No.: Fi. 6, EŞ 2799 (present location: Arkeoloji Müzeleri, Istanbul)

Primary Publications: Hrozný 1905: 37–38 (photo, pl. 1; copy, pl. 3); Maisler 1937: 52–54; Albright 1944: 24–25; Rainey 1999: 159*–60*

Studies: Hrozný 1906 (photo, pl. 124, obverse only); Lambdin 1953: 150; Landsberger 1954: 59; Malamat 1961: 218–27; Galling 1968: 14; Rainey 1977: 64 and *passim*; Glock 1983: 61–62; Zadok 1996: 106, 108–9; Izreʾel 1998b: 424; Horowitz and Oshima 2004: 34–35; Cochavi-Rainey 2005: 306; Berlejung 2006: 232–33; Horowitz, Kreuzer, and Oshima 2006: 92–93

Language: Akkadian

Date: Late Bronze Age, fifteenth century BCE

Find Information: Glock 1983: 58–59; Sellin 1905: 34–35

22. For two examples from Ugarit, see Izreʾel 1991: II, 127.

Taanach 6 is in parts badly damaged. Our restorations are not as bold as those of Rainey 1999.

	Edition	**Translation**
	Obverse	
1	[*a-na Ta*]*l-wa-šur*	[To Ta]lwašur
2	[*um-ma A*]*-ma-an-ḫa-at-pa*	[Message of A]manhatpa:
3	[^{d}IM] ZI-*ta-ka li-*[*iṣ-ṣur*]	[May the Storm God gu]ard your life.
4	[*pa-n*]*a-nu-um Ba-az-ú-nu*	[For]merly, Baz'unu
5	⸢DUMU⸣ *Na-ar-sí tu-wa-še-ru*	son of Narsi is whom you were sending
6	*a-na ia-a-ši ša-ni-tam la-a-mi*	to me. Furthermore,
7	⸢*i*⸣*-na ma-an-ṣa-ar-ti i-*⸢*ba-šu*⸣	your retainers are not on guard and
8	⸢*ḫa*⸣*-na-ku-u-ka ù la-a-mi*	
9	*ti-il*$_5$*-la-ku en-na at-t*[*a*]	you yourse[lf] do not come
10	*a-na maḫ-ri-ia ù šum-ma-mi*	before me nor do you
11	*tu-wa-še-ru-na* ŠEŠ-*ka*	send your brothers here
12	*ša-ni-tam i-na* URU *Ḫa-za-t*[*i*]	Furthermore, in Gaza
13	*i-ba-ša-ti ù la-a-mi*	I was, but
14	*ti-il*$_5$*-la-ku-na a-na ma*[*ḫ-ri*]*-ia*	you did not come t[o m]e.
	Reverse	
15	*a-nu-*[*m*]*a a-*⸢*na*⸣*-*[*ku uṣ-ṣu-n*[*a*]	Now I [am going fort[h]
16	*a-na nu-kur-t*[*i . . .*	to wa[r . . .]
17	[*i*]*-ba-ša-*⸢*ta*⸣ [× × × × *-k*]*a*	you are [. . . . of yo[urs
18	[*š*]*a-ni-tam* ⸢ŠEŠ⸣.M[EŠ-*ka ù* L]Ú.MEŠ	[F]urthermore [your] brothers [and your y[oung men - you do [no]t
19	[*ṣ*]*e*$^{?}$*-eḫ-ru-t*[*i-ka la-a*]*-mi*	
20	[*ta-w*]*a-*⸢*še*⸣*-ru-u*[*š-šu-nu a-na m*]*aḫ-ri-*⸢*ia*⸣	[s]end [them t]o me.
21	[. . . *-k*]*a*	[. . .] of yours
22	[*a-na*] *maḫ-*⸢*ri*⸣*-ia u*[*š-še-ra-šu-nu*]	s[end them to] me
23	[*a-nu-u*]*m-ma!* LÚ.MEŠ *ḫu-ub-t*[*e*]	[No]w, in regard to the captiv[es]
24	[*š*]*a ap-ta-aṭ-tu*	[w]hom I have redeemed,
25	[*uš-š*]*e-ra-šu-nu* ⸢ŠEŠ.MEŠ⸣*-ka ù*	[se]nd them. As for [your] broth-er[s] and
26	[× ×] × ×*-šu-nu* [.	[. .] their . . [. . . . .
27	[× × × *š*]*a-ni-tam* × [. . .	[. . . F]urthermore . [. . .]
28	[*uš-še-ra*] *a-na m*[*aḫ-ri-ia i-na*]	[send] to m[e]
29	[*u*$_4$*-mi ma-ḫ*]*a-ri ù* × [. . .	[tomo]rrow and . [. . .

Commentary

Lines 6, 8, 10, 13, and 19

For the Northwest Semitic enclitic *-mi* in Taanach 5–6, see the introduction to Taanach 5.

Line 8

ḫa-na-ku is most probably an Egyptian loan word that also appears in Genesis 14:14; see Rainey 1999: 159* and Berlejung 2006: 233 n. 9.

Line 14

The first word is complete in Hrozný's copy and in Shaffer's photograph.

Rev. 15

The trace at the end of the line may confirm Rainey's restoration.

TAANACH 7: ADMINISTRATIVE TABLET WITH LIST OF PERSONAL NAMES

Basics: Clay tablet; 7.6 × 6.3 cm; copy, p. 220; photos, p. 239
Reg. No.: Fi. 7, EŞ 2800 (present location: Arkeoloji Müzeleri, Istanbul)
Primary Publication: Hrozný 1905: 38–39 (photo, pl. 2; copy, pl. 3); Maisler 1937: 62–64
Studies: Landsberger 1954: 59; Galling 1968: 14; Zadok 1996: 109; Horowitz and Oshima 2004: 35; Horowitz, Kreuzer, and Oshima 2006: 93–94
Language: Akkadian
Date: Late Bronze Age, fifteenth century BCE
Find Information: See Glock 1983: 58–59

The shape of the present fragment indicates that what we have is from the right half of the original, i.e., the obverse col. ii and reverse col. i. The horizontal ruling at the start of obverse col. ii would be most unusual at the beginning of a document. Most, but not all, of the personal names are assigned a numeral of uncertain significance.

Edition		Translation
Obverse, col. ii		
1	*⸢a⸣-wa-ti*	(By) the word
2	[^{m}]×*-zu-*[*r*]*a-mi*	(of) PN
3	[^{m}]ÌR-*⸢šar⸣-ru-ma* 1	Abdi-šarruma 1

4	⸢^{m}⸣*Zi-ir-wa-ša* 2	Zirwaša 2
5	^{m}*Ga-ma-lu* 2	Gamalu 2
6	^{m}DUMU-*D*[*a*]-*ni-ya* 1	Bin-D[a]niya 1
7	^{m}DUMU-*Ḫu-n*[*i*]-*ni* 3	Bin-Hun[i]ni 3
8	^{m}*Bi-il*-×-×-×-× ⸢1⸣	PN 1
9	^{m}*Ak-ti-m*[*i*(-) . . .	P[N . . .
10	^{m}*Ia-an-d*[*i*- . . .	Yand[i- . . .
11	^{m}DUMU-*Ya-y*[*a*- . . .] × (×)	Bin-Yay[a- . . .] . .
12	^{m}ÌR-^{d}I[M . . .	Abdi-Ad[du . . .
13	^{m}*A-b*[*i* . . .	Ab[i . . .

Reverse, col. i

1'	^{m}⸢*Ḫi*⸣-*bi*-[*ya* . . .	Hibi[ya . . .
2'	^{m}*Za-wa-ia* 3	Zawaya 3
3'	^{m}*E-lu-ra-ma* 1	Elurama 1
4'	^{m}DUMU-*Ia-ma*-× × ⸢1⸣	Bin-Yama- . . 1
5'	^{m}*Ze-ra*-[. . .	P[N . . .]
6'	^{m}BE.LUM-*i*[a_5 . . .	Baʿaliy[a . . .
7'	^{m}ÌR-*Ḫe-b*[*a* . . .	Abdi-Heb[a . . .
8'	^{m}DUMU-*Id*-×-× ⸢1⸣	Bin- . . . 1
9'	^{m}*Ir-ze-e-tu* 1	Irzetu 1
10'	^{m}*Ḫa-ba*-⸢*du*⸣ 1	Habadu 1
11'	^{m}*Zi-q*[*u*]-*un-bu* 1	Ziq[u]nbu 1

Commentary

Obverse, col. ii, line 11

At the end of the line, ×(×) is most likely for the end of a sign and the bottom of the numeral 1, but other readings are possible.

Line 12

Hrozný: ^{m}ÌR-^{d}I[M]-*du*

Reverse, col. i, line 1'

For the name, see Taanach 14:9; and Hess 1993: 76–77.

Line 3'

The name also occurs in Taanach 4, 12, and 14; see Index of Personal Names.

Line 6'

The writing ^{m}BE.LUM-*ia*$_5$ is an *Akkadogram* with phonetic ending for the hypocoriston *Baʿaliya*. Cf. Hazor 11:2: ^{m}*Ba*-⸢ʾ⸣-*li-ia*$_5$.

TAANACH 8: LETTER FRAGMENT

Basics: Clay tablet; 3.4 × 4.1 × 1.5 cm; copy, p. 221
Reg. No.: Fi. 14, EŞ 2801?[23] (present location: Arkeoloji Müzeleri, Istanbul)
Primary Publication: Hrozný 1905: 39–40 (photo, pl. 2; copy, pl. 3); Maisler 1937: 58
Studies: Galling 1968: 14; Zadok 1996: 109; Horowitz and Oshima 2004: 36; Horowitz, Kreuzer, and Oshima 2006: 94–95
Language: Akkadian
Date: Late Bronze Age, fifteenth century BCE
Find Information: See Glock 1983: 58–59

No physical join between fragments 8 and 8a is possible. Moreover, it is highly unlikely that they belong to the same original since the hand of the two pieces seems to be different. Here too, some signs along the broken edges of the fragment have been lost over the past century.

	Edition	**Translation**
	Obverse	
1'	. . .] × ×	. . .] . .
2'	. . . *a-nu-u*]*m-*˹*ma*˺ LÚ-*ia*	. . . No]w my man.
3'	. . .] × ˹*ut*˺-*ta-šìr ù*	. . .] . has sent and
4'	. . .] ^{m}*Ra-ba-ia it-ti-šu*	. . .] Rabaya with him
5'	. . . P]AP KÙ.BABBAR.ḪÁ *i-na*	. . . sum t]otal of the monies in
6'	. . .] *ù-lu i-te-na*	. . .] or should he give$^{?}$
7'	. . .] *ù šum-ma la-*[*a-mi*]	. . .] and if no[t]
8'	. . . *il-l*]*a-kam ù t*[*i-*×-(×)]	. . . will c]ome here and you$^{?}$ [. . .]
	Reverse	
1'	. . .] *Ù* [×] ×	. . . [ ] .
2'	. . .]-*mu* ˹A˺.AN.MEŠ	. . .] . rain
3'	. . . *a*]-*na ia-ši*	. . . t]o me
4'	. . .]-*la-ta*	. . .] . .
5'	. . . -*m*]*a*	. . .] .
6'	. . .] ×-˹BAL˺-*n*[*i*]	. . .] . . .

Commentary

Obverse, line 6'

For writings of forms of *nadānu* with *te*/*te*$_7$ at Ugarit and Amarna, see Sivan 1984: 255, 292. Cf. Rainey 1996: II, 56–57.

23. The question mark is that of the museum's identification materials.

Line 7′
Hrozný, at the edge: *la*-⌜*a*⌝-[*mi*].

Reverse, line 2′
Could this be a gloss [*ša*]-*mu* = ŠÈG.MEŠ (A.AN.MEŠ) for *šamû*, "rain"?

TAANACH 8A: LETTER FRAGMENT[24]

Basics: Clay tablet; 3.1 × 1.7 × 1.2 cm; copy, p. 221
Reg. No.: Fi. 15, EŞ 2803 (present location: Arkeoloji Müzeleri, Istanbul)
Primary Publications: Hrozný 1905: 40 (photo, pl. 2; copy, pl. 3); Maisler 1937: 58
Studies: Galling 1968: 14; Horowitz and Oshima 2004: 36; Horowitz, Kreuzer, and Oshima 2006: 94–95.
Language: Akkadian
Date: Late Bronze Age, fifteenth century BCE
Find Information: See Glock 1983: 58–59

	Edition	**Translation**
1'	*a-nu-*[*um-ma* . . .	No[w . . .
2'	*i-na* [. . .	in [. . .
3'	*uš-te-*[. .	. . [. . . .
4'	[*š*]*a-ni-t*[*am* . . .	[M]oreo[ver . . .
5'	[×] × [. . .	[.] . [. . .

TAANACH 9: LETTER FRAGMENT

Basics: Clay tablet; 2.3 × 2.4 × 1.4 cm; copy, p. 221; photos, p. 239
Reg. No.: Fi. 8, EŞ 2805 (present location: Arkeoloji Müzeleri, Istanbul)
Primary Publication: Hrozný 1905: 40 (photo, pl. 2; copy, pl. 3); Maisler 1937: 58
Studies: Albright 1944: 25; Galling 1968: 14; Zadok 1996: 106, 109; Horowitz and Oshima 2004: 35; Horowitz, Kreuzer, and Oshima 2006: 95
Language: Akkadian
Date: Late Bronze Age, fifteenth century BCE
Find Information: See Glock 1983: 58–59

Hrozný believed that the obverse of the fragment was from the upper edge and so restored his lines 1–2 (our lines 1'–2') as the address formula, with the recipient being the man we know as Talawašur, as in Taanach 1, 2, 5, and 6. Based on this assumption,

24. As previously mentioned, there is no join between Taanach 8a and Taanach 8.

Albright 1944: 25, n. 94, proposed a reading *Ki-su-na* for the sender.[25] Our inspection of the tablet cannot confirm either proposal. The only word that may be gleaned from the surviving signs is the conjunction "and" in rev. 2'.

Edition

Obverse

1'	. . .] ×	
2'	. . .] *TU ZU*$^{!}$	
3'	. . .] *TI*	*Too fragmentary for translation*
4'	. . .] ×-*at u* [. . .	
5'	. . .] × [. . .	

Reverse

1'	. . .] × *RA* × [. . .
2'	. . .] × *ù* [. . .
3'	. . .] × × *UD* [. . .

TAANACH 10: LETTER FRAGMENT

Basics: Clay tablet; 3.3 × 4.0 × 3.0 cm; copy, p. 221; photo, p. 239
Reg. No.: Fi. 9, EŞ 2802 (present location: Arkeoloji Müzeleri, Istanbul)
Primary Publication: Hrozný 1905: 41 (photo, pl. 2; copy, pl. 3)
Studies: Galling 1968: 14; Horowitz and Oshima 2004: 35; Horowitz, Kreuzer, and Oshima 2006: 95
Language: Akkadian
Date: Late Bronze Age, fifteenth century BCE
Find Information: See Glock 1983: 58–59

	Edition	**Translation**
1'	. . .]-×-*mi zi-r*[*i* . . .	. . .] . . . . [. . .
2'	. . . -*u*]*t*$^{?}$-*te AN* × [. . .	. . .] . . . . [. . .
3'	. . .]-×-*ka a-n*[*a* . . .	. . .] your . [. .] t[o . . .
4'	. . .] ˹*DA*˺ [. . .	. . .] . [. . .

TAANACH 11: LETTER FRAGMENT

Basics: Clay tablet; 3.3 × 4.0 × 3.0 cm; copy, p. 222; photo, p. 240
Reg. No.: Fi. 10, EŞ 2804 (present location: Arkeoloji Müzeleri, Istanbul)

25. We saw no sign NA along the edge.

Primary Publication: Hrozný 1905: 41 (photo, pl. 2; copy, pl. 3)
Studies: Galling 1968: 14; Horowitz and Oshima 2004: 35; Horowitz, Kreuzer, and Oshima 2006: 95
Language: Akkadian
Date: Late Bronze Age, fifteenth century BCE
Find Information: See Glock 1983: 58–59

After inspection of the tablet it seems certain to us that Hrozný's obverse? is the reverse and vice versa.

Edition	**Translation**
Obverse	
1' . . . *ša*] ⸢*ad-bu-bu*⸣	. . . which] I spoke out (about)
2' . . . *at*?]*-tu-nu-ma*	. . . y]ou (*pl.*)
3' . . . *a*]*t-tu-ma*	. . . y]ou
———	———

Reverse	
1' . . . *t*]*e*-⸢*du*⸣ [. . .	. . .] . . [. . .
———	———
2' . . .] *i-nu-te*^m^[^eš^	. . .] equipmen[t . . .
3' . . .]*-ia*	. . .] my [. . .

Commentary

Reverse, line 2'

We take this to be an unusual writing of *AHw* 1422 *u/e/anūtu*, "tools, equipment, household utensils, etc.," with i.

TAANACH 12: FRAGMENT OF ADMINISTRATIVE TABLET WITH LIST OF PERSONAL NAMES

Basics: Clay tablet; 3.5 × 3.5 cm[26] (location unknown)
Primary Publication: Hrozný 1905: 41 (photo, pl. 2; copy, pl. 3); Maisler 1937: 64–65
Studies: Galling 1968: 14; Zadok 1996: 110; Horowitz, Kreuzer, and Oshima 2006: 96
Language: Presumed Akkadian, but only parts of PNs survive
Date: Late Bronze Age, fifteenth century BCE
Find Information: See Glock 1983: 58–59

26. Thus Hrozný 1905: 41.

This small fragment, like Taanach 4a, is no longer with the Fi. collection in the Arkeoloji Müzeleri.

Edition		Translation
1'	[^{m}×]-*EN*$^{?}$-×	[P]N
2'	^{m}*A-bi-ra-*[. . .	Abi-ra[. . .
3'	^{m}*E-lu-ra-m*[*a*/*a*[*m-ma* . . .	Eluram[a/a[mma . . .
4'	^{m}*Mu-ut-*[. . .	Mut-[. . .
5'	^{m}×-[. . .	P[N]

Commentary

Line 3'

This is probably the same name as the one in Taanach 4, 7, and 14 (see Index of Personal Names).

Line 4'

Cf. the name of the famous Mut-Baʿal from Pella in the Amarna letters (Hess 1993: 114–15).

TAANACH 13: INSCRIBED CYLINDER SEAL

Basics: Dark syenite; height: 3.0 cm; diameter: 4.1 cm (present location: Arkeoloji Müzeleri, Istanbul)
Primary Publications: Sellin 1904: 27–28 (copy, p. 28; fig. 22); Nougayrol 1939: 37–39 (copy, pl. 12, TT. 1)
Studies: Gressman 1927: 164, no. 577; Galling 1968: 14 A 8b; Horowitz, Kreuzer, and Oshima 2006: 96
Language: Akkadian (Sumerograms)
Date: Late Bronze Age, fifteenth century BCE
Find Information: See Glock 1983: 58–59

Edition		Translation
1	*A-ta-na-aḫ-ì-lí*	Atanahili
2	[D]UMU *Ḫa-ab-si-im*	[the s]on of Habsim
3	ÌR ^{d}NÉ$^{!}$.ERI$_{11}$.GAL	the servant of Nergal

Commentary

Line 1

For this type of name, see *CAD* A$_{II}$ 103 *anāhu* A 2b.

TAANACH 14: ADMINISTRATIVE TABLET WITH LIST OF PERSONAL NAMES

Basics: Clay tablet; 5.1 × 3.0 × 1.1 cm; photos, p. 240
Reg. No.: TT 950 (present location: Israel Museum)
Primary Publication: Glock 1971 (photo, pp. 18–20; copy, p. 21)
Studies: Mayrhofer 1972; Zadok 1996: 119; Hess 2003: 39–40; Horowitz, Kreuzer, and Oshima 2006: 96–97; *NEAEHL*: 1431 (photo)
Language: Presumably Akkadian; only PNs survive
Date: Late Bronze Age, fifteenth century BCE
Find Information: See Glock 1971: 17

	Edition	**Translation**
1	[^{m}]⸢ÌR⸣-LUGAL	Abdi-milki
2	⸢^{m}⸣*Ša-ba-ya*	Šabaya
3	^{m}*Pu*-^{d}IM	Pu-Baʿal
4	^{m}*Zi-bi-lu*	Zibilu
5	^{m}DUMU-*A-ya*	Bin-Aya
6	^{m}DUMU-*An*-[*t*]*a*-⸢*ma*$^{?}$⸣	Bin-Antama
7	^{m}ÌR-⸢*da*⸣-*ya*	Abdaya
8	^{m}*Pu-ri-iz*-⸢*zu*⸣-*ya*	Purizzuya
9	^{m}*Ḫi-bi-ya*	Hibiya
10	^{m}DINGIR-*ra-ma*	Elurama
11	^{m}*Zi-ni-ta-ba-an-di*	Zinitabandi
12	^{m}*Bi-ir-ya-ma-aš-da*	Biryamašda
13	[^{m}*N*]*a-ṣi-ib-ti*	[N]aṣibti
14	[13 *ṣ*]*a-bu* LÚ × [. . .	[13 (men), the wo]rk group . . [. . .
15	[× ×] × × × É	[. .] . . . temple/estate$^{?}$

Commentary

Line 1

This is but one of a number of possible renderings of the name; see Hess 2003: 39, n. 18.

Line 3

For this name at El-Amarna with a possible phonetic writing of the DN, see Hess 1993: 126–27.

Line 6

Glock 1971 suggests this could be a phonetic writing for *Bīn-Anat*. If so, cf. Hazor 5:1, *Bīn-Ha-nu-ta* in our corpus.

Line 9
See comment to Taanach 7, rev. i 1.

Line 10
This may be the same person as the one in Taanach 4, 7, and 12 (see Index of Personal Names).

Line 11
The second sign in the name is clearly NI. GLock 1971 proposes a correction to IR and then compares the name with Taanach 7 ii 4: ⸢m⸣*Zi-ir-wa-ša*.

Line 12
This is an older form of an Indo-Aryan name attested in the Rig-Veda; see Mayrhofer 1972: 119–21, and more recently Pruzsinszky 2006: 108.

Line 13
Cf. Shechem 2:2': *Na-ṣí-ib-ti*.

TAANACH 15: ALPHABETIC CUNEIFORM TEXT

For an edition with bibliography and discussion, see Part III, pp. 165–67, and Horowitz, Kreuzer, and Oshima 2006: 97–99.

Tabor

1. Alphabetic Cuneiform Inscription on Knife Blade

For an edition with bibliography and discussion, see Part III, pp. 168–71.

Wingate

1. Inscribed Cylinder Seal Found near Wingate Institute

WINGATE 1: INSCRIBED CYLINDER SEAL FOUND NEAR WINGATE INSTITUTE

Basics: White chalcedony; length: 38 mm; diameter: 16 mm
Reg. Nos.: Seal impression: IAA 60-1355, Cast IAA 60-1356 (unknown location)[1]
Primary Publications: Tadmor and Tadmor 1967 (photo, pl. 6:1–2; copy p. 69); 1995 (photo, p. 347, pls. 2–3, copy, 348, figs. 1–2)
Studies: Stern 2001: 17–18 (photo, p. 18); *PNAE*: 287
Date: Neo-Assyrian period
Language: Akkadian written in Sumerograms
Find Information: See Tadmor and Tadmor 1995: 345

Edition	Translation
1 NA$_4$.KIŠIB ^{m}EN.MAŠ	The seal of Bel-ašared
2 GAL É.GAL (*rab ēkalli*)	the palace overseer

1. The object was lost in tragic circumstances; see Tadmor and Tadmor 1995: 355. "The young man who had found the seal did not agree to part from it, believing that it was his lucky amulet. Unfortunately, he was killed some years later on the banks of the Suez Canal and the present location of the seal is unknown again." An impression and cast are held at the Israel Antiquities Authority.

PART III

Alphabetic Cuneiform Texts

Beth Shemesh 1

ALPHABETIC CUNEIFORM ABECEDARY

Basics: Clay tablet; 14.8 × 5.2 × 2.9 cm
Reg. No.: IAA 33.1867 (present location: Israel Antiquities Authority storerooms, Rockefeller Museum, Jerusalem)
Primary Publications: Grant 1933 (photo, p. 4); 1934: 27 (photo, pl. 20; copy, p. 29, no. 1); Barton 1933 (photo, p. 4; copy, p. 5); Albright 1934 (copy, p. 19); 1964: 51–53; Loundine 1987 (copy, p. 244); Puech 1991; Sass 1991 (photo and copy, p. 326); Sanders 2009: 92–93 (copy).
Studies: Virolleaud 1960; Weippert 1966: 313–14; Cross 1967 14*; Galling 1968: 14; Naveh 1982: 28–30 (copy, p. 28, fig. 22); Puech 1986: 207–8 (copy, p. 202); Dietrich and Loretz 1988a, 1988b: 277–96, 303, 305–7; 1989: 104; Ryckmans 1988; Pardee and Bourdreuil 1995; 2001; Zadok 1996: 115; *NEAEHL*: 250 (photo)[1]
Date: Late Bronze Age; thirteenth century BCE
Language: West-Semitic alphabet
Find Information: Room 526, Stratum IVa; see Grant 1934: 27

The Beth Shemesh tablet was the first alphabetic cuneiform text to be discovered outside Ugarit. The tablet is distinctive in physical format, mode of inscription, and content.

The tablet was found in 1933 in a stratum dated to the end of the Late Bronze Age (Grant 1934: 27). This stratum seems to have been destroyed around 1200 BCE. Since the tablet's script is unlikely to pre-date that of Ugarit, a thirteenth-century date is indicated. Barton 1933 has noted that the tablet appeared to have been made in a mold. It has an anomalous shape for an alphabetic cuneiform tablet: a smooth texture, flat sides, and a marked flare on the back right edge. Further, it has a distinct taper towards the left, giving it a sharper edge on the left (0.7 cm) than on the right (1.3 cm), where it flares towards the end.[2]

1. The articles by Dietrich and Loretz give some further general bibliography.

2. The shape most resembles that of an adze, and given the extensive metalwork that went on at Beth-Shemesh one possibility is that the object was shaped in a mold for an iron tool. Obviously one of the three alphabetic cuneiform inscriptions is found on a weapon, the Tabor knife (see below). A second possibility is that it is a ritual object shaped like a tongue.

Second, our alphabetic clay axe bears a unique type of inscription: it is inscribed in a single counterclockwise arc along the outer limit of the flat of the "blade," running from the top right to the top left, down along the "edge" and then from the bottom left to the bottom right, so that it could be read continuously by rotating the tablet 180°. The letters are executed loosely and display noncanonical "southern" letter forms, such as *d* with symmetrical heads.

The Beth Shemesh tablet was unearthed by Grant in 1933 in a broken condition; one photograph was taken, but the tablet was further damaged that year and has suffered further damage since then.[3] Consequently, the photograph in the initial report (Grant 1933: 4) is the first and best witness to the tablet.[4] Written in the opposite direction from the alphabetic cuneiform texts then known and bearing a chain of letters with no obvious significance, a wide range of interpretations were proposed. None, however, was convincing. In 1987, Loundin cut the Gordian knot by demonstrating that the text had no "meaning" at all, showing that instead it was an abecedary of a new type, with its first eight letters clearly displaying an order corresponding to that found in South Arabian epigraphic inscriptions of the first few centuries CE.[5] Puech 1991 confirmed that this alphabetic order continued in the bottom portion of the text. Today, over 80 years after its discovery, it is clear that the tablet bears an abecedary of some 27 letters.

Scholars gave this discovery an ethnic interpretation, postulating connections between nomadic South Arabian tribes and Syria in the Late Bronze Age.[6] However, while the order underlying this text is so close to the order chosen by later South Arabian scribes that their common ancestry is clear, the text has no distinctively "South Arabian" features. That is, while it shares a common proto-Semitic sound inventory and a few possible letter forms with later epigraphic South Arabian, there is no evidence of any broader structural correspondence.[7]

3. Autopsy in 2004 reveals that a small chunk of clay on the bottom of the recto, which in 1933 bore most of the ġ, has since fallen off.

4. Albright 1934: 18 reports as follows: "The surface has suffered considerably since the photograph published in the Bulletin (*BASOR* 52: 4) was made by Grant." Later photographs, such as the one appearing in Grant 1934: p. 20, were made after the tablet was already damaged. Courtois 1969: pl. facing p. 79, gives a color photograph of the damaged tablet.

5. The most complete order is, according to Irvine and Beeston 1988, known from Qatabanian. It must be emphasized, however, that *all* existing South Arabian abecedaries are defective, missing the *ẓ* and sometimes the *h*, and varying in the order of *b* and *ġ*. The complete "South Arabian alphabetic order" is in fact the work of modern scholarship. This should caution us against attributing a fully worked-out, fixed, and unchanging order to what appears to have been an evolving ancient tradition.

6. Note the title of Dietrich and Loretz 1988a: "Die Alphabettafel aus Bet Šemeš und die ursprüngliche Heimat der Ugariter." Cf. their discussion of possible "ethnic, linguistic, social and political differences" (four categories assumed to go together) between two different alphabetic "traditions" carried by two separate "language groups" (Dietrich and Loretz 1989: 110–12). For important counter-arguments, see, primarily, Sass 1991: "The fact that the Sabaeans chose the *hlḥ* and not the *ʾbg* order is in itself no confirmation of the former being South Semitic in Palestine" (Sass 1991: 319) and Knauf 1989. For some other fundamental issues, see Sanders 2004.

7. Most importantly, the distinctive South Arabian sibilant s^2, corresponding to Hebrew *ś* but unattested in Ugaritic, as well as the *ẓ* phoneme, are both absent. Attempts to directly connect this text with any specific

In 1995, Pardee and Bordreuil published a parallel text, unearthed in 1988 at Ugarit (published in full by them in 2001). This text, RS 88.2215, is an abecedary, written like the canonical alphabet of Ugarit from left to right on a standard tablet, taller than it is wide, at the hands of a more skilled scribe than that of the Beth Shemesh tablet. Reasonably well preserved, it allows us for the first time to reconstruct the entire contents of the Beth Shemesh text.[8] All of the preserved signs on the Beth Shemesh tablet correspond to the signs of RS 88.2215, and the two texts share distinct features, such as the 90° rotation of sibilants, although letters such as *ǵ* and *ṭ* show distinctive forms, as opposed to both the Beth Shemesh tablet and the canonical letter forms of Ugaritic. Both texts preserve the same alphabetic order, and the size of the breaks on the Beth Shemesh tablet fits the number of missing letters attested in the Ras Shamra text precisely. There are two letters missing from the Beth Shemesh tablet where one would expect them on the basis of the Ras Shamra text.[9] These absences can be explained by variance in letter order or scribal error.[10]

The Beth Shemesh tablet, when deciphered with the help of the new abecedary, allows us to make two important observations. First, there was a language variety being taught in the southern Levant at the end of the Late Bronze Age which contained as wide a phoneme inventory as standard Ugaritic. It renders implausible the idea that the south possessed a single, reduced "southern" or "Canaanite" alphabet which was closer to the Phoenician linear alphabet in its inventory.[11] Second, there are now two main branches of the alphabetical order known from the second millennium BCE, the *ʾbgd* order first known from thirteenth-century Ugarit and the *hlḥm* order, first known from a recently deciphered fifteenth-century Theban ostracon that combines alphabetic and hieratic signs (Haring 2015; Fischer-Eifert and Krebernik 2016). Thus, the Beth Shemesh abecedary represents what may be the older and more original of the two. The order of our tablet, while it did not persist into the first millennium Levant (where all documented abecedaries are in the linear alphabet and follow the *ʾbgd* order), also traveled more widely. While the *hlḥm* order is best known from Epigraphic South Arabian and Classical Ethiopic,

South Arabian language, let alone ethnic identity, are therefore dubious. Furthermore, a closely similar sequence of consonants is found in Egyptian; see Quack 1993.

8. The uncertainty of interpretation before Pardee and Bordreuil's publication, even after Loundin's discovery, is described by Sass 1991: 317: "only the first eight or nine letters belong unequivocally to an abecedary."

9. These letters are the *b*, expected in ninth position, and the *ḏ*, found in eleventh position in the Ras Shamra text.

10. As the *ḏ* is found near the end of the alphabet in the South Arabian exemplars, third to last in the attested abcedaries, it is quite plausible that it would have appeared in a similar position in the Beth Shemesh tablet, in the break at the end. The absence of *b* is more problematic, but admits two possible explanations: (1) scribal error: the tablet is sloppily written, though no obvious copying error, such as dittography, comes to mind considering the shape of the characters; (2) variant letter order: in the South Arabian texts, *b* and *ǵ* exchange position between ninth and twenty-third place. It is also plausible that the place of the *b* was not yet fixed in the tradition our text represents, and it appeared near the end or in one of the medial breaks.

11. For analysis of the noncanonical alphabet cuneiform texts, see Bordreuil 1979; 1981; and above all, 1983.

it appears in later Egyptian texts (of the late first millennium BCE through the early Roman period; Quack 2003) which are not in an alphabet at all but rather use this sequence to order lists of items such as personal names or birds by the initial sound of their names. It thus connects the Late Bronze Age Southern Levant more closely with Egypt through alphabetic traditions.

Edition

h l ḥ m q w ṯ r t š k n ⸢ḫ⸣ [. . .] ʿ⸢ḍ g⸣ d ⸢ġ ṭ z⸣ [. . .

Taanach 15

ALPHABETIC CUNEIFORM TEXT

Basics: Clay tablet; 22 × 12.5 × 48 mm
Reg. No.: TT 433 (location unknown)[12]
Primary Publications: Hillers 1964 (photo, pp. 46–47; copy, p. 48); Cross 1968 (copy, p. 45)
Studies: Weippert 1966: 314–15; 1967; Galling 1968: 14; Rainey 1969; Dietrich, Loretz, and Sanmartin 1974; Janowski 1982: 62–63; Naveh 1982: 29–30; Puech 1986: 203–6 (copy, p. 202); Dijkstra 1986: 122, n. 7; Zadok 1996: 115–16; Dietrich and Loretz 1988b: 246–47; *NEAEHL*: 1431 (photo); Cogan 2007: 247
Date: Twelfth century BCE
Language: West Semitic
Find Information: Found in 1963 north of the center of the southwest quadrant in the destruction of a large roofed building dated by Lapp to the early twelfth century BCE; see Lapp 1964: 23

Unlike most alphabetic cuneiform tablets from the southern Levant and the other two examples from Israel, the Taanach tablet is written from left to right. Sloppily inscribed and difficult to decipher, it nonetheless displays sufficient distinctive features to place it firmly with the noncanonical southern texts: an absence of word dividers; paleographic distinctions, such as the symmetrical writing of the *b* (both also found in the Tabor knife); a symmetrical *d*, found in the Beth Shemesh tablet; and a *ṯ* sign to be read *š*, with the phonological merger found in some southern alphabetic cuneiform texts.

The text was published by Hillers in 1964. An improved edition with a superior copy was published by Cross in 1968. Both Hillers and Cross worked from a plaster squeeze and a photograph, rather then from the original. In 1986, Puech published a study which made further progress on epigraphic problems in the text. Since then,

12. The current whereabouts of the tablet are unknown. It appears that the tablet was taken to Oxford by D. R. Hillers for at least some time after excavation, since a case of the tablet was prepared by Ms. A. C. Western of the Ashmolean Museum (Hillers 1964: 45). However, we have been informed that the tablet is not at the Ashmolean Museum at present. Nor could the tablet be found at the museums in Jerusalem, or in the collections of the Israel Antiquities Authority.

a number of other interpretations have appeared, proposing new sign values and readings, none based on autopsy.

We still lack a broad enough epigraphic base to judge whether the tablet's difficulty of interpretation is due mainly to poor writing or script variance. In the absence of autopsy, the treatment here is nothing more than an interpretive suggestion and bibliographic aid. On current evidence, the presence of at least two personal names, a noun for "ransom/fee" and a verb for "fix, decide," are the most epigraphically and grammatically plausible proposals. Our provisional conclusion is that this is a legal notice of remittance.

Edition	**Translation**
Obverse	
1 *k k b ʾ l*! *p ʿ ṣ*	KKBʾ , for PʿṢ
———————————	———————————
2 *k p r š y ḫ t k*	The fee/ransom which was fixed
Edge	
3 *l*	for
Reverse	
4 *d w*	him

Commentary

Line 1

The *l* is anomalous, with a uniquely shortened middle stroke. The epigraphically superior reading is that of Puech 1986, who reads *g m*, creating a series of three personal names. His reading, however, generates grammatical difficulties, which are only resolved by assuming a novel writing of a sign in the second line. Three names in the first line would require some sort of plural reference in the second line, which Puech finds by reading the fourth letter of that line as an anomaly, either a rotated *m* or a *t* with an accidental stroke superimposed over it, resulting in either a masculine plural *kprm* or a feminine plural *kprt*. However, in light of the epigraphically preferable reading of a singular noun in the second line (see below), one must choose between the lesser of two anomalies. We prefer to amend the *l*.

At the end of the line, we follow Puech, reading an emphatic sibilant *ṣ*, instead of Cross's epigraphically difficult three-stroke *m*, whose proposal was partly based on a reading of the Beth Shemesh abecedary now ruled out by the Ras Shamra parallel RS 88.2215.

Lines 2–4

Grammatically, we follow Cross and Puech in reading the verb as a 3rd ms passive prefix form with punctual aspect from the root *ḥ t k*, the semantic range of which in West Semitic includes “rule, fix, decide.” Phonologically, a merger between *ḥ* and *ḫ* is implied. For the demonstrative *dw*, see Cross, supported by Puech. It is quite possible to read, with Cross, a predication between the verb and the demonstrative particle, “the fee/ransom which was fixed (has been remitted to) him.”

Tabor 1

ALPHABETIC CUNEIFORM INSCRIPTION ON A KNIFE BLADE

Basics: Bronze knife blade; 14.8 × 2.2 × 0.25 cm
Reg. No.: IAA 44.318 (present location: Israel Museum)
Primary Publications: Yeivin 1945 (enhanced photo, pl. 3, no. 2); Albright 1945: 21; Weippert 1966: 314 (photo, pl. 35 A–B);[13] Puech 1986: 206 (copy, p. 202); Dietrich and Loretz 1988b: 239–46 (copy, p. 242)
Studies: Mazar 1946: 172–73; Herdner 1946–48 (copy, p. 165); Cross 1967: 14*, n. 39; Galling 1968: 14; Naveh 1982: 29–30 (copy, p. 29, fig. 24); Zadok 1996: 115
Date: Thirteenth or twelfth century BCE
Language: West Semitic
Find Information: See Yeivin 1945: 32, summarized in Weippert 1966: 314

This knife blade, found on the surface in the vicinity of the dry riverbed of Naḥal Tabor, was published by Yeivin in 1945. As an inscription on a weapon, it has symbolic affinities with the Beth Shemesh abecedary in the shape of an axe-head and the proto-Phoenician arrowheads known from the Levant.[14] Although two letters near the beginning are damaged, there is no disagreement about its reading. Like the Beth Shemesh text and most other noncanonical southern alphabetic cuneiform texts, the inscription on the knife blade runs from right to left. The Tabor knife fits the pattern of these noncanonical texts in its essential features: the inscription lacks word dividers, and the formation of the letters, in particular the symmetrical formation of the *bet* (like the *dalet* of Beth Shemesh), also fits the noncanonical alphabetic cuneiform style.[15]

13. A is a reprint of Yeivin's photo; B is a new photograph.

14. For the corpus of inscribed linear alphabetic arrowheads, see Cross 2003: 200–202 (originally published in 1996).

15. Herdner 1965–68 notes that, while the letters of the Tabor knife inscription are also apparently noncanonical in that they are formed of triangular head shapes, rather than the full cuneiform nail shape, this (*pace* Dietrich and Loretz) is a function of the medium in which the text is inscribed, as shown by the similar shapes of the letters on the metal artefacts from Ugarit. In fact, the triangular head shape is far more common than many older, Sumero-Akkadian–influenced Ugaritic hand copies would suggest; see Ellison 2002, the definitive work on Ugaritic paleography.

Yeivin's initial reading of the text, *liṢ[ ]Baʿl biPalṣi-Baʿl* as "belonging to PN, in GN," with its oddly formed and otherwise unattested place-name, was improved upon by Albright and Herdner. Both independently suggested reading the second *b* as a shortened form of *bn* "son of," thus *lṣ[l]bʿlb<n>plṣbʿl*, perhaps to be vocalized *li-Ṣillī-Baʿl bu<n>-Palṣī-Baʿl*[16] (or, with assimilation of the *n*, *li-Ṣillī-Baʿl bup-Pilṣī-Baʿl*), "belonging to PN, s<on> of PN," a phraseology well attested in inscribed weapons of the period.[17] Weippert, followed by Dietrich and Loretz, argued that the writing of the second name with *ṣ* suggested a merger between *ṣ* and *s* in the language variety of the writer.[18]

The most plausible reading of the underlying consonants that emerges is thus *l⸢ṣ⸣⸢l⸣bʿlb<n>plṣbʿl*, but this raises a further question. Since the text's publication, scholars have debated whether the absence of the *n* of *bn* is due to omission or assimilation, that is, whether it was caused by a random scribal error or a significant phonological change.[19] If it is a scribal error, it would be unique in the period.

16. The vocalization of *bn* in Phoenician is uncertain, but early and late evidence suggests that both *bun*- and *bin*- existed in West Semitic; see Gelb 1980, *s.v. binu*, *bunu*, with around 53 instances with -*u*- and 45 with -*i*-, and compare Hoftijzer and Jongeling 1995, *s.v. bn* I, where Punic forms transliterated with Greek *u* (if this does indeed correspond to a Punic *u*!) exist alongside forms with *y*.

17. The formula is found in the Phoenician arrowheads of Ruweise, Zakarbaal, Azarbaal, Rapa, Yato, El-Khadr V, ʾAdaʿ, Maharan, Paday, Shallum, Uzzi-Milk, Shemida, Bin-Anat, and Zimmaʾ. This list of mostly unprovenanced arrowheads, judged by Cross to be genuine, is in order of publication and taken from Cross 2003. Note that there is no evidence of the use of *b* as an *abbreviation* for "son of" in West-Semitic inscriptions. For the use of abbreviations in ancient West Semitic, see Driver 1960.

18. The WS root *plṣ* "tremble, quake" is only certainly attested in Hebrew, where it appears, e.g., in Job 9:6, in which God is said, storm god–like, to shake the earth's foundations till they "quake." It is difficult to find in names, but most probably does appear in the Late Bronze Age Southern Levant in the name Palṣi (from the relatively nearby Late Bronze Age text Shechem 2 3'). Thus the most plausible reading is Palṣi-Baʿl "Quake-of-Baal." Because names with *pls* are better attested, one could follow scholars like Weippert, Dietrich, and Loretz and apply the epigraphic principle of banality of content and read it here. There are three ways one could argue for a reading Palsi-Baʿlu. (1) *Systematic collapse of voiceless/emphatic distinction*: Weippert points to a reasonably broad distribution of names with a *pls* root in West-Semitic languages of the Late Bronze and early Iron Ages; Gröndahl's study of Ugaritic names (1967) registers examples in Amorite, Ugaritic, and Phoenician, including several instances of *pls* + *bʿl*, presumably with a sense like "Baal opened the way" or the like. But this produces a difficulty of its own: the phonological novelty of the neutralization of the voiceless/emphatic distinction in West Semitic, a collapse unattested in any of the first-millennium dialects of which this text's language is presumably an ancestor. (2) *Phonetic influence of adjacent phonemes in PN*: Tropper points to a well-attested variety of mutations that emphatic consonants undergo in PNs (Tropper 2000: § 32.134), but those these are usually assimilation or dissimilation, and this is neither. (3) *Scribal error*: The scribe may have accidentally omitted the third wedge of an original *s* (Pardee: personal communication, January 2005).

19. Previous discussions noted the absence of *n* in the *bn* of other Canaanite dialects, generally referred to as "Phoenician," as well as sometimes in a Hebrew name known in a number of places from the Bible: *baʿanâ* (spelled with a final ʾ or *h*) appears in 1 Kings 4:12, 16; 2 Sam. 4:2, 5f, etc. and Nabatean *bʿnw*. This name appears on a Phoenician arrowhead in standard Phoenician (unassimilated) form; see Milik 1956, with discussion of the name on p. 5. Linguistically this is a different phenomenon, since if in fact the *n* has assimilated across word boundaries to a following ʿ it is assimilating in the one type of environment that Old Byblian *n* would not! Not mentioned in these discussions are possible examples from Hebrew epigraphy

If, on the other hand, it is a phonological change, it would fit a coherent pattern found in the oldest extended inscriptions in the linear alphabet.[20]

The assimilation of the final *n* to the initial, nonlaryngeal, consonant of the following word is found in only one other West-Semitic language variety,[21] the archaic Old Byblian dialect of Phoenician of the tenth century BCE.[22] Thus, the most plausible explanation of our text's spelling is that it shares affinities with the Phoenician dialect of Byblos, as opposed to standard Ugaritic. It has long been known that there is more than one language variety underlying the alphabetic cuneiform texts at Ugarit. That the alphabetic cuneiform texts from the southern Levant also reflect more than one language variety has more recently become clear.[23] While there is no reason to believe that the Tabor knife originated in the precise place it was found,[24] its only plausible place of manufacture and use is in the immediate region. This is because it belongs to a type—prestige artefacts inscribed in noncanonical alphabetic cuneiform—known only from the southern Levant.[25] This text is therefore a

---

such as the seal excavated at Beth Shemesh, Avigad, and Sass 1997: no. 52, p. 68, where again the putative assimilation would be to a laryngeal.

20. Dietrich and Loretz 1988b mention three possible Ugaritic parallels, of which one is a plausible, if uncertain, example of assimilation of *n*. Examples 4.178:2 and 4.178:4 are from a fragmentary text of uncertain content and apparently not yet published according to *KTU*²; 4:696:9 attests *yny*, a known place-name but also a known personal name, in the formula "*b* X, *b* Y," requiring either the odd "from X, from Y" or the easier "son of X, from Y."

21. For nonassimilation of *n* in Ugaritic inscriptions, see *KTU* 6.16, 61, 62, and for earlier West Semitic, cf. Sivan 1984: 212, which registers four certain and three possible Alalakh names and one Amarna name. The further question of whether one should describe this assimilation as a frozen feature of the name, or of the language of the inscription itself, reduces itself to whether the epithet "son of PN" is to be considered a semantically opaque proper name or a linguistically transparent phrase. Within Byblian itself the answer is clear: these epithets are transparent to the phonology of the language, spelled in the early period with assimilation of the *nun* but later on in the standard nonassimilating orthography (Yehawhilk 1). Thus, it is best to interpret the language of the inscription as a whole as sharing a distinctive feature with Old Byblian, a feature not recognized, for example, in Tropper 2000 (see § 22.8).

22. Attested in *KAI* 6:1, 7:3, 8 and Byblos Graffito B, published by Cross and McCarter (see Gibson 1971–82: III 3). The phenomenon is restricted to cases in which the initial consonant of the second word is nonlaryngeal. This pattern also lines the Naḥal Tabor variety up with Phoenician, against Ugaritic, in not preserving the case vowels of nouns in construct position. Garr 1985: 40–42, 44 with n. 166, cf. Guzzo et al. 1999: § 92b with n. 1. As noted by Guzzo, unlike in Ugaritic and Arabic, case vowels in Byblian must have already been lost, at least in construct position, in order for this assimilation to take place.

23. This important pattern was first recognized by Greenstein and expanded by Bordreuil. Several other alphabetic cuneiform inscriptions from south of Ugarit are written in a West-Semitic language variety that shares distinctive features with Phoenician. In 1976, Greenstein argued that the jar inscription from Sarepta was not in Ugaritic; with his readings confirmed by Bordreuil's re-examination, he was able to recognize two features of syntax and lexicon well attested in Phoenician as opposed to Ugaritic: the use of the demonstrative particle *z*, as opposed to Ugaritic *d*, and the taxonomically Phoenician verb *pʿl* "to make." See Greenstein 1976, with additional comments in Bordreuil 1979. See also Bordreuil's re-examination of the Hala Sultan Tekke bowl in Bordreuil 1983: 13, where he finds, as in standard Phonenician, the verb *pʿl*, as well as the standard form of *bun* "son of." Puech 1986: 208–11 raises significant, though not decisive, counterarguments to Bordreuil's readings.

24. As pointed out by Alan Millard (personal communication, April 2004).

25. For this point, see Dietrich and Loretz 1988b: 244.

significant piece of a larger cultural puzzle: the map of language and writing in the Levant at the dawn of the Iron Age.

Edition	**Translation**
l⸢ṣ l⸣ b ʿ l b p l ṣ b ʿ l	Belonging to Ṣillī-Baʿl, s<on> of Palṣī-Baʿl

Commentary

The text was collated by E. Greenstein on January 18, 2005. In a personal communication, he confirms the established reading and adds that the most recent copy (Puech 1986: 202) is good, although the rendering can make it "seem that the lines are thick while they are actually thinly but clearly etched, very apparently by a professional scribe or artisan." He notes, "Almost all the signs are very clear." As for the damaged second and third signs, the second sign, *ṣ*, "is not as clear as one might like: the second vertical wedge is far shorter than the first and it is fainter. This may be a consequence of the damage/corrosion to the left of this sign on the third letter, *l*." In contrast to the straight top of the first *l*, the top of the second *l* "is curved and the vertical triangular wedges crunched together, the apparent result of the damage/corrosion that affects that sign." In the second name, "the letters are very clear. A *p* immediately follows the *b*, with less space than is usual between letters in this inscription."

The name is best read Palṣi-Baʿl "Quake-of-Baal," or perhaps more idiomatically "Thunder of the Storm God." In addition to avoiding the emendations or poorly attested sound changes suggested by previous scholars (including us in the first edition!), it would fit with another Late Bronze Age name of the same type from this region, Shechem 2's hypocoristic *Palṣī*[0] (see p. 129).

ABBREVIATIONS

AAA	Annals of Archaeology and Anthropology
AASOR	Annual of the American Schools of Oriental Research
ADAJ	Annual of the Department of Antiquities of Jordan
AfO	Archiv für Orientforschung
AHw	Soden, W. von, *Akkadisches Handwörterbuch*, Wiesbaden: Harassowitz
AJSL	American Journal of Semitic Languages
AOAT	Alter Orient und Altes Testament
ARM	Archives Royales de Mari
BA	Biblical Archaeologist
Bagh. Mitt.	Baghdader Mitteilungen
BASOR	Bulletin of the American Schools of Oriental Research
BiOr	Bibliotheca Orientalis
BN	Biblische Notizen
CAD	Chicago Assyrian Dictionary
CDA	Black, J., George, A., and Postgate, N. (eds.), *A Concise Dictionary of Akkadian*, Wiesbaden: Harrassowitz, 1995
CRAI	Compte rendu, Rencontre Assyriologique International
CT	Cuneiform Tests from Babylonian Tablets in the British Museum
DDD	Van der Toorn, K., Becking, B., and Van der Horst, P. W. (eds.), *Dictionary of Deities and Demons*, Leiden: Brill, 1995
DNWSI	*Dictionary of Northwest Semitic Inscriptions*
EI	Eretz-Israel
IEJ	Israel Exploration Journal
IOS	Israel Oriental Studies
JANES	Journal of Ancient Near Eastern Studies
JAOS	Journal of the American Oriental Society
JBL	Journal of Biblical Literature
JCS	Journal of Cuneiform Studies
JEOL	Jaarbericht van het Vooraziatisch-Egyptisch Genootschap "Ex Orient Lux"
JNES	Journal of Near Eastern Studies
JPOS	Journal of the Palestine Oriental Society
JSS	Journal of Semitic Studies
MSL	Materials for the Sumerian Lexicon
NABU	Nouvelles Assyriologiques Brèves et Utilitaires
OA	Oriens Antiquus
OLZ	Orientalistische Literaturzeitung
Or	Orientalia
PEFQSt	Palestine Exploration Fund Quarterly Statement
PEQ	Palestine Exploration Quarterly
PJb	Palästinajahrbuch
PNAE	The Prosopography of the Neo-Assyrian Empire of the Neo-Assyrian Text Corpus Project
PSAS	Proceedings of the Society for Arabian Studies
RA	Revue d'Assyriologie et d'Archéologie Orientale
RB	Revue Biblique
RGTC	Répertoire géographique des textes cunéiformes
RIA	Reallexicon der Assyriologie

SAA	State Archives of Assyria
SAAB	State Archives of Assyria Bulletin
SAAS	State Archives of Assyria Studies
SEL	Studi Epigrafici e Linguistici sul Vicino Oriente Antico
TA	Tel Aviv
TUAT	Texte aus der Umwelt des Alten Testaments
UF	Ugarit-Forschungen
WO	Die Welt des Orients
ZA	Zeitschrift für Assyriologie
ZDPV	Zeitschrift des Deutschen Palästina-Vereins

BIBLIOGRAPHY

Aharoni, Y.
1973 *Beer-Sheba 1: Excavations at Tel Beer-Sheba, 1969–1971 Seasons*, Tel Aviv: Tel Aviv University

Aḥituv, S.
1984 *Canaanite Toponyms in Ancient Egyptian Documents*, Jerusalem: Magnes Press

Albright, W. F.
1924 *Excavations and Results at Tell el-Fûl (Gibeah of Saul) by the Director of the School in Jerusalem* (= *AASOR* 4)
1932 "The Fourth Joint Campaign of Excavation at Tell Beir Mirsim," *BASOR* 47: 3–17
1934 "The Cuneiform Tablet from Beth-Shemesh," *BASOR* 53:18–19
1935 "Palestine in the Earliest Historical Period," *JPOS* 15: 193–234
1938 *The Excavation of Tell Beit Mirsim* II. *The Bronze Age* (= AASOR 17)
1942a "A Teacher to a Man of Shechem About 1400 B.C.," *BASOR* 86: 28–31
1942b "A Case of Lèse-Majesté in Pre-Israelite Lachish, with Some Remarks on the Israelite Conquest," *BASOR* 87: 32–38
1943 "A Tablet of the Amarna Age from Gezer," *BASOR* 92: 28–30
1944 "A Prince of Taanach in the Fifteenth Century B.C.," *BASOR* 94: 12–27
1945 "Some Publications Received by the Editor," *BASOR* 99: 21–23
1955 "Recent Books on Archaeology and Ancient History," *BASOR* 139: 14–25
1956 *The Archaeology of Palestine*, Harmondsworth, Middlesex: Penguin Books
1960 "Reports on Excavations in the Near and Middle East," *BASOR* 159: 37–39

Alt, A.
1941 "Lesefrüchte aus Inschriften, 4. Briefe aus der assyrischen Kolonie in Samaria," *PJb* 37: 102–4

Amiet, P.
1955 "Cylindres-Sceaux Conservés à Jérusalem," *RB* 62: 407–13

Anbar, M., and Na'aman, N.
1986 "An Account Tablet of Sheep from Ancient Hebron," *TA* 13–14: 3–12

Arnaud, D.
1998 "Hazor à la fin de l'age du Bronze d'après un document méconnu: *RS* 20.225," *Aula Orientalis* 16: 27–35

Astour, M. C.
1991 "The Location of *Haṣurā* of the Mari Texts," *Maarav* 7: 51–65

Avigad, N., and Sass, B.
1997 *Corpus of West Semitic Stamp Seals*, Jerusalem: Israel Exploration Society

Barton, G. A.
1933 "Notes on the Ain Shems Tablet," *BASOR* 52: 5–6

Beck, P.
1973 "A Votive Cylinder Seal," in Aharoni 1973, 56–60

Becking, B.
1981–82 "The Two Neo-Assyrian Documents from Gezer in Their Historical Context," *JEOL* 27: 76–89
1992 *The Fall of Samaria: An Historical and Archaeological Study*, Leiden: Brill

Beckman, G.
1997 "Tablet Fragments from Sepphoris," *NABU* 1997/3: 81–82, no. 86

Beitzel, B. J.
1997 "Did Zimri-Lim Play a Role in Developing the Use of Tin-Bronze in Palestine?," in Young, G. D., et al. (eds.), *Crossing Boundaries and Linking Horizons, Studies in Honor of Michael C. Astour on His 80th Birthday*, Bethesda, MD: Capital Decisions, 121–44

Ben-Tor, A.
1992a "The Hazor Tablet: Foreword," *IEJ* 42: 17–20

1992b "Tel Hazor, 1992," *IEJ* 42: 254–60
2016 *Hazor: Canaanite Metropolis, Israelite City*, Jerusalem: Israel Exploration Society

Berlejung, A.
2006 "Briefe aus dem Archiv von Taanach," in Janowski, B., and G. Wilhelm (eds.), *Briefe* (= TUAT.NF 3), Gütersloh: Gütersloher Verlagshaus Mohn, 230–34

Bezold, C., and Budge, E. A. W.
1882 *The Tell El-Amarna Tablets in the British Museum*, London: Longmans

Bienkowski, P.
1991 *Treasures from an Ancient Land: The Art of Jordan*, Wolfeboro Falls: National Museums and Galleries

Bliss, F. J.
1894 *A Mound of Many Cities, or Tell El Hesy Excavated*, London: Macmillan

Böhl, F. M. Th.
1926 "Die bei den Ausgrabungen von Sichem gefundenen Keilschrifttafeln," *ZDPV* 49: 321–27
1974 "Der Keilschriftbrief aus Sichem (Tell Balâṭa)," *Bagh. Mitt.* 7: 21–30

Bonechi, M.
1992 "Relations amicales Syro-Palestiniennes: Mari et Haṣor au XVIIIe siècle av. J.C.," *Florilegium marianum, Recueil d'études en l'honneur de Michel Fleury, Mémoires de NABU* 1: 9–22

Bordreuil, P.
1979 "L'inscription phénicienne de Sarafand en cunéiformes alphabétiques," *UF* 11: 63–68
1981 "Cunéiformes alphabétiques non canoniques I: La tablette alphabétique senestroverse RS 22.03," *Syria* 58: 301–10
1983 "Cunéiformes alphabétiques non canoniques II: A propos de l'épigraphe de Hala Sultan Tekké," *Semitica* 33:7–15

Bottéro, J.
1992 *L'Épopée de Gilgameš, Le grand homme qui ne voulait pas mourir*, Paris: Gallimard

Brinkman, J. A.
1965 "Appendix 3, Two Cuneiform Tablets from Shechem," in Wright, G. E., *Shechem: The Biography of a Biblical City*, New York: McGraw-Hill, 208–13
1971 "Mu-ús-sa Dates in the Kassite Period," *WO* 6: 153–56

Campbell, E., Jr., Ross, J. F., and Toombs, L. E.
1971 "The Eighth Campaign at Balāṭa (Shechem)," *BASOR* 204: 2–17

Charpin, D.
2004 "Histoire Politique du Proche-Orient Amorrite (2002–1595)," in Charpin, D., Edzard, D. O., and Stol, M., *Mesopotamien: Die altbabylonische Zeit* (= Orbis Biblicus et Orientalis 160/4), Göttingen: Vandenhoeck & Ruprecht, 5–480
2007 "*Cuneiform in Canaan*," *RA* 101: 187–88 (Review)

Charpin, D., and Ziegler, N.
2004 "Une Lettre de Šamši-Addu découverte à Hazor?," *NABU* 2004/4: 85–86, no. 84

Cochavi-Rainey, Z.
2005 *To the King My Lord: Letters from El-Amarna, Kumidu, Taanach, and Other Letters from the Fourteenth Century BCE*, Jerusalem: Bialik (Hebrew)

Cogan, M.
1995 "A Lamashtu Plaque from the Judaean Shephela," *IEJ* 45: 155–61
2007 Review of *Cuneiform in Canaan*, *IEJ* 57/2: 246–48
2008 "The Assyrian Stela Fragment from Ben-Shemen," in Cogan M. and Kahn D. (eds.), *Treasures on Camels' Humps: Historical and Literary Studies from the Ancient Near East Presented to Israel Eph'al*, Jerusalem: Hebrew University Magnes Press, 66–69
2013a *Bound for Exile: Israelites and Judeans Under Imperial Yoke, Documents from Assyria and Babylonia*, Jerusalem: Carta
2013b "A New Cuneiform Text from Megiddo," *IEJ* 63/2: 131–34

Cogan, M., and Tadmor, H.
1988 *The Anchor Bible: II Kings; A New Translation with Introduction and Commentary*, Garden City, NY: Doubleday

Cohen, M. E.
1993 *The Cultic Calendars of the Ancient Near East*, Bethesda, MD: CDL Press

Cohen, Y.
2008 Review of *Cuneiform in Canaan*, *BASOR* 349, 83–86

Collon, D.
1987 *First Impressions: Cylinder Seals in the Ancient Near East*, London: British Museum

Conder, C. R.
1904 "Remarks on the Gezer Tablet," *PEFQSt* 36: 400–401
1905 "Note on the Gezer Tablet," *PEFQSt* 37: 74

Courtois, J.-C.
1969 "The Excavations at Ugarit, 1929–1966," *Qadmoniot* 2: 74–83 (Hebrew)

Cross, F. M.
1967 "The Origin and Early Evolution of the Alphabet," *EI* 8: 8*–24*
1968 "The Canaanite Cuneiform Tablet from Taanach," *BASOR* 190: 41–46
2003 "The Arrow of Suwar, Retainer of ʿAbday," in *Leaves from an Epigrapher's Notebook*, Winona Lake, IN: Eisenbrauns

Crowfoot, J. W., et al.
1957 *The Objects from Samaria*, London: Palestine Exploration Fund

Dalley, S.
1984 "The Cuneiform Tablets from Tell Tawilan," *Levant* 16: 19–22
1991 *Old Babylonian Texts in the Ashmolean Museum: Texts from Kish and Elsewhere* (= Oxford Cuneiform Texts 13), Oxford: Oxford University Press
1998 "The Influence of Mesopotamia upon Israel and the Bible," in Dalley, S., et al. (eds.), *The Legacy of Mesopotamia*, Oxford: Oxford University Press, 58–83
2000 "Hebrew TAḤAŠ, Akkadian DUHŠU, Faience and Beadwork," *JSS* 45: 1–19
2013 "Gods from North-eastern and North-western Arabia in Cuneiform Texts from the First Sealand Dynasty, and a Cuneiform Inscription from Tell en-Naṣbeh, c. 1500 BC," *Arabian Archaeology and Epigraphy* 24: 177–85

Dalley, S., and Goguel, A.
1997 "The Selaʿ Sculpture: A Neo-Babylonian Rock Relief in Southern Jordan," *ADAJ* 41: 169–76

Demsky, A.
1976 "Literacy in Israel and Among Neighboring Peoples in the Biblical Period" (Ph.D. diss., Hebrew University of Jerusalem), Jerusalem (Hebrew)
1990 "The Education of Canaanite Scribes in the Mesopotamian Cuneiform Tradition," in Klein and Skaist 1990: 157–70

Dhorme, P.
1909 "A Note on the New Cuneiform Tablet from Gezer," *PEQ* 41: 106

Dhorme, P., and Harper, R. F.
1912 *apud* Macalister 1912: 29–31

Dietrich, M., and Loretz, O.
1988a "Die Alphabettafel aus Bet Šemeš und die ursprüngliche Heimat der Ugariter," in Mauer, G., and Magen, U. (eds.), *Ad bene et fideliter seminandum: Festgabe für Karlheinz Dell zum 21. Februar 1987* (= AOAT 220), Neukirchen-Vluyn: 61–85
1988b *Die Keilalphabete: Die phönizisch-kanaanäischen und altarabischen Alphabete in Ugarit*, Münster: Ugarit-Verlag
1989 "The Cuneiform Alphabets of Ugarit," *UF* 21: 101–12

Dietrich, M., Loretz, O., and Sanmartin, J.
1974 "Zu TT 433," *UF* 6: 469–70

Dijkstra, M.
1986 "Another Text in the Shorter Cuneiform Alphabet (KTU 5.22)," *UF* 18: 121–23

Donbaz, V.
1988 "Some Neo-Assyrian Contracts from Girnavaz and Vicinity," *SAAB* 23–30
1998 "Once Again Fi.16 (= Samaria 1825)," *NABU* 1998/1: 24–26, no. 22

Dothan, M.
1964 "Ashdod: Preliminary Report on the Excavation in Season 1962/1963," *IEJ* 14: 79–95
1971 *Ashdod II–III: The Second and Third Seasons of Excavations 1963, 1965, Soundings in 1967; Text, Figures and Plates* (= ʿAtiqot 9–10), Jerusalem: Department of Antiquities and Museums in the Ministry of Education and Culture; Department of Archaeology, Hebrew University; Israel Exploration Society

1972 "Ashdod—Seven Seasons of Excavation," *Qadmoniot* 17: 2–13 (Hebrew)

Driver, G. R.
1944 *Semitic Writing, From Pictograph to Alphabet*, London: Oxford University Press
1960 "Abbreviations in the Massoretic Text," *Textus* 1: 112–31

Durand, J.-M.
2006 "La Date des textes de Hazor," *NABU* 2006/4, 88–89, no. 86

Edzard, D. O.
1985 "Amarna und die Archive, seiner Korrespondenten zwischen Ugarit und Gaza," in *Biblical Archaeology Today: Proceedings of the Intenational Congress of Biblical Archaeology Jerusalem 1984*, Jerusalem: Israel Exploration Society; Israel Academy of Sciences and Humanities in cooperation with the American Schools of Oriental Research, 248–50

Elat, M.
1998 "Die wirtschaftlichen Beziehungen der Assyrer mit den Arabern," in Maul, S. (ed.), *Festschrift für Rykle Borger zu seinem 65. Geburtstag am 24. Mai 1994*, Groningen: Styx, 39–57

Ellison, J. L.
2002 "A Paleographic Study of the Alphabetic Cuneiform Texts from Ras Shamra/Ugarit" (Ph.D. diss., Harvard University), Cambridge, MA

Eph'al, I.
2005 "Esarhaddon, Egypt, and Shubria: Politics and Propaganda," *JCS* 57: 99–111
2010 "Assyrian Imperial Rule in Non-literary Documents Relating to the Territory 'Beyond the River,'" in Talshir, Z. (ed.), *Israel and Its Land: Inscriptions and History; Proceedings of a Conference in Honor of Shmuel Aḥituv on the Occasion of His Retirement* (Beer-Sheva 19), Beer Sheva: 31–69 (Hebrew)

Fales, F. M., and Postgate, J. N.
1995 *Imperial Administrative Records, Part II: Provincial and Military Administration* (= SAA 11), Helsinki: Helsinki University Press

Feigin, S. I.
1934 "The Captives in Cuneiform Inscriptions," *AJSL* 50: 217–45

Finkelstein, I.
2002 "Gezer Revisited and Revised," *TA* 29: 262–96

Fischer-Elfert, H.-W. and Krebernik, M.
2016 "Zu den Buchstabennamen auf dem *Halaḥam*-Ostrakon aus TT 99 (Grab des Sennefri)," *Zeitschrift für ägyptische Sprache und Altertumskunde* 143: 169–76

Frame, G.
1999 "The Inscription of Sargon II at Tang-I Var," *Or* 68: 31–57

Freedman, D. N.
1963 "The Second Season at Ancient Ashdod," *BA* 26: 134–39

Fuchs, A.
1994 *Die Inschriften Sargons II, aus Khorsabad*, Göttingen: Cuvillier

Galil, G.
2001 "Two Neo-Assyrian Tablets from Tel-Hadid," *NABU* 2001/3: 68–69, no. 70

Galling, K.
1935 "Assyrische und persische Präfekten im Geser," *PJb* 31: 75–93

Galling, K., Edel, E., and Borger, R.
1968 *Textbuch zur Geschichte Israels*, Tübingen: Mohr (Siebeck)

Garr, R. W.
1985 *Dialect Geography of Syria-Palestine, 1000–586 B.C.E.*, Philadelphia: University of Pennsylvania Press

Garstang, J.
1934 "Jericho: City and Necropolis, Fourth Report," *AAA* 21: 99–116

Gelb, I. J.
1980 *Computer-Aided Analysis of Amorite* (= Assyriological Studies 21), Chicago:

Oriental Institute of the University of Chicago

Geller, M.
1997 "The Last Wedge," *ZA* 87: 43–95

George, A. R.
1999 *The Epic of Gilgamesh, the Babylonian Epic Poem, and Other Texts in Akkadian and Sumerian*, London: Penguin Books
2003 *The Babylonian Gilgamesh Epic: Introduction, Critical Edition, and Cuneiform Text*, Oxford: Oxford University Press

Gerson, S. N.
2001 "Fractional Coins of Judea and Samaria in the Fourth Century BCE," *Ancient Near Eastern Archaeology* 64: 106–21

Gianto, A.
1995 "Amarna Lexicography: The Glosses in the Byblos Letters," *SEL* 12: 65–73

Gibson, J. C. L.
1971–82 *Textbook of Syrian Semitic Inscriptions*, 3 vols., Oxford: Clarendon Press

Glock, A. E.
1971 "A New Ta'annek Tablet," *BASOR* 2004: 17–30
1983 "Texts and Archaeology at Tell Ta'annek," *Berytus* 31: 57–66

Goetze, A., and Levy, S.
1959 "Fragment of the Gilgamesh Epic from Megiddo," *'Atiqot* 2: 121–28

Goren, Y.
2000 "Provenance Study of the Cuneiform Texts from Hazor," *IEJ* 50: 29–42

Goren, Y., Finkelstein, I., and Na'aman, N.
2004 *Inscribed in Clay: Provenance Study of the Amarna Letters and Other Ancient Near Eastern Texts*, Tel Aviv: Emery and Claire Yass Publications in Archaeology

Goren, Y., Mommsen, H., Finkelstein, I., and Na'aman, N.
2009 "A Provenance Study of the Gilgamesh Fragment from Megiddo," *Archaeometry* 51/5: 763–73

Goren, Y., Na'aman, N., Mommsen, H., and Finkelstein, I.
2006 "Provenance Study and Re-evaluation of the Cuneiform Documents from the Egyptian Residency at Tel Aphek," *Ägypten und Levante* 16: 161–72

Görg, M.
1988 "Zum Namen der Fürsten von Taanach," *BN* 41: 15–18

Grant, E.
1933 "Beth Shemesh in 1933," *BASOR* 52: 3–5
1934 *Rumeileh: Being Ain Shems Excavations (Palestine), Part III*, Haverford: Haverford College

Greenfield, J. C.
1991 "Of Scribes, Scripts, and Languages," in Baurain, C., et al. (eds.), *Phoinikeia Grammata: Lire et écrire en Méditerranée* (= Studia Phoenicia 9), Liège-Namur: Société des études classiques, 173–85

Greenfield, J. C., and Shaffer, A.
1983 "Notes on the Akkadian-Aramaic Bilingual Statue from Tell Fekherye," *Iraq* 45: 109–16

Greenstein, E.
1976 "A Phoenician Inscription in Ugaritic Script?," *JANES* 8: 49–57
2004 "Another Case of Hiphil in Amarna Age Canaanite," in Cohen, C., Hurvitz, A., and Paul, S. M. (eds.), *Sefer Moshe: The Moshe Weinfeld Jubilee Volume; Studies in the Bible and the Ancient Near East, Qumran, and Post-Biblical Judaism*, Winona Lake, IN: Eisenbrauns

Gressman, H.
1909 *Altorientalische Texte und Bilder zum Alten Testament*, erster Band, *Texte*, Tübingen: J. C. B. Mohr
1926 *Altorientalische Texte zum Alten Testament*, Berlin: W. de Gruyter
1927 *Altorientalische Bilder zum Alten Testament*, Berlin: W. de Gruyter

Gröndahl, F.
1967 *Die Personennamen der Texte aus Ugarit* (= Studia Pohl 1), Rome: Pontifical Biblical Institute

Gustavs, A.
1927 "Die Personennamen in den Tontafeln von Tell Ta'annek," *ZDPV* 50: 1–18
1928 "Die Personennamen in den Tontafeln von Tell Ta'annek II," *ZDPV* 52: 169–218

Guy, P. L. O., and Engberg, R. M.
1938 *Megiddo Tombs*, Chicago: University of Chicago Press

Guzzo, M. G. A., Friedrich, J., and Röllig, W.
1999 *Phönizisch-Punische Grammatik*, Rome: Pontifical Biblical Institute

Halévy, J.
1904 "Les Habiri et les inscriptions de Ta'annek," *Revue Sémitique* 12: 246–58

Hallo, W. W.
1981 "A Letter Fragment from Tel Aphek," *TA* 8: 18–24 (reprinted in Owen et al. 1987: 18–24)
2002 *The Context of Scripture*, vol. 3, *Archival Documents from the Biblical World*, Leiden: Brill

Hallo, W. W., and Tadmor, H.
1977 "A Lawsuit from Hazor," *IEJ* 27: 1–11

Haring, B.
2015 "*Halaḥam* on an Ostracon of the Early New Kingdom?" *JNES* 74: 189–96

Harris, R.
1955 "The Archive of the Sin Temple in Khafajah (Tutub)," *JCS* 9: 31–88, 91–120

Hecker, K.
1994 "Das Akkadische Gilgamesch-Epos," *TUAT* III/4: 646–744

Heltzer, M.
1981 *The Suteans*, Naples: Istituto universitario orientale

Herdner, A.
1946–48 "A-t-il existé une variété palestinienne de l'écriture cunéiforme alphabétique?," *Syria* 25: 165–68

Hess, R. S.
1993 *Amarna Personal Names*, Winona Lake, IN: Eisenbrauns
2001 "Typology of a Late Bronze Age Administrative Tablet from Hazor," *UF* 33: 237–43
2003 "Preliminary Perspectives on Late Bronze Age Culture from the Personal Names in Palestinian Cuneiform Texts," *Dutch Studies of the Near Eastern Languages and Literatures Foundation* 5: 35–57
2007 "Personal Names in Cuneiform Texts from Middle Bronze Age Palestine," in Watson, W. G. E. (ed.), *"He Unfurrowed His Brow and Laughed": Essays in Honour of Nicolas Wyatt* (= AOAT 299), Münster: Ugarit-Verlag: 153–61

Hestrin, R., et al.
1972 *Inscriptions Reveal: Documents from the Time of the Bible, the Mishna, and the Talmud*, Jerusalem: Israel Museum (Hebrew edition published the same year)

Hillers, D. R.
1964 "An Alphabetic Cuneiform Tablet from Taanach (TT 433)," *BASOR* 173: 45–50

Hilprecht, H. V.
1896 *Old Babylonian Inscriptions, Chiefly from Nippur*, Part II (= BE I/2), Philadelphia: American Philosophical Society

Hoftijzer, J., and Jongeling, K.
1995 *Dictionary of the North-West Semitic Inscriptions*, Leiden: Brill

Holma, H.
1914 "Zum ersten Ta'anek-Brief," *ZA* 28: 102–3

Horowitz, W.
1994 "Trouble in Canaan—A Letter of the el-Amarna Period on a Clay Cylinder from Beth-Shean," *Qadmoniot* 27: 84–86 (Hebrew)
1996a "An Inscribed Clay Cylinder from Amarna Age Beth Shean," *IEJ* 46: 208–18
1996b "The 360 and 364 Day Year in Ancient Mesopotamia," *JANES* 24: 35–44
1997a "The Amarna Age Inscribed Clay Cylinder from Beth-Shean," *BA* 60: 97–100
1997b "A Combined Multiplication Table on a Prism Fragment from Hazor," *IEJ* 47: 190–97
2000 "Two Late Bronze Age Tablets from Hazor," *IEJ* 50: 16–28
2011 *Mesopotamian Cosmic Geography* (Mesopotamian Civilizations 8), 2nd printing, Winona Lake, In.: Eisenbrauns

2012 "New Bronze Age Documents from Hazor," *Qadmoniot* 143: 34–35 (Hebrew)
2018 "The Last Days of Cuneiform in Canaan: Speculations on the Coins from Samaria," in Aster, S. Z. and Faust, A. (eds.), *The Southern Levant under Assyrian Domination*, University Park, Penn.: Eisenbrauns, 236–45

Horowitz, W., Kreuzer, S., and Oshima, T.
2006 "Die Keilschriftexte von Taanach / Tell Ta'annek," in Kreuzer 2006: 85–99

Horowitz, W., Mazar, E., Goren, Y., and Oshima, T.
2010 "A Cuneiform Tablet from the Ophel in Jerusalem," *Israel Exploration Journal* 60/1: 4–21
2014 "Jerusalem 2: A Fragment of a Cuneiform Tablet from the Ophel Excavations," *Israel Exploration Journal* 64: 129–38

Horowitz, W., and Ornan, T.
2014 "Cylinder Seals: A Clay Cylinder with Cuneiform Signs," with T. Ornan, in Ben-Shlomo, D., and Van Beek, G. W., *The Smithsonian Institution Excavation at Tell Jemmeh, Israel 1970–1990* (= Smithsonian Contributions to Anthropology 50), Washington, DC.: SISP, 2014, 1017–19

Horowitz, W., and Oshima, T.
2002 "Two More Cuneiform Finds from Hazor," *IEJ* 52: 179–86
2005 "Cuneiform Tablets from Canaan in the Arkeoloji Müzerli," *Colloquium Anatolicum* 3: 31–39
2006 "The Taanach Cuneiform Tablets, A Retrospective," in Kreuzer 2006: 77–84
2007 "Hazor 15: A Letter Fragment from Hazor," in *IEJ* 57: 34–41
2008 "New Light on an Old Find from Hazor," in Cogan, M., and D. Kahn, D. (eds.), *Treasures on Camels' Humps: Historical and Literary Studies from the Ancient Near East Presented to Israel Eph'al*, Jerusalem: Hebrew University Magnes Press, 99–103
2010a "Hazor 16: Another Administrative Docket from Hazor," *Israel Exploration Journal* 60, 129–32
2010b "Hazor: A Cuneiform City in Canaan, A Retrospective and Look Forward," with Takayoshi Oshima, in P. Matthiae, P., Pinnock, F., et al. (eds.), *Proceedings of the 6th International Congress on the Archaeology of the Ancient Near East, May, 5th–10th, "Sapienza"—Università di Roma*, vol. 3, *Islamic Session, Poster Session, The Ceremonial Precinct of Canaanite Hazor*, 483–90

Horowitz, W., Oshima, T., and Sanders, S.
2002 "A Bibliographical List of Cuneiform Inscriptions from Canaan, Palestine/Philistia, and the Land of Israel," *JAOS* 122: 753–66

Horowitz, W., Oshima, T., and Vukosavović, F.
2012 "Hazor 18: Fragments of a Cuneiform Law Collection from Hazor," *Israel Exploration Journal* 62/2: 158–76

Horowitz, W., Oshima, T., and Winitzer, A.
2010 "Hazor 17: Another Clay Liver Model," *IEJ* 60: 133–45

Horowitz, W., and Shaffer, A.
1992a "An Administrative Tablet from Hazor: A Preliminary Edition," *IEJ* 42: 21–33
1992b "A Fragment of a Letter from Hazor," *IEJ* 42: 165–67

Horowitz, W., and Vanderhooft, D.
2002 "The Cuneiform Inscription from Tell En-Naṣbeh: The Demise of an Unknown King," *TA* 29: 318–27

Horowitz, W., and Wasserman, N.
2000 "An Old Babylonian Letter from Hazor with Mention of Mari and Ekallātum," *IEJ* 50: 169–74
2004 "From Hazor to Mari and Ekallātum: A Recently Discovered Old-Babylonian Letter from Hazor," *Amurru* 3: 335–44

Hrozný, F.
1904 "Keilschrifttexte aus Ta'anek," in Sellin, E., *Tell Ta'annek*, Vienna: Gerold, 113–22
1905 "Die neugefundenen Keilschrifttexte von Ta'annek," in Sellin, E., *Eine Nachlese auf dem Tell Ta'annek in Palästina*, Vienna: A. Hoelder, 36–41
1906 "Amanhašir," *Vienna Oriental Journal* 20: 123–24

Huehnergard, J.
1989 *The Akkadian of Ugarit*, Atlanta: Scholars Press

Huehnergard, J., and Van Soldt, W.
1999 "A Cuneiform Lexical Text from Ashkelon with a Canaanite Column," *IEJ* 49: 184–92
2008 "A Cuneiform Lexical Text with a Canaanite Column," in Stager, L., et al. (eds.), *Ashkelon 1: Introduction and Overview (1985–2006)*, Winona Lake, IN: Eisenbrauns, 327–32

Irvine, A. K. and Beeston, A. F. K.
1988 "New Evidence on the Qatabanian Letter Order," *PSAS* 18: 35–38

Izreʾel, Sh.
1991 *Amurru Akkadian: A Linguistic Study*, Atlanta: Scholars Press
1995 "The Amarna Glosses: Who Wrote What for Whom? Some Sociolinguistic Considerations," *IOS* 15: 101–22
1997 *The Amarna Scholarly Tablets*, Groningen: Styx
1998a *Canaano-Akkadian*, Munich: Lincom Europa
1998b "A New Dictionary of Northwest Semitic and the Amarna Glosses," *IOS* 18: 421–29

Jajan, M.
2009 "Studies in Lamashtu: A Demon or an Icon of Evil?" (M.A. thesis, University of Leiden)

James, F. W., and McGovern, P. E.
1993 *The Late Bronze Egyptian Garrison at Beth Shean: A Study of Levels VII and VIII*, 2 vols., Philadelphia: University Museum

Janowski, B.
1982 *Sühne als Heilsgeschehen* (= Wissenschaftliche Monographien zum Alten und Neuen Testament 55), Neukirchen-Vluyn: Neukirchener Verlag

Jas, R.
1996 *Neo-Assyrian Judicial Procedures* (= SAAS 5), Helsinki: Neo-Assyrian Text Corpus Project

Jewish Museum
1986 *Among Ancient Empires* (Museum Exhibition Catalogue), New York

Johns, C. H. W.
1904a "Note on the Gezer Contract Tablet," *PEFQSt* 36: 237–44
1904b "Remarks on the Gezer Tablet," *PEFQSt* 36: 401–2
1905 "The New Cuneiform Tablet from Gezer," *PEFQSt* 37: 206–10

Johns, C. H. W., et al.
1912 *apud* Macalister 1912: vol. 1, 23–31
1924 *Assyrian Deeds and Documents*, Cambridge: Deighton, Bell

Kienast, B.
1978 *Die altbabylonischen Briefe und Urkunden aus Kisurra*, Wiesbaden: Franz Steiner

Klein, J., and Skaist, A.
1990 (eds.), *Bar-Ilan Studies in Assyriology Dedicated to Pinḥas Artzi*, Ramat Gan: Bar Ilan University Press

Klengel, H.
1992 *Syria: 3000 to 300 B.C.*, Berlin: Akademie Verlag

Knauf, E. A.
1989 "The Migration of the Script and the Formation of the State in South Arabia," *PSAS* 19: 79–91

Knudtzon, J. A.
1915 *Die El-Amarna Tafeln mit Einleitung und Erläuterungen*, Leipzig: Hinrichs

Koch, J.
1989 *Neue Untersuchungen zur Topographie des babylonischen Fixsternhimmels*, Wiesbaden: Otto Harrassowitz

Koch-Westenholz, U., and Westenholz, A.
2000 "Enkidu—The Noble Savage?," in George, A. R., and Finkel, I. L. (eds.), *Wisdom, Gods, and Literature: Studies in Assyriology in Honour of W. G. Lambert*, Winona Lake, IN: Eisenbrauns, 437–51

Kochavi, M.
1977 "The Canaanite Palace at Aphek and Its Inscriptions," *Qadmoniot* 10: 62–68 (Hebrew)

1981 "The History and Archaeology of Aphek-Antipatris: A Biblical City in the Sharon Plain," *BA* 44: 75–86

Kochavi, M., et al.
1978 *Aphek-Antipatris, 1974–1977: The Inscriptions*, Tel Aviv: Tel Aviv University, Institute of Archaeology

Kreuzer, S.
2006 (ed.), *Taanach/Tell Taʿannek: 100 Jahre Forschungen zur Archäologie, zur Geschichte, zu den Fundobjekten und zu den Keilschriftexten* (= Wiener Altestamentliche Studien 5), 85–99

Lambdin, T. O.
1953 "Egyptian Loan Words in the Old Testament," *JAOS* 73: 145–55

Lamon, R. S., and Shipton, G. M.
1939 *Megiddo I: Seasons of 1925–34, Strata I–V*, hicago: University of Chicago Press

Landsberger, B.
1954 "Assyrische Königsliste und 'Dunkles Zeitalter,'" *JCS* 8: 31–45, 47–73, 106–33
1967 "Über Farben im Sumerisch-Akkadischen," *JCS* 21: 139–73
1968 "Zur vierten und siebenten Tafel des Gilgamesh-Epos," *RA* 62: 97–135

Landsberger, B., and Gurney, O. R.
1958 "Practical Vocabulary of Assur," *Archiv für Orientforschung* 18: 328–41

Landsberger, B., and Tadmor, H.
1964 "Fragments of Clay Liver Models from Hazor," *IEF* 14: 201–18

Langdon, S.
1936 "Note on the Cuneiform Tablet Found at Samaria," *Journal of the Royal Asiatic Society*, 501–2

Lapp, P. W.
1964 "The 1963 Excavation at Taʿannek," *BASOR* 173: 4–44
1967 "The 1966 Excavations at Tell Taʿannek," *BASOR* 185: 2–39

Leichty, E.
2011 *The Royal Inscriptions of Esarhaddon, King of Assyria (680–669 BC)* (= RINAP 4), Winona Lake, IN: Eisenbrauns

Lemaire, A., and Joannès, F.
1994 "Premières Monnaies avec signes cunéiformes: Samarie, IVème s. av. n.è," *NABU* 1994/4: 84–86, no. 95

Limet, H.
1971 *Les légendes des sceaux cassites*, Brussels: Palais des Académies

Lipiński, E.
1976 "Apladad," *Or* 45: 53–73

Loud, G.
1948 *Megiddo II: Seasons of 1935–1939, Plates*, Chicago: University of Chicago Press

Loundine, A.
1987 "L'Abécédaire de Beth Shemesh," *Le Muséon* 100: 243–50

Macalister, R. A. S.
1904 "Eighth Quarterly Report on the Excavation of Gezer," *PEFQSt* 36: 194–228
1905 "Twelfth Quarterly Report on the Excavation of Gezer," *PEFQSt* 37: 183–99
1909 "Twenty-First Quarterly Report on the Excavation of Gezer," *PEQ* 41: 87–105
1912 *The Excavation of Gezer, 1902–1905 and 1907–1909*, 3 vols., London: J. Murray

Magnusson, M.
1977 *BC: The Archaeology of the Biblelands*, New York: Book Club Associates

Maisler, B.
1937 "The Taanach Tablets," in Torczyner, N. H., et al. (eds.), *Sefer Klausner*, Tel Aviv: Vaad HaYovel, 44–66 (Hebrew)
1946 "The Phoenician Inscriptions from Byblos and Chain of Development of the Phoenician-Hebrew Alphabet," *Lešonenu* 14: 166–81 (Hebrew)

Malamat, A.
1960 "Hazor: The Head of All Those Kingdoms," *JBL* 79: 12–19

1961 "Campaigns of Amenhotep II and Thutmose IV to Canaan," *Scripta Hierosolymitana* 8: 218–31
1989 *Mari and the Early Israelite Experience*, Oxford: Oxford University Press

Matthews, D. M.
1990 *The Kassite Glyptic of Nippur, Inscriptions by W. G. Lambert* (= Orbis Biblicus et Orientalis 116), Göttingen: Vandenhoeck & Ruprecht; Freiburg, Switzerland: Universitätsverlag

Maul, Stefan
2012 "Tontafelschriften des 'Kodex Hammurabi' in altbabylonischer Monumentalschrift," *ZA* 102: 76–99
2013 *Die Wahrsagekunst im Alten Orient. Zeichen des Himmels und der Erde*, Munich: C. H. Beck, 2013

Mayrhofer, M.
1972 "Eine neue Ta'anach-Tafel und ein indoarischer Name," *Anzeiger der Österreischischen Akademie der Wissenschaften in Wien* 109: 119–21

Mildenberg, L.
1996 "Yĕhūd und šamryn. Über das Geld der persischen Provinzen Juda und Samaria im 4. Jahrhundert," in Cancik, H., et al. (eds.), *Geschichte—Tradition—Reflexion. FS Martin Hengel*, Tübingen: Mohr Siebeck, 119–46

McCown, C. C.
1947 *Tell En-Naṣbeh I: Archaeological and Historical Results*, Berkeley: Palestine Institute of Pacific School of Religion

Meshorer, Y., and Qedar, S.
1991 *The Coinage of Samaria in the Fourth Century BCE*, Jerusalem: Numismatic Fine Arts International
1999 *Samarian Coinage*, Jerusalem: Israel Numismatic Society

Meshorer, Y., Bijovsky, G., and Fischer-Bossert, W.
2013 *Coins of the Holy Land: The Abraham and Marion Sofaer Collection at the American Numismatic Society and the Israel Museum*, New York: American Numismatic Society

Meyers, C. L., and Meyers, E. M.
2009 "The Persian Period at Sepphoris," in *Eretz-Israel* 29: 136*–44*

Milik, J. T.
1956 "An Unpublished Arrow-head with Phoenician Inscription of the 11th–10th Century B.C.," *BASOR* 143: 3–6

Millard, A.
1994 *The Eponyms of the Assyrian Empire, 910–612 BC* (= SAAS 2), Winona Lake, IN: Eisenbrauns

Moran, W. L.
1963 "A Note on the Treaty Terminology of the Sefire Stelas," *JNES* 22: 173–76
1992 *The Amarna Letters*, Baltimore: Johns Hopkins University Press

Na'aman, N.
1988 "Pharaonic Lands in the Jezreel Valley in the Late Bronze Age," in Heltzer, M., and Lipiński, E. (eds.), *Society and Economy in the Eastern Mediterranean (c. 1500–1000 B.C.)*, Leuven: Peeters, 177–85
1994 "The Hurrians and the End of the Middle Bronze Age in Palestine," *Levant* 26: 175–87
1996 "The Coming Forth of the 'Life' of the Pharaoh (EA 227:9–11)," *NABU* 1996/3: 73, no. 82
2004 "The *Ṣuhāru* in the Second-Millennium BCE Letters from Canaan," *IEJ* 54: 92–99
2007 "The Contribution of the Suḫḫu Inscriptions to the Historical Research of the Kingdoms of Israel and Judah," *JNES* 66/2: 107–22

Na'aman, N., and Zadok, R.
2000 "Assyrian Deportations to the Province of Samerina in the Light of Two Cuneiform Tablets from Tel Hadid," *TA* 27: 159–88

Naveh, J.
1982 *Early History of the Alphabet*, Jerusalem: Magnes Press (Hebrew version: 1989)

Niehr, H.
2011 Review of *Cuneiform in Canaan*, *OLZ* 106: 250–51

Nissen, H., Damerow, P., and England, R. K.
1993 *Archaic Bookkeeping: Early Writing and Techniques of Economic Administration in the Ancient Near East* (translated by Paul Larsen), Chicago: University of Chicago Press

Nougayrol, J.
1939 *Cylindres-sceaux et empreintes de cylindres trouvés en Palestine*, Paris: P. Geuthner

Ornan, T.
1997 "Mesopotamian Influence on the Glyptic of Israel and Jordan in the First Millennium" B.C." (Ph.D. diss., Tel Aviv University), Tel Aviv (Hebrew with English abstract)
2003 "On the Dating of Some Middle Assyrian Cylinder Seals," *NABU* 2003/3: 71–73, no. 63

Oshima, T.
2003 "Hymns and Prayers to Marduk and the Descriptions of His Divine Aspects in the Texts" (Ph.D. diss., Hebrew University of Jerusalem), Jerusalem

Owen, D. I.
1981 "An Akkadian Letter from Ugarit at Tel Aphek," *TA* 8: 1–17 (reprinted in Owen et al. 1987: 1–17)

Owen, D. I., et al.
1987 *Aphek-Antipatris, 1978–1985*, Tel Aviv: Tel Aviv University

Paley S. M., Spar, I, and Stieglitz, R. R.
Forthcoming "A Cuneiform Contract Fragment from Tel Mikhmoret," in press IEJ

Pardee, D., and Bordrueil, P.
1995 "Un abécédaire du type sud-sémitique découvert en 1988 dans les fouilles archéologiques françaises de Ras Shamra-Ougarit," *CRAI*: 855–60
2001 "RS 8.2215, Abécédaire," in Yon, M., and Arnaud, D. (eds.), *Études Ougaritiques I: Travaux 1985–1993* (= Ras Shamra-Ougarit XIV), Paris: Éd. Recherche sur les civilisations, 341–48

Parker, B.
1949 "Cylinder Seals from Palestine," *Iraq* 11:1–43
1961 "Administrative Tablets from the North-West Palace, Nimrud," *Iraq* 23: 15–67

Parpola, S.
1970 *Neo-Assyrian Toponyms* (= AOAT 6), Neukirchen-Vluyn: Butzon und Bercker Kevelaer

Peiser, F.
1903 "Zu den Ta'annek-Tafeln," *OLZ* 6: 321–23

Pettinato, G.
1992 *La Saga di Gilgamesh*, Milan: Rusconi

Pfeiffer, C. F.
1966 *The Biblical World: A Dictionary of Biblical Archaeology*, Grand Rapids, MI: Baker Book House

Pinches, T. G.
1904 "The Fragment of an Assyrian Tablet Found at Gezer," *PEFQSt* 36: 229–36

Porada, E.
1965 "Appendix F, Cylinder Seas," in Kenyon, K. M., *Excavations at Jericho*, vol. 2, *The Tombs Excavated in 1955–1958*, London: British School of Archaeology in Jerusalem , 656–61

Postgate, J. N.
1974 *Taxation and Conscription in the Assyrian Empire* (= Studia Pohl: Series Maior 3), Rome: Biblical Institute Press
1976 *Fifty Neo-Assyrian Legal Documents*, Warminster: Aris and Phillips
1978 "An Inscribed Jar from Tell al Rimah," *Iraq* 40: 71–75

Powell, M. A.
1984 "On the Absolute Value of Assyrian *qa* and *emār*," *Iraq* 46: 57–61

Pritchard, J. B.
1969 (ed.), *Ancient Near Eastern Texts Relating to the Old Testament*, 3rd ed., Princeton: Princeton University Press

Pruzsinszky, R.
2006 "Das Onomastikon der Texte von Tell Ta'annek/Taanach," in Kreuzer 2006: 101–17

Puech, E.
1986 "Origine de l'alphabet," *RB* 93: 161–213
1991 "La Tablette cunéiforme de Beth Shemesh. Premier témoin de la séquence des lettres du sud-sémitique," in Baurain, C., et al. eds., *Phoinikeia Grammata: Lire et écrire en Méditerranée*, Namur: Société des études classiques

Quack, J. F.
1993 "Ägyptisches und südarabisches Alphabet," *Revue d'Égyptologie* 44: 141–51
2003 "Die spätägyptische Alphabetreihenfolge und das 'südsemitische' Alphabet," *Lingua Aegyptia* 11: 163–84

Rabinovich, A., and Silberman, N. A.
1998 "The Burning of Hazor," *Archaeology* 51 (May/June): 50–55

Radner, K.
1995 "Samaria 1825 = Fi. 16. Zum Verbleib einer nA Urkunde aus Sāmirīna" (Samaria), *NABU* 1995/4: 90, no. 100
1997 *Die neuassyrischen Privatrechtsurkunden, als Quelle für Mensch und Umwelt* (= SAAS 6), Helsinki: Neo-Assyrian Text Corpus Project
1998 "Traders in the Neo-Assyrian Period," in Dercksen, J. (ed.), *Trade and Finance in Mesopotamia: Proceedings of the First MOS Symposium (Leiden 1997)*, Istanbul: Nederlands Historisch-Archeologisch Instituut te Istanbul

Rainey, A. F.
1969 "A Clay Tablet from Taanach—A Ray of Light on Eretz-Israel on the Eve of Joshua's Conquest," *Qadmoniut* 2: 89–90 (Hebrew)
1973 "The Cuneiform Inscription on a Votive Cylinder from Beer-Sheba," in Aharoni 1973: 61–70
1975 "Two Cuneiform Fragments from Tel Aphek," *TA* 2: 125–29 (reprinted in Kochavi et al. 1978: 8–16)
1976 "A Tri-Lingual Cuneiform Fragment from Tel Aphek," *TA* 3: 137–40
1977 "Verbal Usages in the Taanach Texts," *IOS* 7: 33–64
1996 *Canaanite in the Amarna Tablets: A Linguistic Analysis of the Mixed Dialect Used by the Scribes from Canaan*, Leiden: Brill
1998 "Syntax, Hermeneutics, and History," *IEJ* 48: 239–51
1999 "Taanach Letters," *EI* 26: 153*–62*

Rainey, A. F., Schniedewind, W., and Cochavi-Rainey, Z.
2015 *The El-Amarna Correspondence*, Leiden: Brill

Reisner, G. A., Fisher, C. S., and Lyon, D. G.
1924 *Harvard Excavations at Samaria, 1908–1910*, vol. 1, *Text*; vol. 2, *Plans and Plates*, Cambridge, MA: Harvard University Press

Rollston C.
2010 "A Fragmentary Cuneiform Tablet from the Ophel (Jerusalem): Methodological Musings About the Proposed Genre and *Sitz im Leben*," *Antiguo Oriente* 8: 11–21

Rothenbusch, R.
2000 *Die kasuistische Rechtssammlung im "Bundesbuch" (Ex. 21,2–11, 18–22, 16), und ihr literarischer Kontext im Licht altorientalischer Parallelen* (= AOAT 259), Münster: Ugarit-Verlag

Rowe, A.
1930 *The Topography and History of Beth-Shan, with details of the Egyptian and other Inscriptions Found on the Site* Philadelphia: University of Pennsylvania Press
1936 *A Catalogue of Egyptian Scarabs: Scaraboids, Seals, and Amulettes in the Palestine Archaeological Museum*, Cairo: Imprimerie de l'Institut français d'archéologie orientale

Ryckmans, J.
1988 "A. G. Lundin's Interpretation of the Bet Shemesh Abecedary: A Presentation and Commentary," *PSAS* 18: 123–29

Sachs, A. J.
1937–39 "Two Notes on the Taanach and Amarna Letters," *AfO* 12: 371–73
1953 "The Late Assyrian Royal-Seal Type," *Iraq* 15: 167–70

Sanders, S.
2004 "What Was the Alphabet For? The Rise of Written Vernaculars and the Making of Israelite National Literature," *Maarav* 11: 1–32
2011 *The Invention of Hebrew*, Champaign: University of Illinois Press

2016 "The Two Dialects of the Jerusalem Scribes of the Amarna Tablets," *NABU* 2016/4: 21–22, no. 98

Sass, B.
1991 "The Beth Shemesh Tablet and the Early History of the Proto-Canaanite, Cuneiform, and South Semitic Alphabets," *UF* 23: 315–26

Sayce, A. H.
1893 "The Cuneiform and Other Inscriptions Found at Lachish and Elsewhere in the South of Palestine," *PEQ* 25: 25–32
1904 "Note on the Assyrian Tablet," *PEFQSt* 36: 236–37
1905 "The New Cuneiform Tablet from Gezer," *PEFQSt* 37: 272

Scheil, V.
1894 "La Tablette de Lachis," *RB* 3: 433–36

Schneider, T.
1992 *Asiatische Personennamen in ägyptischen Quellen des Neuen Reiches*, Freiburg, Switzerland: Universitäts Verlag

Schröder, O.
1915a *Vorderasiatische Schriftdenkmäler der Königlichen Museen zu Berlin*, Heft 11, *Die Tontafeln von El-Amarna, Erster Teil*, Leipzig
1915b *Vorderasiatische Schriftdenkmäler der Königlichen Museen zu Berlin*, Heft 12, *Die Tontafeln von El-Amarna, Zweiter Teil*, Leipzig

Schumacher, G.
1908a *Tell el-Mutesellim*, Band 1, Fundbericht A, *Text*, Leipzig: Haupt
1908b *Tell el-Mutesellim*, Band 1, Fundbericht B, *Tafeln*, Leipzig: Haupt

Sellin, E.
1904 *Tell Ta^{c}annek, Bericht über eine mit Unterstützung der Kaiserlichen Akademie der Wissenschaften und des K.K. Ministeriums für Kultus und Unterricht unternommene Ausgrabung in Palästina*, Vienna: C. Gerold's Sohn

Shaffer, A.
1970 "Fragment of an Inscribed Envelope (Appendix B)," in Dever, W. G., et al., *Gezer I. Preliminary Report of the 1964–66 Seasons*, Jerusalem: Hebrew Union College, 111–13
1971 "The Ashdod Cylinder Seal," in Dothan 1971: 198–99
1988 "Cuneiform Tablets from Palestine I: The Letter from Shechem," *Beer Sheva* 3: 163–69 (Hebrew), 13* (English summary

Shanks, H.
2013 "More Treasures from a Dump," *Biblical Archaeology Review* 39/4: 18

Sigrist, R. M.
1982 "Une Tablette cunéiforme de Tell Keisan," *IEJ* 32: 32–35
2008 "Cunéiformes en Canaan," *RB* 115: 307–8 (Review)

Singer, I.
1983 "Takuḫlinu and Ḫaya: Two Governors in the Ugarit Letter from Tel Aphek," *TA* 10: 3–25 (reprinted in Owen et al. 1987: 25–57)
1999 "A Political History of Ugarit," in Watson, W. G. E., and Wyatt, N. (eds.), *Handbook of Ugaritic Studies*, Leiden: Brill
2008 "Purple-Dyers in Lazpa," in Collins, J. C., et al. (eds.), *Anatolian Interfaces: Hittites, Greeks, and Their Neighbours*, Oxford: Oxbow Books

Sivan, D.
1984 *Grammatical Analysis and Glossary of the Northwest Semitic Vocables in Akkadian Texts of the 15th–13th C.B.C. from Canaan and Syria* (= AOAT 213), Neukirchen-Vluyn: Neukirchener Verlag

Smith, M. S.
2008 *God in Translation: Deities in Cross-Cultural Discourse in the Biblical World*, Tübingen: Mohr Siebeck

Smith, S.
1934 "Report on Tablet from Jericho," *AAA* 21: 116–17

von Soden, W.
1963 "Assyrisch *ana ʿini<ana mīni und suʿʿu<summu*," *AfO* 20: 82

Stern, E.
2001 *Archaeology of the Land of the Bible*, vol. 2, *The Assyrian, Babylonian, and*

Persian Periods 732–332 BCE, New York: Doubleday
2003 "The Assyrian Impact on the Material Culture of Palestine," in Eph'al, I., Ben-Tor, A., and Machinist, P. (eds.), *Hayim and Miriam Tadmor Volume* (= Eretz-Israel 27), Jerusalem: 218–29

Stolper, M. W.
1980 Review of M. Mayrhofer, *Supplement zur Sammlung der altpersischen Inschriften*, *AfO* 27: 174–76
1996 In Nagy, R. M., Meyers, C. M., Weiss, Z., and Meyers, E. M. (eds.), *Sepphoris in Galilee: Crosscurrents of Culture*, Raleigh: North Carolina Museum of Art

Streck, M. P.
2000 *Das amurritische Onomastikon der altbabylonischen Zeit*, Band 1, *Die Amurriter, die onomastische Forschung, Orthographie und Phonologie, Nominalmorphologie*, Münster: Ugarit-Verlag

Tadmor, H.
1966 "Philistia Under Assyrian Rule," *BA* 29: 86–102
1967 "Fragments of a Stele of Sargon II from the Excavations of Ashdod," *EI* 8: 241–45 (Hebrew), 75* (English summary)
1971 "Fragments of an Assyrian Stele of Sargon II," in Dothan 1971: 192–97
1973 "On the History of Samaria in the Biblical Period," in Aviram, J. (ed.), *Eretz Shomron*, Jerusalem: Israel Exploration Society, 67–74 (Hebrew), XV (English summary)
1977 "A Lexicographical Text from Hazor," *IEJ* 27: 98–102

Tadmor, H,. and Tadmor, M.
1967 "The Seal of Bēlu-ašarēdu, Majordomo," *Bulletin of the Israel Exploration Society* 31: 68–79 (Hebrew)
1995 "The Seal of Bel-Asharedu—A Case of 'Migration,'" in Van Lerberghe, K., and Schoors, A. (eds.), *Immigration and Emigration Within the Ancient Near East. Festschrift E. Lipiński*, Leuven: Uitgeverij Peeters en Departement Oriëntalistiek, 345–55

Tallqvist, K.
1914 *Assyrian Personal Names*, Helsingfors: Soc. Litterariae Fennicae (published same year as *Acta Societas Scientarum Fennicae* 43/1)

Thureau-Dangin, F.
1931 "Vocabulaires de Ras-Shamra," *Syria* 12: 225–66

Tigay, J.
1982 *The Evolution of the Gilgamesh Epic*, Philadelphia: University of Pennsylvania Press

Tournay, R. J., and Shaffer, A.
1994 *L'Épopée de Gilgamesh*, Paris: Cerf

Tropper, J.
2000 *Ugaritische Grammatik* (= AOAT 273), Münster: Ugarit-Verlag

Ussishkin, D.
2017 *Biblical Megiddo: The Story of the Canaanite and Israelite City*, Jerusalem: Yad Ben-Zvi (Hebrew)

Van Beek, G. W.
1993 "Tell Jemmeh," in *The New Encyclopedia of Archaeological Excavations in the Holy Land*, Jerusalem: Israel Exploration Society, 667–74
1983 "Digging up Tell Jemmeh," *Archaeology* 36/1, 1983, 12–19

Vanderhooft, D.
1999 *The Neo-Babylonian Empire and Babylon in the Latter Prophets* (= Harvard Semitic Museum Monographs 59), Atlanta: Scholars Press
2003 "Babylonian Strategies of Imperial Control in the West: Royal Practice and Rhetoric," in Lipschits, O., and Blenkinsopp, J. (eds.), *Judah and Judeans in the Neo-Babylonian Period*, Winona Lake, IN: Eisenbrauns, 235–62

Van der Toorn, K.
2000 "Cuneiform Documents from Syria-Palestine: Texts, Scribes, and Schools," *ZDPV* 116: 97–113

Van Soldt, W. H.
1991 *Studies in the Akkadian of Ugarit: Dating and Grammar* (= AOAT 40), Neukirchen-Vluyn: Neukirchener Verlag

Virolleaud, C.
1969 "L'Alphabet sénestogyre de Ras Shamra (Ugarit)," *CRAI*: 85–90

Von Dassow, E.
2004 "Canaanite in Cuneiform," *JAOS* 124: 641–74

Watzinger, C.
1929 *Tell el-Mutesellim*, Band 2, *Die Funde*, Leipzig: Haupt

Weippert, H.
1998 "Kumidi, Die Ergebnisse der Ausgrabungen auf dem *Tell Kāmid el-Lōz* in den Jahren 1963 bis 1981," *ZDPV* 114: 1–38

Weippert, M.
1966 "Archäologischer Jahresbericht," *ZDPV* 82: 274–330
1967 "Zur Lesung der alphabetischen Keilschrifttafel vom Tell Ta'annek," *ZDPV* 83: 82–83
2010 *Historisches Textbuch zum Alten Testament* (= Grundrisse zum Alten Testament), Göttingen: Vandenhoeck & Ruprecht

Winckler, H.
1896 *Die Thontafeln von Tell-el-Amarna*, Berlin: Reuter & Reichard

Worschech, U.
1991 "Eine Keilalphabetische Inschrift von el-Bālū'?," *UF* 23: 395–99

Yadin, Y., et al.
1959 *The James A. De Rothschild Expedition at Hazor: Hazor II; An Account of the Second Season of Excavations, 1956*, Jerusalem: Magnes Press (Hebrew
1960 *The James A. De Rothschild Expedition at Hazor: Hazor II; An Account of the Second Season of Excavations, 1956*, Jerusalem: Magnes Press
1961a *The James A. De Rothschild Expedition at Hazor: Hazor III–IV: An Account of the Third and Fourth Seasons of Excavations, 1957–1958*, Jerusalem: Magnes Press
1961b *The James A. De Rothschild Expedition at Hazor: Hazor III–IV; An Account of the Third and Fourth Seasons of Excavations, 1957–1958*, Jerusalem: Magnes Press (Hebrew)

Yeivin, S.
1945 "A New Ugaritic Inscription from Palestine," *Kedem* 2: 32–41 (Hebrew), viii (English summary)

Yener, A.
1995 "Amor, Figurines, and Weapons," *BA* 58: 101–7

Zadok, R.
1977 "*On West Semites in Babylonia During the Chaldean and Achaemenian Periods: An Onomastic Study*. Jerusalem: H. J. & Z. Wanaarta
1977–78 "Historical Onomastic Notes," *WO* 9: 35–56
1985 "Samarian Notes," *BiOr* 42: 567–72
1991 "On the Onomasticon of the Old Aramaic Sources," *BiOr* 48: 25–40
1996 "A Prosopography and Ethno-Linguistic Characterization of Southern Canaan in the Second Millennium BCE," *Michmanim* 9: 97–145

Zawadzki, S.
2009–10 "AMAR, *Bēr*, *Būru*, and *Apladad*: One or Many?," *SAAB* 18: 205–14

Zilberg, P.
2015 "A New Edition of the Tel Keisan Cuneiform Tablet," *IEJ* 65/1, 90–95

Zorn, J. R.
1997 "Mizpah: Newly Discovered Stratum Reveals Judah's Other Capital," *Biblical Archeology Review* 23/5: 28–38, 66

INDEX OF PERSONAL NAMES IN THE SOURCES

This index contains the personal names in the sources edited in this volume. All complete names are included, as well as all names for which at least three complete signs have been preserved, not counting the *Personnenkeil*. On a few occasions, names with fewer than three complete signs are given, particularly in the case of the Taanach tablets, where signs belonging to a number of names have been lost since the time of Hrozný's copies. Syllabic names or portions of names are given as in the editions, while Sumerograms are rendered into Akkadian with what we consider to be the most likely reading. Names that include Sumerograms are transliterated in full in parentheses after the main entry. Variant renderings for what we consider to be the same name are listed together under the first complete version of the name in alphabetical order.

A-a-*ahhē* (^{m}A-a-PAP.MEŠ)	Samaria 2:3
^{m}A-˹a˺-še-eb-š[i	Hadid 1:6
ʿAbdaya (^{m}ÌR-˹da˺-ya)	Taanach 14:7
Abdi-Addu (^{m}ÌR-^{d}I[M . . .	Taanach 7 ii 12
Abdi-He-b[a] (ÌR-He-b[a])	Taanach 7 rev. i 7'
[^{m}]Ab-di-˹ia˺-du	Hazor 5 rev. 2'
Abdi-milki ([^{m}]˹ÌR˺-LUGAL)	Taanach 14:1
[^{m}]*Abdi*-˹šar˺-ru-ma (ÌR-˹šar˺-ru-ma	Taanach 7 ii 3
Abdi-ša-ru-na (^{m}ÌR-ša-ru-na)	Taanach 4 rev. 7', son of Zi-˹ib˺-[. . .
A-bi-*Erah* (A-bi-30)	Hazor 7 rev. 4
^{m}A-bi-ra-[. . .	Taanach 12:2'
A-bi-ra-pí	Hazor 7 Lower Edge 1
Abu-erība (^{m}AD.SU)	Gezer 3:2
Adda-id-r[i] (^{md}IM-id-r[i])	Beer Sheva 1:3, father of Re-mut-*ilāni*
^{m}Ad-du-ap-˹di?˺	Hazor 10:3
^{m}Ad-du-ia	Aphek 7:15, 21
^{m}Ad-du-ya	Aphek 7:32, 34
A-gi-[i]a	Taanach 4:12', father of [^{m}R]A?-BE-šu
Ah-ab-be	Hadid 2:3
Ahi-ia-mi (^{m}ŠEŠ-ia-mi)	Taanach 2:2
Ahu-ilāya (^{m}PAP-DINGIR-a-a)	Gezer 4 Lower Edge 1–2, governor of Carchemish
^{m}*Aḫu-nū*[*rī*] (^{m}ŠEŠ-*nu*-[*ri* . . .	Keisan 1 obv. 3'
[^{m}A-i]a-˹ri˺	Taanach 3 rev. 11'
^{m}Ak-ti-m[i(-) . . .	Taanach 7 ii 9
^{m}Al-tu-un-šu	Megiddo 5:1
A-ma-an-ha-at-pa	Taanach 5:2, 6:2
[^{m}AN]-ya-mu-˹na˺	Taanach 4:6'
^{m}Ar-ta-a[k-šá-as-su]	Sepphoris 1:2, Arta[xerxes] (Akkadian)
Assur-dūru-uṣur (^{m}AŠ+ŠUR.BÀD.PAP)	Gezer 3 rev. 6', governor of Barhalzi
A[*ssur*- . . . -*i*]*n* (^{md}A[Š+ŠUR-×-(×)-i]n)	Samaria 1:1
A-ta-na-ah-ì-lí	Taanach 13:1, son of Ha-ab-si-im
^{m}Ba˹ʾ˺-li-ia$_{5}$	Hazor 11:2
^{m}BE.LUM-i[a$_{5}$]	Taanach 7 rev. i 6'
Ba-az-ú-nu	Taanach 6:4, son of Na-ar-sí
^{m}Ba-ṣi!-ir-da	Gezer 2:9'
Ballas-su-i[q-bi . . .	Sepphoris 3:1'

^{m}Ba-ʾ-lu-pá-di	Shechem 2 rev. 4
Bēl-ahhē (^{md}EN.ŠEŠ)	Mikhmoret 1:1
Bēl-apla-iddina (^{m}EN.A.AŠ)	Gezer 3 rev. 8'
Bēl-ašarēd (^{m}EN.MAŠ)	Wingate 1:1, the palace overseer
^{m}*Bēl-Dūrī* (^{m}EN.BAD)	Tel Keisan 1 obv. 2'
[B]i-il-lu-lum	Ashdod 1:2, father of [Ì-l]í-ab-num
^{m}Bi-ir-ya-ma-aš-da	Taanach 14:12
Bīn-An-t[a]-⸢ma$^{?}$⸣: (^{m}DUMU-AN-[t]a-⸢ma$^{?}$⸣)	Taanach 14:6
Bīn-A-ya (^{m}DUMU-A-ya)	Taanach 14:5
Bīn-⸢Ba⸣-wa-za-en-zi (^{m}DUMU-⸢Ba⸣-wa-za-en-zi)	Taanach 3 rev. 6'
Bīn-D[a]-ni-ya (^{m}DUMU-D[a]-ni-ya)	Taanach 7 ii 6
Bīn-E-ze-e-[..] (^{m}DUMU-E-ze-e-[× ×])	Taanach 3 rev. 3'
Bīn-Ha-nu-ta (^{m}DUMU-Ha-nu-ta)	Hazor 5:1
Bīn-Hu-bi-ri (^{m}DUMU-Hu-bi-ri)	Taanach 3:8'
Bīn-Hu-[n]i-ni (^{m}DUMU-Hu-[n]i-ni)	Taanach 7 ii 7
Bīn-Ia-ma-×-× (^{m}DUMU-Ia-ma-×-×)	Taanach 7 rev. i 4'
[*Bī*]*n*-Ra-ba-ya (^{m}[DUM]U-Ra-ba-ya)	Taanach 3:9'
^{m}*Bīn*-Ya-ya[. . . (^{m}DUMU-Ya-y[a . . .	Taanach 7 ii 11
Bīn-Za-nu-⸢qí ⸣-ma (^{m}DUMU- Za-nu-⸢qí ⸣-ma)	Taanach 4:4'
Bu-nu-ma-nu	Hazor 7 rev. 7
^{m}BU.SIK.SUKKAL.GIŠ	Gezer 4 rev. 2'
Bur-ra-pi-Iʾ	Gezer 3 rev. 10'
^{m}⸢Da⸣-ni-bé-li	Hazor 11:1
DUMU-	See *Bīn*-
^{m}Dup-da-ya	Taanach 4 rev. 6', son of Za-gu-[. . .
Eh-li-*Tešub* (^{m}Eh-li-^{d}IM)	Taanach 1:3
Eh-lum-ma-an-ti	Gezer 1 Outer Surface 4–5, 8, son of Ab-d[i?. . ., the overseer of the shepherds
[^{m}]⸢E⸣-li-tu	Taanach 3:7'
E-lu-ra-ma	
^{m}DINGIR-ra-ma	Taanach 14:10
^{m}E-lu-ra-am$^{!}$-ma	Taanach 4:9'
^{m}E-lu-ra-ma	Taanach 7 rev. i 3'
^{m}E-lu-ra-m[a/a]m-ma	Taanach 12:3'
Elu-ra-pí-i	Geezer 2:21
^{m}En-ki-du	Megiddo 1 rev. 11'
^{m}Ga-ma-lu	Taanach 7 ii 5
Gilgameš (^{m}PAN.MAŠ)	Megiddo 1 rev. 3', 12'
^{m}Ha-a-ia	Aphek 7:1, the Great Man
[H]a-ab-da-du	Hazor 7:11'
Ha-ab-si-im	Taanach 13:2, father of A-ta-na-ah-ì-lí
^{f}Ha-am-ma-a-a	Hadid 2:5
^{m}Ha-ba-du	Hazor 7 Right Edge, Shechem 2:2', son of ^{m}Na-ṣí-ib-ti, Taanach 7 rev. i 10'
Ha-ma-din-nu	Keisan 1:6'
^{m}Ḫattā[iu] (^{m}*Ḫat-a-a-*[*a* . .)	Keisan 1 obv. 4'
^{m}Hi-bi-ya	Taanach 14:9
Hi-in-ni-Èl	Hazor 7:7'
Hi-li-Èl	Hebron 1 passim
^{md}Hum-ba-ni-[ga-aš]	Ashdod 4:1
^{m}Hur-ú-a-ṣi	Gezer 3:9'
Ia-da-⸢da⸣	Hazor 7 rev. 8

[^{m}Ia-d]i-in-nu	Taanach 3 rev. 12'
^{m}Ia-id-[da]-⸢du⸣	Shechem 2:4'
Ia-ah-tuq-*Addu* (Ia-ah-tuq-^{d}IM)	Hazor 7:6'
^{m}Ia-an-d[i- . . .	Taanach 7 ii 10
Ia-an-ṣur-*Addu* (Ia-an-ṣur-^{d}IM)	Hazor 7 Lower Edge 2
^{m}Ia-an-ti-na-du	Shechem 2 rev. 3
Ib-lu-ṭà -du	Hazor 7 rev. 3
Ib-lu-uṭ-Èl	Hazor 7 rev. 6
Ib-ni-[. . .	Hazor 8:1
^{m}I-ia-ri-ma	Hazor 10:9, 16
[Ì-l]í-ab-num	Ashdod 1:1, son of [B]i-il-lu-lum
I-lu-⸢ka-a-num⸣	Hazor 7:4'
^{m}I-lu-lu	Taanach 4:3', son of Su-bi-ir-ri
In-te-du	Hazor 7 rev.1, the smith
In-te-du-*Addu* (In-te-du-^{d}IM$^{!}$)	Hazor 7 rev. 2
In-ti	Hebron 1:8
ÌR-	see *Abdu*
^{m}Ir-pa-⸢a⸣-du	Hazor 5:1 (cf. Hazor 8: ^{m}Ir-p[a . . .
^{m}Ir-tak-i[k-šá-iš-šá]	Sepphoris 1:1, Artaxerxes (Elamite)
^{m}Ir-ze-e-tu	Taanach 7 rev. i 9'
I[š-me-*Addu* (^{m}I[š]-me-^{d}IM$^{!}$)	Hazor 1:1
Iš-me-Èl	Hazor 7:5'
Iš-ni-du	Hazor 7:8'
Iš-pu-uṭ-*Addu* (Iš-pu-uṭ-^{d}IM)	Hazor 7:10'
[I]z$^{!}$-kùr-*Addu* ([I]z$^{?}$-kùr-^{d}IM)	Megiddo 3:1, the scribe
[^{m}Ka-m]a-ru	Taanach 3 rev. 8'
[^{m}]Ka-n[a]-pé-⸢el⸣	Shechem 2:1'
Kanūnāia (^{itu}AB-a-a)	Gezer 3 rev. 7', 11', father of *Zēra-ukīn*
La-ab-a-⸢ya⸣	Beth Shean 2:1
^{m}Le-⸢še⸣-r[u . . .	Hadid 1 rev. 14
Lu-*ahhê* (Lu-PAP.MEŠ)	Gezer 3:4
Ma-a-nu-um	Beth Shean 1:1, the diviner, the servant of Ea
Ma-ni-ti- ìl/^{d}[(×)	Shechem 1:3
Man-nu-ki-*Arbaʾil* (^{m}Man-nu-ki-LÍMMU-ìl)	Gezer 3 rev. 13'
Marduk-bēla-[*uṣur*] (^{md}KU.EN.[PAP])	Hadid 1:10, rev. 6
Marduk-erība (^{md}ŠÚ.SU)	Gezer 3:1
Marduk-nāṣir (^{md}ŠÚ.PAP-ir)	Gezer 3 rev. 8'
Marduk-ni-šu (^{d}AMAR.UTU-ni-šu)	Jericho 3:1, son of *Sîn*-re-me-ni, servant of Adad (for another Marduk name, see Samaria 3:4 md⸢AMAR⸣.U[TU × ×])
Me-na-ni	Kusiya 1:5'
Mi-i[s-ki]	Taanach 4: rev. 3', father of [^{m}×]-×-a-nu
^{m}Mi-ta-[ti] . . .	Taanach 3 rev. 2'
^{f}Mu-na-hi-ma-a	Hadid 2:6
^{m}Mu-ut-[. . .	Taanach 12:4'
Na-ar-sí	Taanach 6:5, father of Ba-az-ú-nu
Na-ba-ṭi	Taanach 4:5', father of [^{m}×]-el-zu$^{?}$-na
^{md}*Nabû*-[. . .] ($^{md+⸢}$AG⸣ [. . .])	Keisan 1 rev. 4'
Nabû-ahhē-iddina	Mikhmoret 1 rev. 6'
Nabû-erība	Mikhmoret 1 rev. 4'
Nabû-za-qi[p]-e[n$^{?}$-ši] (^{md}PA-za-qi[p]-e[n$^{?}$-ši])	Samaria 3:2 (for this name, see *PNAE* 905)
Na-di-n[u . . .	Hadid 1: 16
$^{m⸢}$Na⸣-[g]u-na-zu	Taanach 4:11'

^{m}Na-ṣi/ṣí-ib-ti	Shechem 2:2', father of ^{m}Ha-ba-du, Taanach 14: 13
^{m}Na-ši-m[a ...	Taanach 4a:3'
^{m}Na-tan-ia-u	Gezer 4:1
Nergal-šal-lim (^{m}U+GUR-šal-lim)	Samaria 2:2
Nergal-šarra-uṣur (^{m}U+GUR.MAN.PAP)	Gezer 4 rev. 4'
⸢^{m}⸣Pa-a-pu	Ḥesi 1:22
[^{m}P]a-a-pí	Ḥesi 1:2
Pá-al-ṣí-i	Shechem 2:3', father of ^{m}Su-ar-mu-hu
Pá-di-da	Hebron 1:1
^{m}Pa-di-i	Hadid 2 rev. 6
^{m}*Pān-Ištar* (^{m}IGI-^{d}15)	Keisan 1 obv. 5'
Pí-ra-aš-še/-×	Shechem 1:1
Pu-*Baʿal* (^{m}PU-^{d}IM)	Taanach 14:3
^{m}Pu-ra-at-pur-ta	Hazor 10:1
[^{m}P]u-ra-gu-uš	Taanach 3 rev. 10'
^{m}Pu-ri-i[š ...	Taanach 3 Left Edge ii 4
^{m}Pu-ri-iz-⸢zu⸣-ya	Taanach 14:8
^{m}Pu[r]-ri-i-di	Hazor 11:3
^{m}Pu-ur-da-ya	Taanach 2:12
Qāta-ṣa-bat	Mikhmoret 1 rev. 5'
[^{m}]Qa-ti-na-×	Taanach 4 rev. 5'
^{m}Ra-ba-ia	Taanach 8:4'
Rab-ba-n[a ...	Gezer 1: 3'
[^{m}R]A$^{?}$-BE-šu	Taanach 4:12', son of A-gi-[i]a
^{m}Ra-bi-Èl	Ḥesi 1:24
Re-mut-*ilāni* (^{m}Re-mut-DINGIR.MEŠ)	Beer Sheva 1:2, son of *Adda*-id-r[i]
^{m}Ša-ba-ya	Taanach 14:2
^{m}*Šad-d*[*in*$^{?}$-*nu*$^{?}$]	Keisan 1 obv. 10'
Sa-[G]I/[Z]I-IG-ni	Jericho 1:3, son of Ta-[g]u-ta-ka
Šamaš-aha-[... (^{md}UTU.PAP.[...	Hadid 1 rev. 13
Šamaš-zēr[*a*$^{?}$- ... (^{md}UTU.NUM[UN$^{?}$...	Hadid 1 rev. 12
Šarru-lu-⸢dà-ri⸣ (^{m}MAN-lu-⸢dà-ri⸣)	Hadid 2 rev. 8, see also Keisan 1 rev. 3'
⸢^{m}Šá⸣-áš-ma-a-a	Hadid 2 rev. 4, the Egyptian
Sí-ib-li-du	Hazor 7:9'
Ṣil-Bēl (^{m}GISSU.EN)	Hadid 2 rev. 3
^{m}Si-li-mu	Hadid 2 rev. 2
^{m}⸢*Ṣil*$^{?}$-*šarri*$^{?}$⸣ (^{m}Ṣil$^{?}$-LUGAL$^{?}$)	Hadid 1 rev. 17
Sîn-re-me-ni (^{d}EN-ZU-re-me-ni)	Jericho 3:2, father of *Marduk*-ni-šu
^{m}Si-ni-i	Gezer 4:3–4
Šipṭī-Baʿlu (^{m}DI.KU$_{5}$.^{d}IM)	Ḥesi 1:5, 9
^{m}Su-ar-mu-hu	Shechem 2:3', son of Pá-al-ṣí-i
Su-bi-ir-ri	Taanach 4:3', father of I-lu-lu
Su-ku-hu	Hebron 1:8
Šulmu-šarri (⸢^{m}⸣DI-mu-MAN)	Hadid 1 Left Edge
^{mf}Su-mu-la-*ilum* (^{mf}Su-mu-la-DINGIR-lum)	Hazor 5:3, 7
Šu-mu-pa-ah	Hazor 7 rev. 5
^{m}Su-um-Ha-nu-ta	Hazor 5:2
^{m}Ta-a-gu	Taanach 3 rev. 5'
^{m}Ta-aš-ru-mu	Taanach 4 rev. 8'
Ta-gi	Beth Shean 2:4
Ta-[g]u-ta-ka	Jericho 1:3, father of Sa-[G]I/[Z]I-IG-ni
^{m}Ta-gu$_{5}$-uh-li-na	Aphek 7:4

^{m}Tal-wa-šur	Taanach 1:1, 2:1, 5:1, 6:1
^{m}Tu-ur-ši-ma-ti	Aphek 7:16
Ṭa-ba-LUGAL	Hazor 4
Ṭabta-uballiṭ (^{m}DÙG-ta.DIN)	Gezer 3 rev. 12'
^{m}Ṭu-ri-^{d}A-a	Gezer 3:5
^{m}⸢Uz⸣-di-a-ša	Taanach 3 rev. 7'
$^{m!}$Ya$^{!}$-ah-zi-ra-d[a]	Hazor 5:10
[^{m}Ya-mi]-ba-an-da-LUGAL	Taanach 3 rev. 13'
[^{m}Ya-ṣ]ur-rù-zi-ir-ta-wa	Taanach 3 rev. 9'
^{m}Zag-gi-i	Gezer 3 rev. 7;, son of *Kanūnāia*
^{m}Za-wa-ia	Taanach 7 rev. i 2'
^{m}Za-za-ku	Hadid 1 rev. 11, L[Ú ...
Zēra-ukīn (^{m}NUMUN.DU)	Gezer 3 rev. 11', son of *Kanūnāia*, Gezer 4 rev. 3'
Zēru-ú-tú (^{m}NUMUN-ú-tú)	Gezer 3 rev. 14'
^{m}Ze-ra-ya	Taanach 3 rev. 4', the Sutean$^{?}$
^{m}Zi-bi-lu	Taanach 14:4
^{m}Zi-im-ri-da	Ḥesi 1:6, 9
⸢^{m}⸣Zi-ir-wa-ša	Taanach 7 ii 4
^{m}Zi-ni-ta-ba-an-di	Taanach 14:11
^{m}Zi-q[u]-un-bu	Taanach 7 rev. i 11'
...]-a-ia-da	Naṣbeh 1
⸢^{m}⸣×-ba-an-du	Taanach 4:13', son of B[A$^{?}$-D]A$^{?}$-na
[^{m}×-×-d]a-bi-di	Taanach 3:5'
^{m}[×]-ru-a-da	Taanach 4:10'
[^{m}... -t]i- ìl-la	Gezer 1 Outer Surface 3'

INDEX OF DIVINE NAMES IN THE SOURCES

Divine names within personal names are not considered in this index.

Adad	Jericho 3:3 (dIM)
Apladda	Beer Sheva 1:1
Aya	Jericho 2:2
Assur	Ashdod 4:4
Assur AN.]ŠAR	Ben Shemen 1:6
Baʿal	Taanach 2:2 (EN), cf. 5:3; 6:3 (restored)
Ea (dEN.KI)	Beth Shean 1:3
Enlil	Shephela 1:3'
dIM	Taanach 5:3 (storm god)
Ištar	Hazor 3 f:1
Išum	Ashdod 1:3
Marduk (dMES)	Megiddo 2:1, Shephela 1:4'
(dŠÀ.ZU)	Megiddo 4:1
(dAMAR.UT[U])	Samaria 3:4, 8
Nabu	Samaria 3:6 (restored)
Nergal	Hazor 3 f:3, Taanach 13:3
Šamaš	Jericho 2:1
Tašmetum	Samaria 3:7
Zarpanitum	Samaria 3:9

INDEX OF GEOGRAPHICAL NAMES IN THE SOURCES

Geographical names are listed in alphabetical order without taking into consideration the geographical indicators KUR (land) and URU (city).

A-ma-ZA-RUM$^{⌜ki!⌝}$	Hazor 11:1
URU Bar-hal-zi	Gezer 3 rev. 6'
Carchemish (Gar-ga-mis)	Gezer 4 Lower Edge 2
Ekallatum (É.GAL.HÁ)	Hazor 12:23'
Gar-ga-mis, see Carchemish	
Gaza (URU Ha-za-t[i])	Taanach 6:12
URU Gi-la-di	Hazor 5:6
Ha-ṣú-ra, see Hazor	
Ha-za-t[i], see Gaza	
Hazor (URU Ha-ṣú-ra)	Hazor 5:5, 11:2
Ia-ap-[p]u-ú / ⌜Ia⌝-[p]u-ú, see Jaffa	
URU Ia-ra-mi	Ḥesi 1:10
Jaffa ([UR]U Ia-ap-[p]u-ú)	Gezer 2:10'
([UR]U ⌜Ia⌝-[p]u-ú)	Aphek 7:17
Karallu ([KUR Kar-a]l-lu)	Ashdod 4:2
URU Ki-id-di-im	Gezer 2:8'
Mari (Má-rí^{ki})	Hazor 12:20'
(URU Má-rí^{ki})	Hazor 12:22'
Media (KUR M]a-ad-a-a	Ashdod 4:3
Megiddo IURU Ma-gi-id-\da)	Taanach 5:15
Mu-[ṣur	Ben Shemen 1:2
Na-A[S]-SUR-[r]a (URU Na-A[S]-SUR-[r]a	Hazor 11:3 (Nazareth?)
URU Ra-ha-bi	Taanach 2:22 (Rehov?)
URU Ru-bu-⌜ti⌝[^{ki}]	Taanach 1:26
KUR Šur-d[a]	Ashdod 4:2
Ugarit (KUR URU Ú-ga-ri-it)	Aphek 7:5, 10

INDEX OF SUMERIAN AND AKKADIAN WORDS DISCUSSED

Summerian in Roman, Akkadian in *italic*

bán, 58
duh.ši.a, 11, 82
ganba, 72
gig, 29, 35
^{mul}iku, 58
^{mul}kak.si.sá, 58
ki.lam. *See* ganba
máš.šu.gíd.gíd, 47
NINDA, (commentary to Keisan 1)
rém, 108
síg.sa$_5$, 35
síg.za.gìn, 35
suhur, 58
udu.máš, 91
udu.níta.amar.ba, 91

agannu, 82
alpu, 28
ālu, 66
aššum mīnum, 53
bārû, See Diviner
dajānu, 83
dekû, 140
duhšû/dušû, See duh.ši.a
erēbu, 70
ha-na-ku, 147
iddan, 66
ikû, 58
inūma, 13, 125
iš-DUM, (under Jerusalem 1)
itti, 137
kibtu, 35
labāṭu/lubbuṭu, 127
nadānu, 66, 149
naṣābu, 128
parīsu, 35
sūtu, 58
ṣuhāru, 69, 126
Šamšī, 28
šamû (rain), 150
šapāṭu/šāpiṭtu, 10, 74, 83
Šūkudu, 58
tabarru, 35
ṭēhu, 58
u, 13
unūtu, 152

INDEX OF SUBJECTS

Abdi-Heba, 99
Adad/Addu/A(H)adad, 42, 47, 64, 74, 94, 98. *See also* storm god
Adapa, 17
administrative texts, Aphek 2, 8, Gezer 1, 3–4, Hadid 1–2, Hazor 5, 7, 11, 14–16, Hebron 1, Jericho 1, Tel Keisan 1, Khirbet Kusiyah 1, Mikhmoret 1, Samaria 1–2, Sepphoris 2–4, Shechem 2, Taanach 3–4, 4a, 7, 12, 14
Alalakh, 145, 170
Aleppo, 24
Alexander the Great, 22
alphabetic cuneiform, 7, 17, 159–71; Beth Shemesh 1, Taanach 15, Tabor 1
Amarna / Amarna letters / Tel el-Amarna, 7, 13–18, 42, 47–48, 53, 65, 79–80, 93, 99–100, 125, 129, 134, 136–37, 141, 144–45, 149, 153–54, 170
  EA 25, 80
  EA 170, 78
  EA 228, 75, 79
  EA 368, 18
Amenophis III, 15
Amenophis IV, 15
Amorite, 169
Anat, 69
antichretic debt, 84
Antipatris, 54
Aphek, 4, 14–15, 17, 27–36
  Aphek 1, 17, 27–29
  Aphek 3, 17, 29–30
  Aphek 7, 17, 29, 32–36, 54, 79, 94
Apladda, 42
Arabic, 170
Aramaic, 22, 139
Artaxerxes, 7, 22, 122
Ashdod, 7, 13, 18, 37–39
  Ashdod 1, 13, 37
  Ashdod 2–4, 19, 38–39
Ashqelon, 7, 40–41
  Ashqelon 1, 17, 29
Assurbanipal, 19, 54, 57, 119

Baal/Baʿlu, 94, 98, 139, 145, 148
Babylon, 4, 11, 63
Babylonians, 101
Beer Sheva, 7, 19, 42–43
  Beer Sheva 1, 7, 21, 118
Beit Anot, 69
Ben Shemen, 19, 44
  Ben Shemen 1, 19, 115
Beth Dagon, 54
Beth Mirsim, 45
  Beth Mirsim 1, 13, 120
Beth Shean, 7, 46–48
  Beth Shean 1, 13, 65
  Beth Shean 2, 7, 15, 42
Beth Shemesh, 7, 45, 49, 161–66, 168, 170
  Beth Shemesh 1, 17, 161–64
blue/purple, 34–35
Boghazköi, 53, 108
Byblos/Byblian, 10, 170

calendar, 127
Cambyses, 22, 112
Carmel, 48
clothing, 81, 126
coins, 4, 22; Samaria 5–7
cylinder seal, Ashdod 1, Beer Sheva 1, Beth Mirsim 1, Beth Shean 1, Tell Jemmeh 1, Jericho 2–3, Megiddo 2–4, Samaria 3, Taanach 13, Wingate 1

Darius, 24
Diri, 18
diviner (*barû*), 46–47, 65

Ea. *See* Enki/Ea
Ebla, 10
Egypt/Egyptian, 3, 7, 17–18, 44–45, 48, 52, 56, 62, 98, 100, 110, 112, 136, 147, 163–64
Ekallatum, 7, 10–11, 63, 80, 82
El-Amarna. *See* Amarna
Elam/Elamite, 7, 104, 122
Emar, 41, 71
Enki/Ea, 47
Enlil, 130
eponym (*limmu*), Gezer 3–4, Hadid 1–2
Esarhaddon, 19, 44, 115
Eusebius, 54

fingernail marks, Hadid 1–2

Gedaliah, 22
Genesis, 147
Gezer, 4, 19, 21, 50–58

Gezer (*cont'd*)
  Gezer 1, 13, 89, 92
  Gezer 2, 17, 35, 52
  Gezer 3, 19, 21
  Gezer 4, 7, 19, 21
  Gezer 5?, 4
Gilead, 70
Gilgamesh / Gilgamesh Epic, 7, 17, 105, 107–8, 134, Megiddo 1
Gitta/Gittaim, 54
gloss, glosses, *Glossenkeil*, 7, 17, 28, 79, 150
grain, 126. *See also* wheat
Greece, 22
Greek, 43, 169

Habuba-Kabira, 10
Hadad. *See* Adad/(H)adad
Hadid, Tel, 19, 59–62
  Hadid 1, 19, 21
  Hadid 2, 19, 21
Hammurabi, 10–11, 63, 87
Hazor, 3–5, 7, 10, 13–15, 17–18, 46, 63–89, 132
  Hazor 1, 11
  Hazor 2–3, 13, 46, 86, 139
  Hazor 4, 11
  Hazor 5, 11, 13–14, 32, 75, 126, 154
  Hazor 6, 13, 17, 40
  Hazor 7, 10, 14, 141
  Hazor 8, 10–11, 14, 75
  Hazor 9, 10, 13
  Hazor 10, 17, 35, 92, 137, 139
  Hazor 11, 17, 97, 128, 148
  Hazor 12, 7, 10–11, 83
  Hazor 13, 17, 41
  Hazor 14, 17, 83, 85
  Hazor 15, 17
  Hazor 16, 3, 83, 85
  Hazor 17, 3, 13
Hazor 18: 3, 11, 13
Hebrew, 7, 58, 66, 78, 91, 117, 120, 162, 169
Hebron, 89–92
  Hebron 1, 13, 51–52
Hellenistic period, 22–24
el-Ḥesi, Tel, 93–95
Hittite/Hittites, 17, 108
Hurrian, 7, 13, 15, 17, 51, 69, 71, 136–37

Ibni-Addu, 10–11, 75
Indo-Aryan / Indo-European / Indo-Iranian, 7, 15, 129, 142, 155

Jaffa, 35, 53–54
Jamnia, 54
Jebel Aruda, 10
Jemmeh, Tell, 96
  Tell Jemmeh 1, 13
Jericho, 7, 97–98
  Jericho 1, 17, 128
  Jericho 2, 13
  Jericho 3, 13
Jerusalem, 17, 22, 99–100
  Jerusalem 1: 3, 17
  Jerusalem 2: 3, 17
Jordan, 24
Judah/Judaean, 3, 19, 21–22, 24, 58

Khafajeh, 37
Keisan, Tel, 19, 101–2
  Tel Keisan 1, 21
Khirbet Kusiya, 19, 103–104
  Khirbet Kusiya 1, 21

Lachish, 93
Lamaštu, 130, Shephela 1
law 4, 11, 13, 55, 60, 63, 68–69, 75, 86–88, Hazor 18
leather, 139
Lebanon, 3
letter, Aphek 7, Beth Shean 2, Gezer 2, Hazor 8, 10, 12, Ḥesi 1, Shechem 1, Taanach 1–2, 5–6, 8, 8a, 9–11
lexical lists, 4–5, 7, 17–18, 49; Aphek 1, 3, Ashqelon 1, Hazor 6
liver model, Hazor 2–3
Lydda, 54

magic, 4
Malku = *šarru*, 119
Marduk, 104, 108–9, 118, 130–31
Mari, 7, 10–11, 13–15, 63, 65, 75, 77, 80–82, 89, 128
mathematics, 4, 10, 13, 75–76; Hazor 9
Megiddo, 4, 7, 19, 46, 104, 105–11, 134, 144–45
  Megiddo 1, 7, 14, 17, 134
  Megiddo 2, 104
  Megiddo 4, 108
Mikhmoret, 112–13
mimmation, 13–14, 52, 65, 68, 70, 84, 86, 89, 125
Mitzpah, 22

Nablus (see Shechem)
Nabonidus, 24
Nabu, 118
en-Naṣbeh, Tel, 114
  en-Naṣbeh 1, 7, 21–22

Nazareth, 79
Nebuchadnezzar II, 24
Nerebu, 24
Neriglessar, 24
Nergal and Ereshkigal, 17
Nile, 100

oil, 30, 126
Ophel exccavations, 99–100

Pegasus, 58
Pella, 145, 153
Petra, 24
Persian / Persian period, 22–24, 112, 121–122
Philistia / Philistines, 3, 18, 21
Phoenician, 139, 163, 168–70
private inscription, Hazor 1, 4, 13, Megiddo 1, Tel en-Naṣbeh 1
Punic, 169

Qaqun, 19, 44, 115
  Qaqun 1, 19, 44
Qatna, 11, 63, 80

Ramesside, 100
Ras Abu Hamid, Tel, 54
Ras Shamr. *See* Ugarit
Rig Veda, 155
Royal Game of Ur, 45
royal inscription, Ashdod 2–4, Ben Shemen 1, Qaqun 1, Samaria 4, Sepphoris 1
Russia, 22

S[a], 18
Sabeans, 162
Samaria, 4, 18–19, 21–22, 48, 116–21
  Samaria 1, 21
  Samaria 2, 21
  Samaria 3, 21, 42
  Samaria 4, 19
  Samaria 5–7, 4, 22, 120
Samsi-Addu, 80
Sarepta, 170
Sargon II, 19, 38, 119
Sargon, King of Battle (*Šar tamhāri*), 17
scribal school / scribes, 13–14, 17, 126–27. *See also* school texts
school texts, 4, 31. *See also* scribal school
seal. *See* cylinder seal, stamp seal
Sennacherib, 19, 119
Semitic / West Semitic, 7, 11, 13–14, 17, 21, 27–30, 40, 52, 66, 82, 92, 128, 144, 147, 161, 165, 167–70
Sepphoris, 22, 122–24
  Sepphoris 1, 5, 7, 22
  Sepphoris 2–4, 5, 7, 21–22, 24
Shamash, 47, 98
Shechem, 48, 125–29
  Shechem 1, 13
  Shechem 2, 15, 92, 97, 110, 155, 169, 171
  Shechem 3, 4
sheep / shepherd, 51–52, 89–91, 111. *See also* Megiddo 6
Shephela, 19, 130–31
  Shephela 1, 19, 104
Shuneh, 98
Sinai, 115
Sirius, 58
South Arabia, 162–63
stamp seal, Hazor 4
storm god, 64, 74, 141, 143–44, 146, 169, 171
Sutean, 140–41
Syria, 3, 7, 10, 13–14, 17, 24, 162

Taanach, 4, 13–15, 53, 65, 93, 132–55, 165
  Taanach 1, 8, 133–34, 136, 144, 150
  Taanach 2, 8, 79, 133–34, 136–37, 144, 150
  Taanach 3, 133–35, 141–43
  Taanach 4, 134, 142, 148, 153, 155
  Taanach 4a, 133–34, 153
  Taanach 5, 8, 133–34, 136, 144, 147, 150
  Taanach 6, 8, 133–34, 136–37, 144, 150
  Taannach 7, 70, 133–34, 141, 143, 153, 155
  Taanach 8, 133–34, 150
  Taanach 8a, 133–34, 150
  Taanach 9, 133–34
  Taanach 10, 133–34
  Taanach 11, 133–34
  Taanach 12, 133–34, 148, 155
  Taanach 13, 134
  Taanach 14, 128, 134, 148, 153
  Taanach 15, 17, 128, 133, 165
  Tabor, 17, 129, 156, 161, 165, 168–71
Tashmetum, 118
textiles, 80, 83. *See also* wool
Tiglath-Pileser III, 19

Ugarit/Ugaritic, 7, 17, 33, 35, 41, 71, 94, 128, 139, 145, 149, 161–63, 168–70
Ur III administrative documents, 10
Urra = *ḫubullu*, 17, 29, 40–41, 63, 70–72, 91

votive inscriptions, 21, 42, 118, Beer Sheva 1, Samaria 3
weights and measures, 35–36, 58, 110, 112, 120
West Semitic. *See* Semitic

wheat, 28–29, 33–35
Wingate, 157
  Wingate 1, 19, 21, 42

Yamm, 143
Yasmah-Addu, 80

Zarpanitum, 118
Zimri-Lim, 10–11

Hand Copies

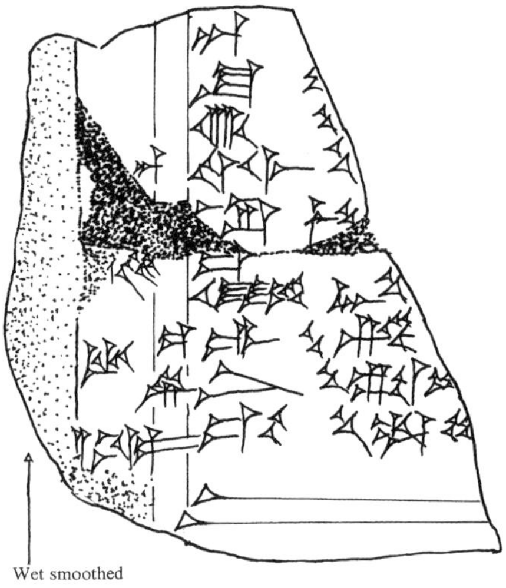

Aphek 1

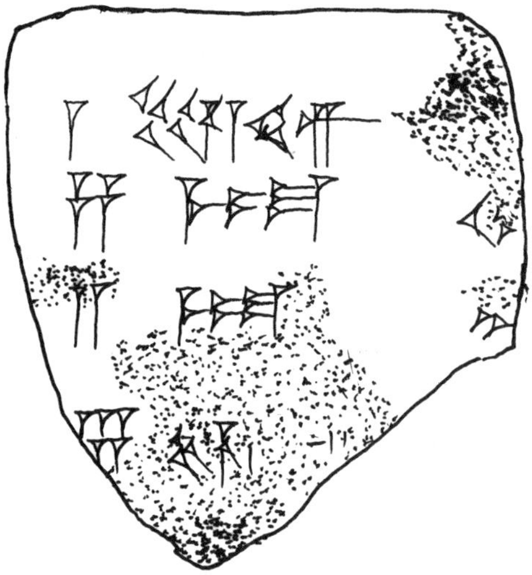

Aphek 2

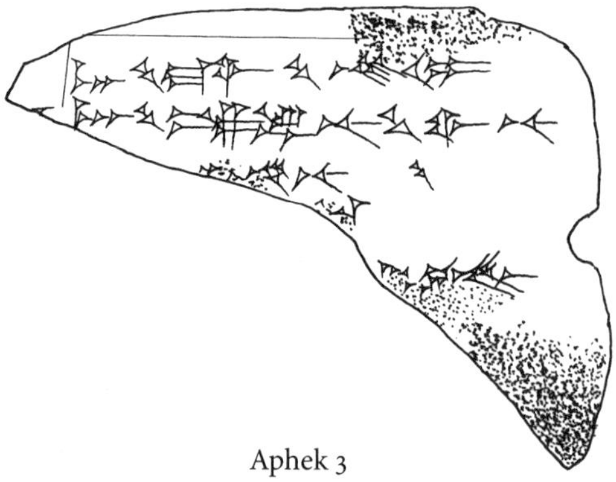

Aphek 3

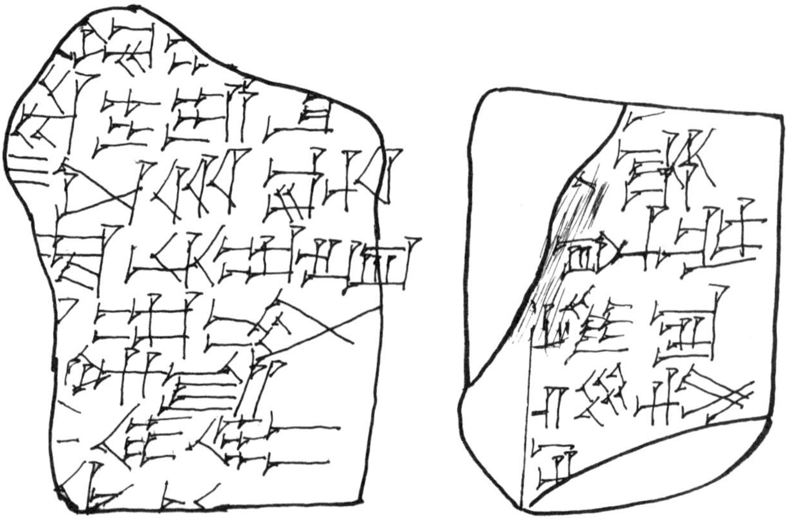

Aphek 6 (left: obverse; right: reverse)

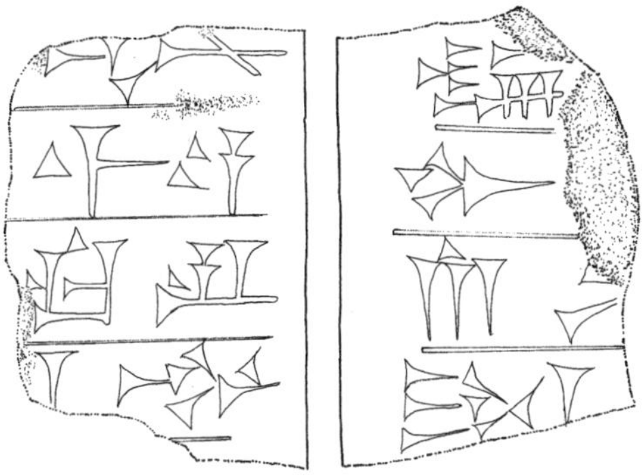

Ashdod 2

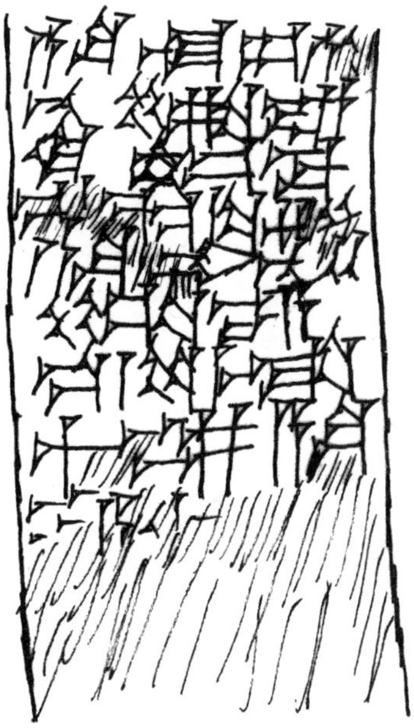

Beth Shean 2

Ashdod 3

Gezer 2

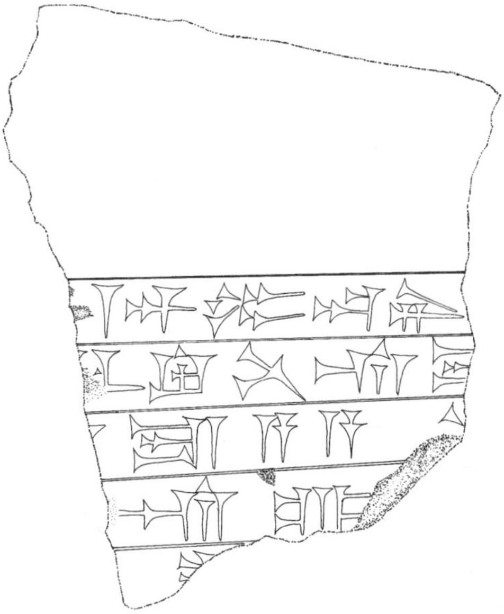

Ashdod 4

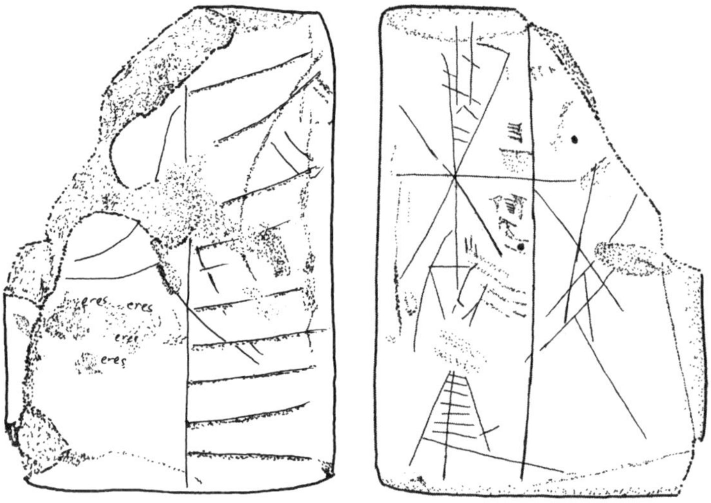

Gezer 5 (left: obverse; right: reverse)

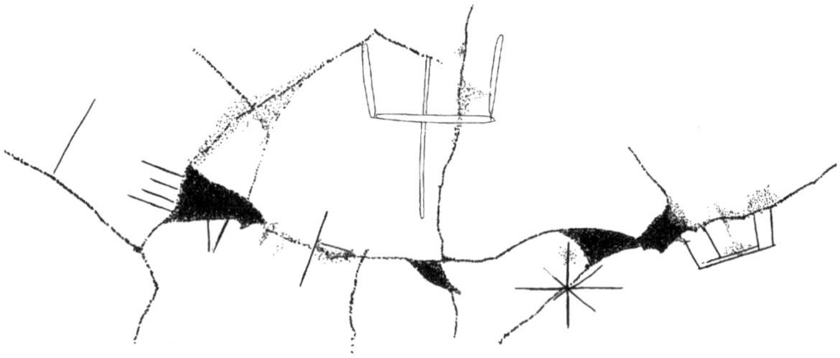

Hazor 1

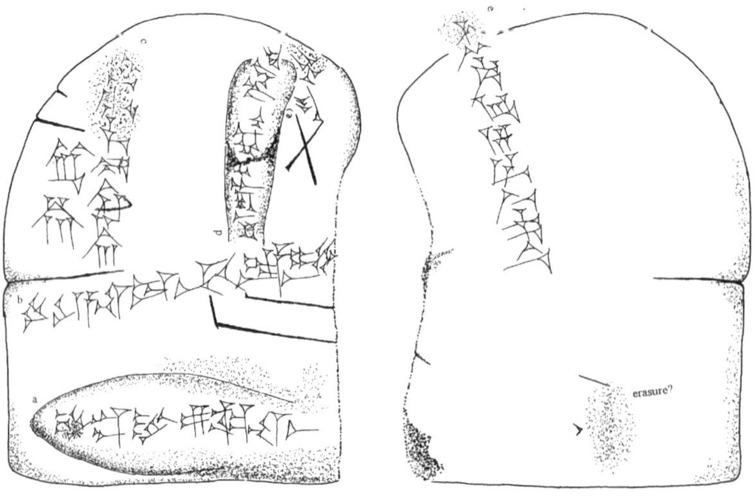

Hazor 2 (left: obverse; right: reverse)

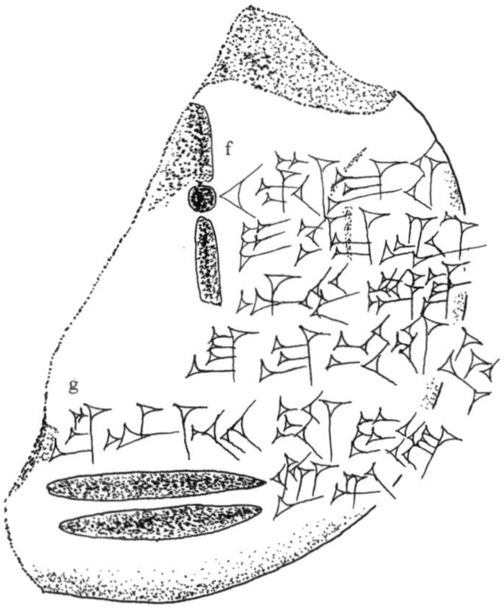

Hazor 3

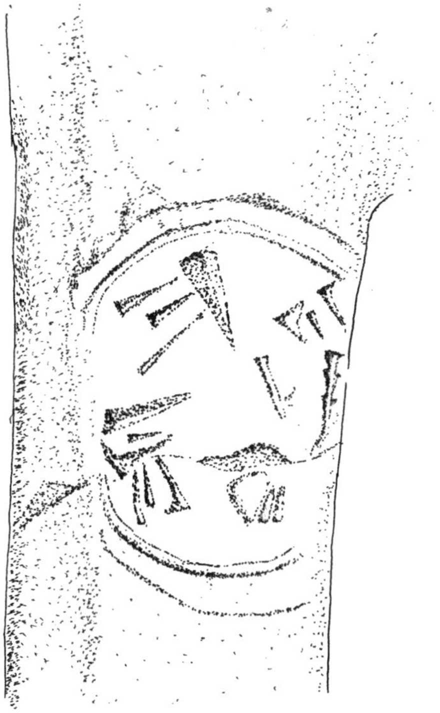

Hazor 4

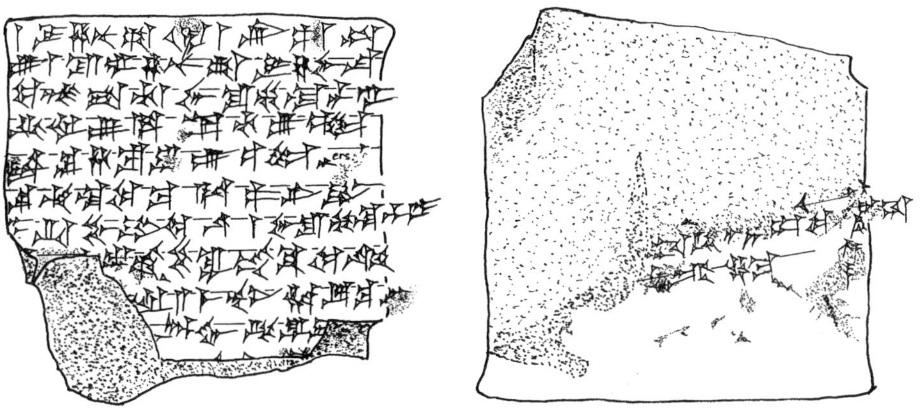

Hazor 5 (left: obverse; right: reverse)

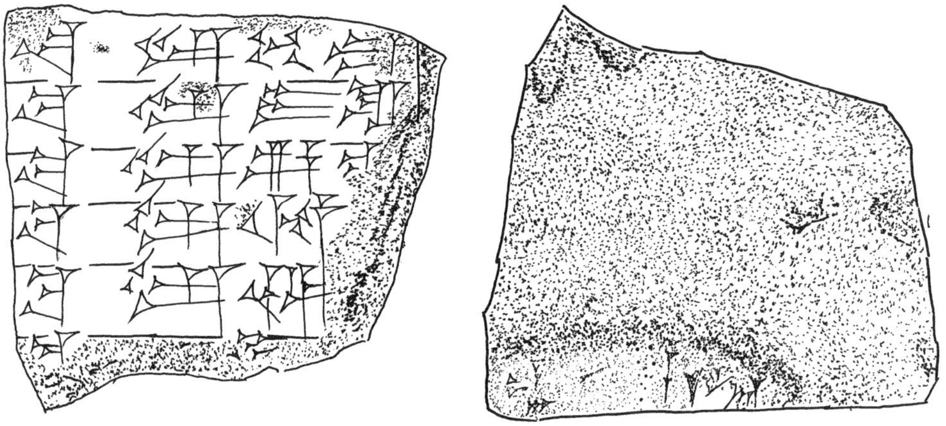

Hazor 6 (left: obverse; right: reverse)

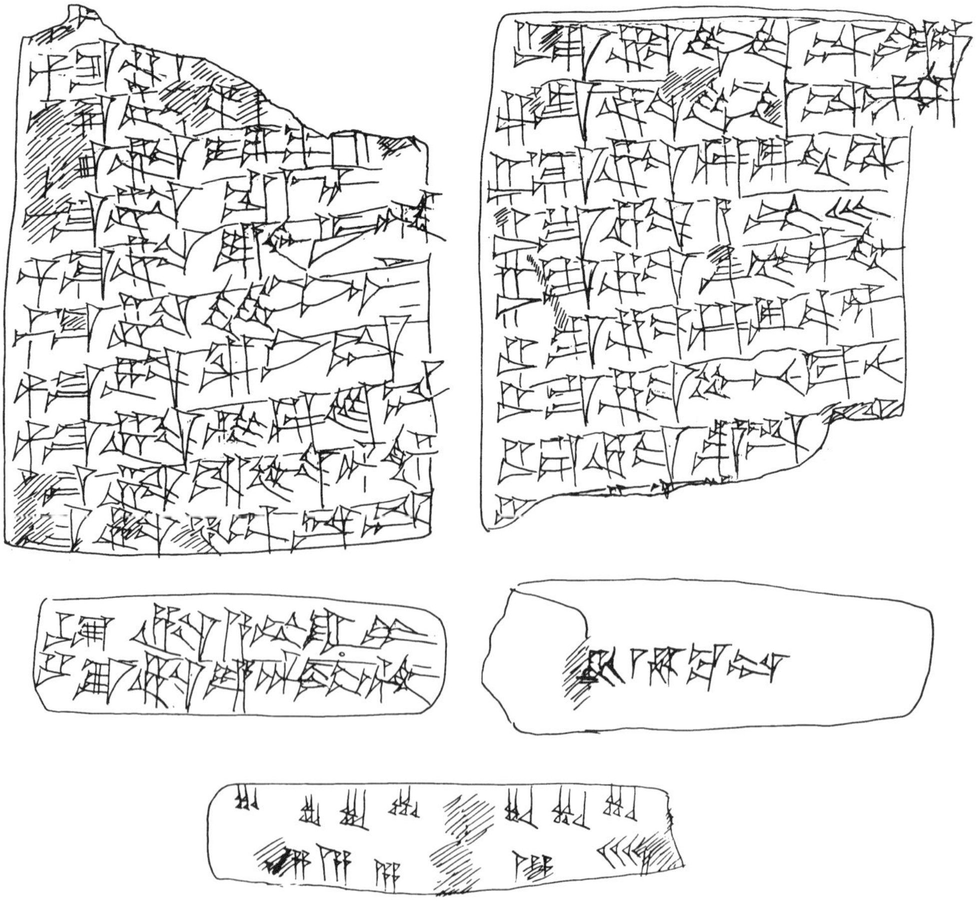

Hazor 7 (top left: obverse; top right: reverse;
middle left: lower edge; middle right: right edge;)
bottom: left edge)

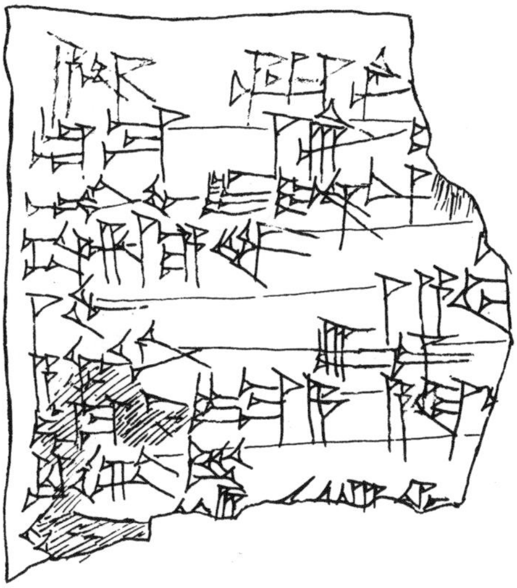

Hazor 8

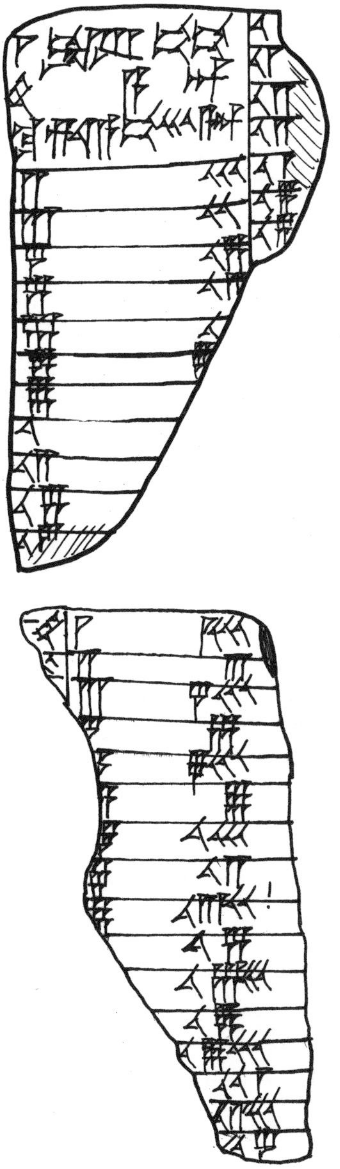

Hazor 9 (top: side I; bottom: side IV)

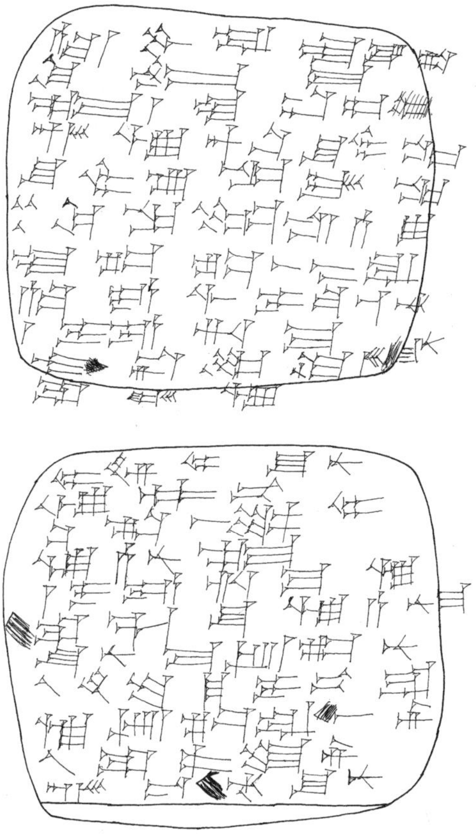

Hazor 10 (top: obverse; bottom: reverse)

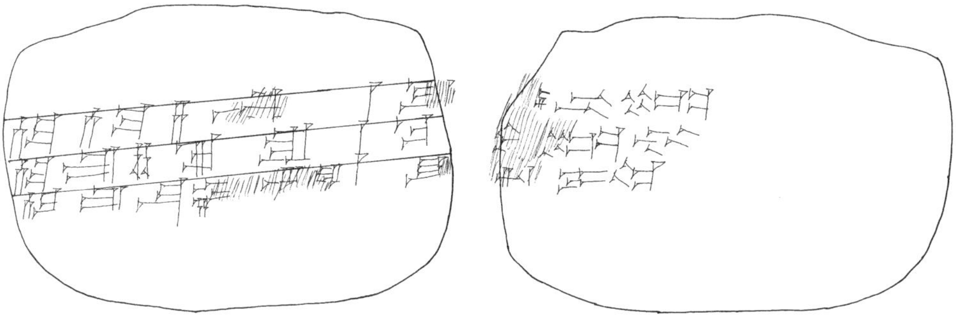

Hazor 11 (left: obverse; right: reverse)

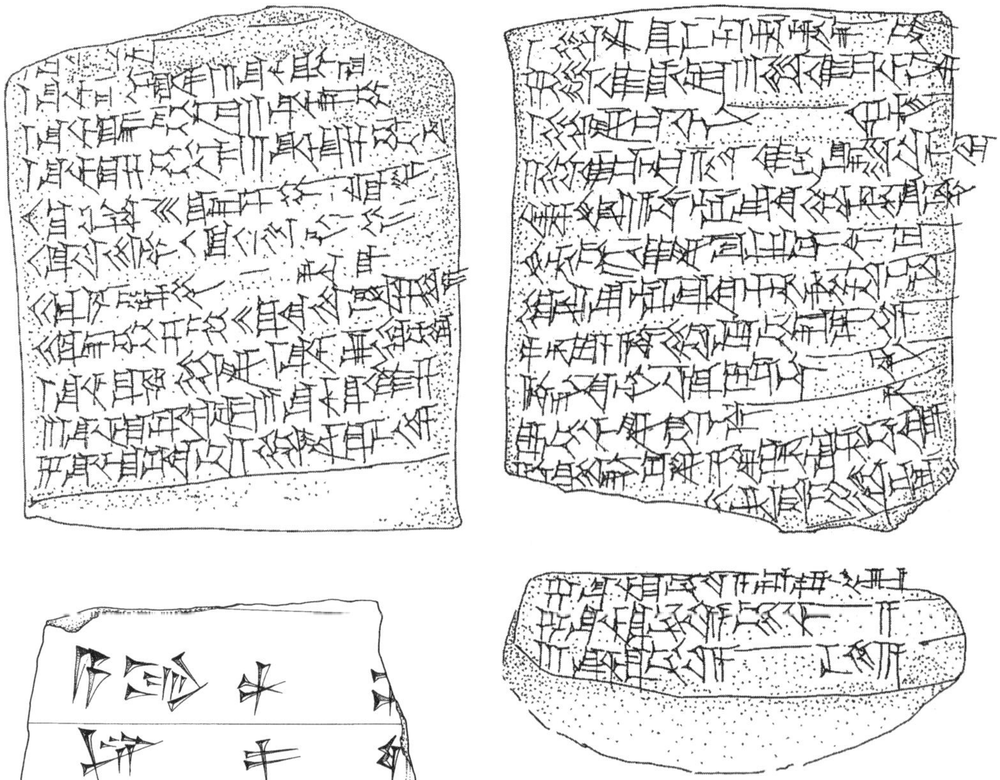

Hazor 12 (left: obverse; right: reverse; bottom right: lower edge)

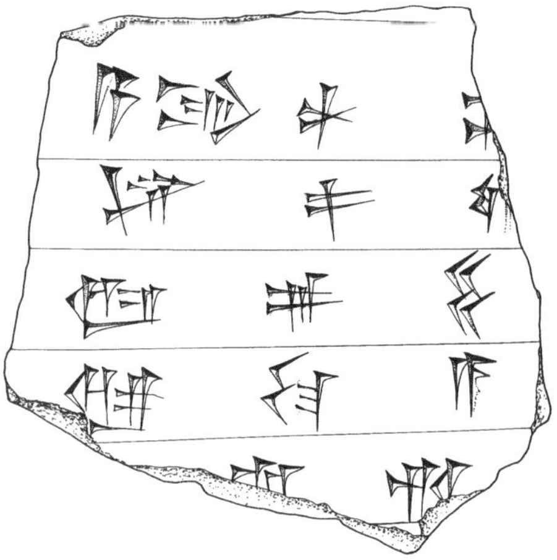

Hazor 13

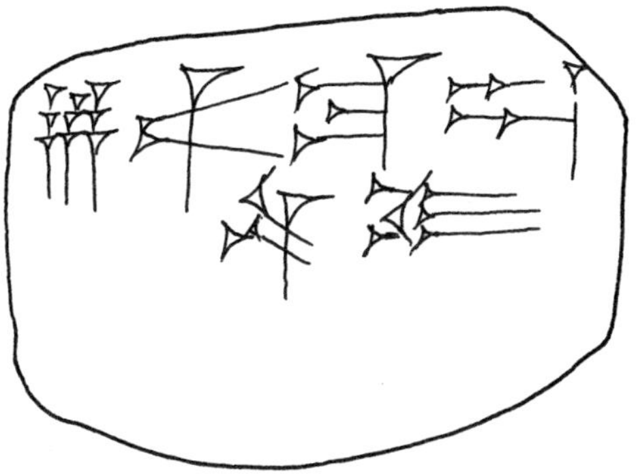

Hazor 14

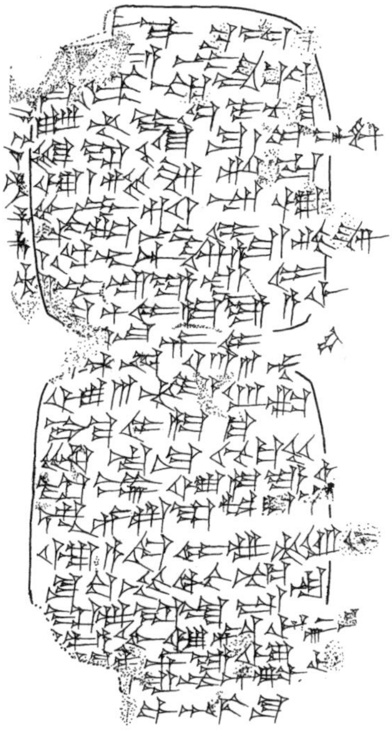

el-Ḥesi 1

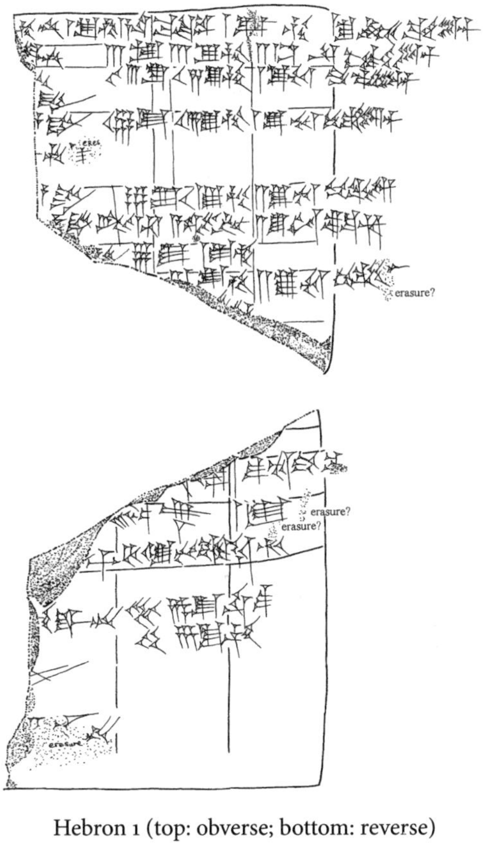

Hebron 1 (top: obverse; bottom: reverse)

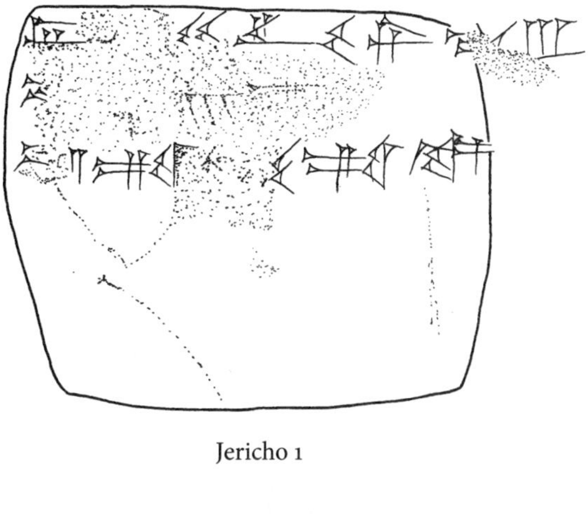

Jericho 1

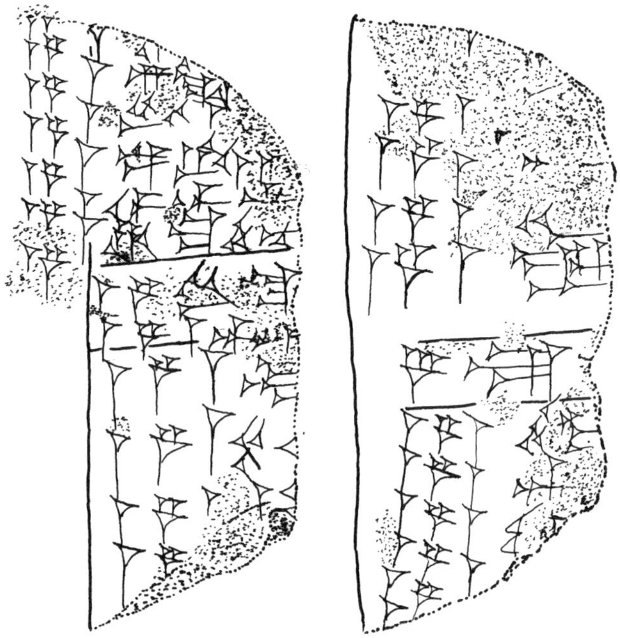

Keisan 1 (left: obverse; right: reverse)

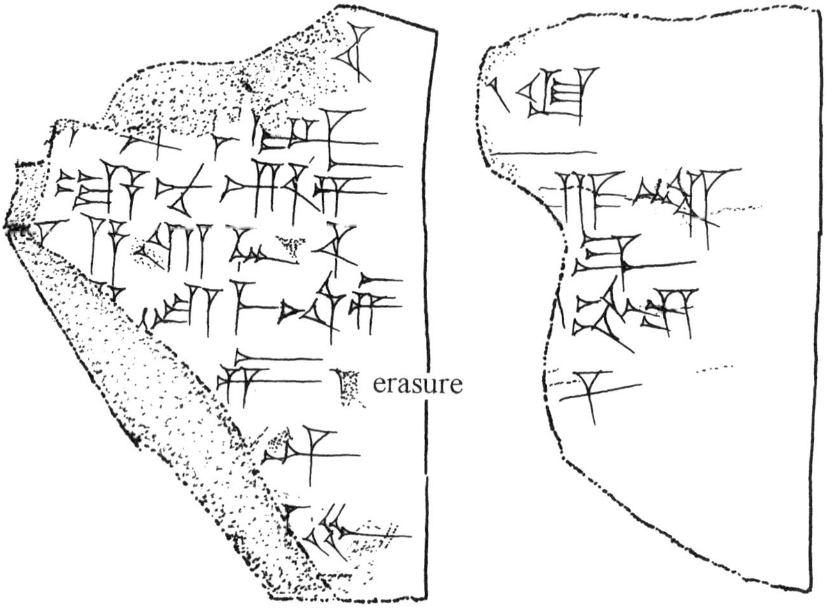

Kusiya 1 (left: obverse; right: reverse)

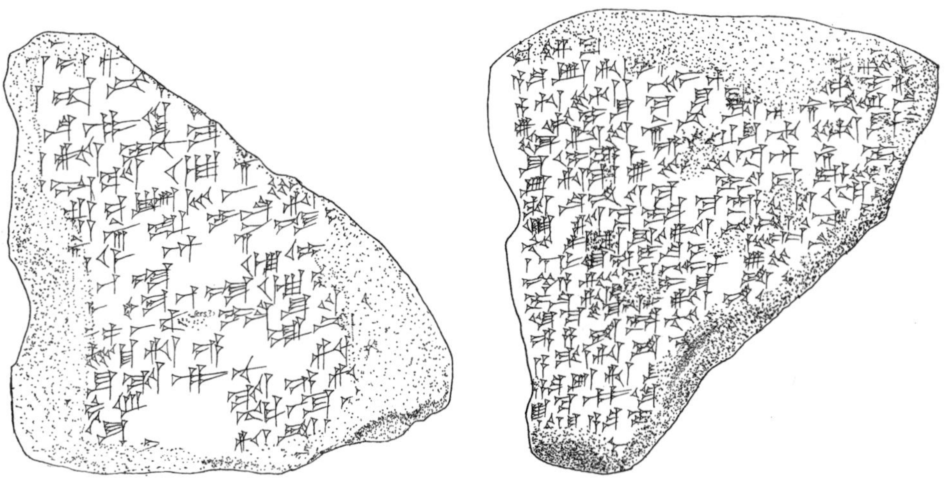

Megiddo 1 (left: obverse; right: reverse)

Megiddo 5 (top left: side view;
top right: inscription; bottom: top of stopper)

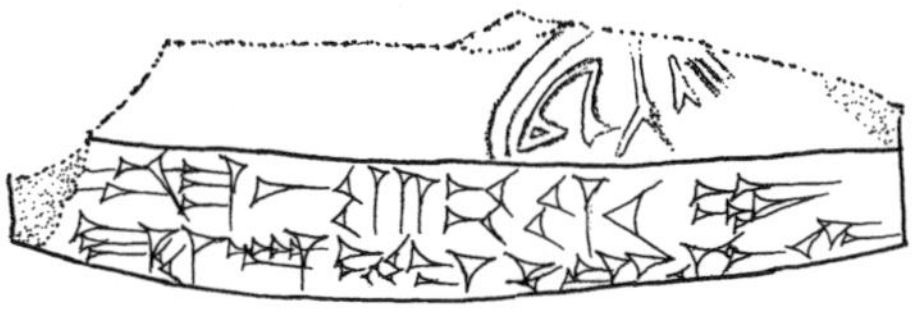

Samaria 2

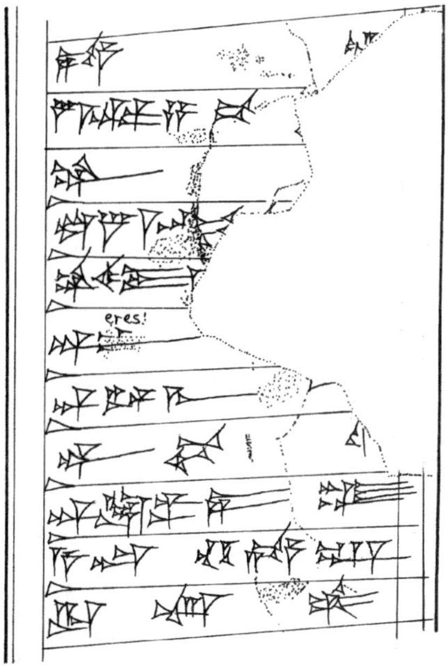

Samaria 3

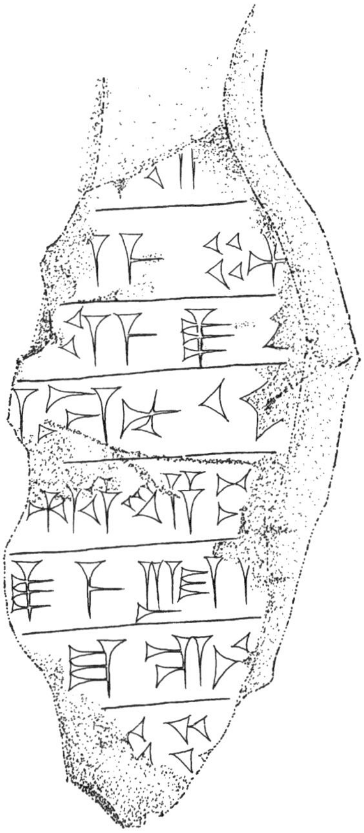

Samaria 4

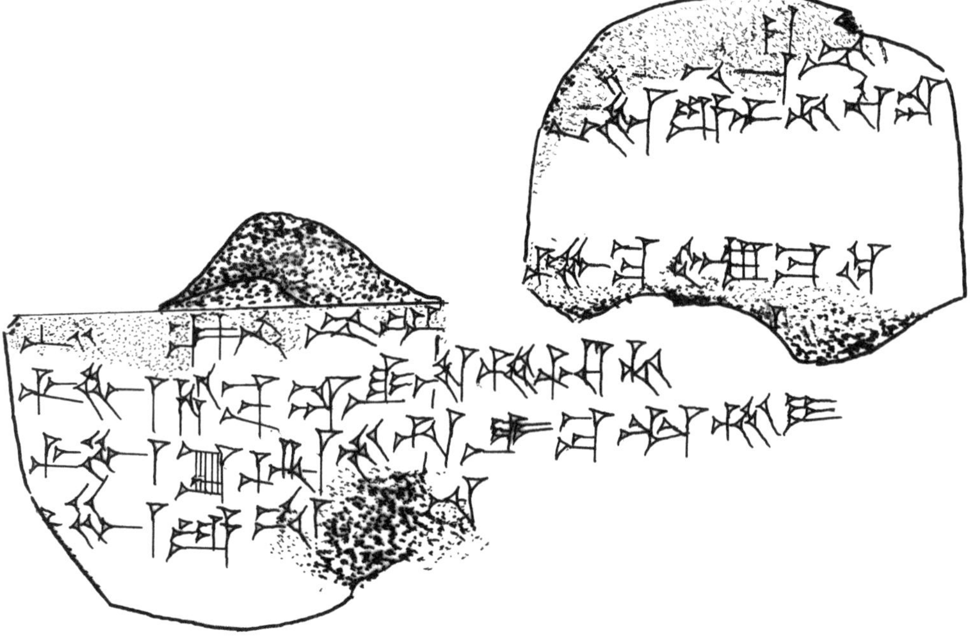

Shechem 2 (left: obverse; right: reverse)

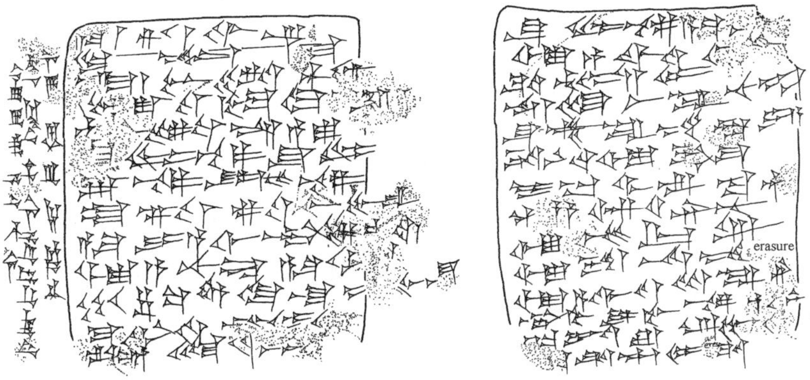

Taanach 1 (left: obverse; right: reverse)

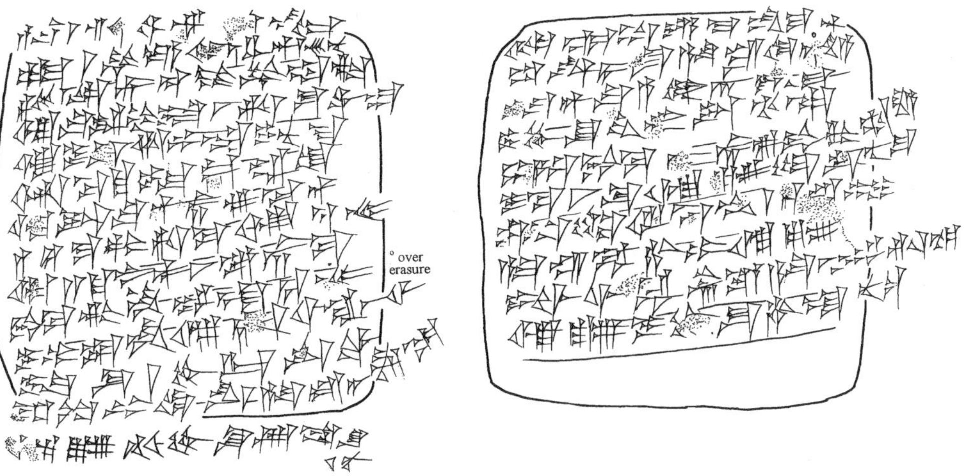

Taanach 2 (left: obverse; right: reverse)

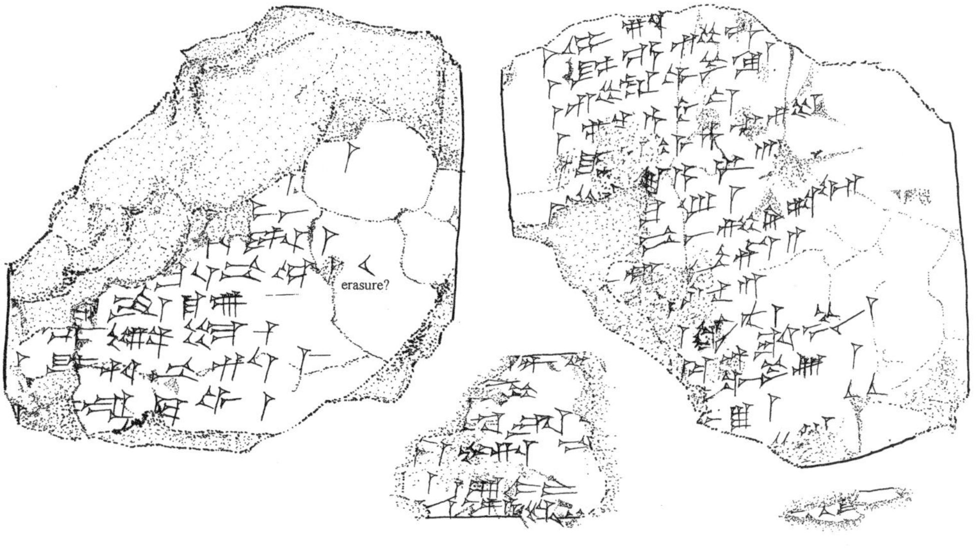

Taanach 3 (left: obverse; middle: left edge; right: reverse)

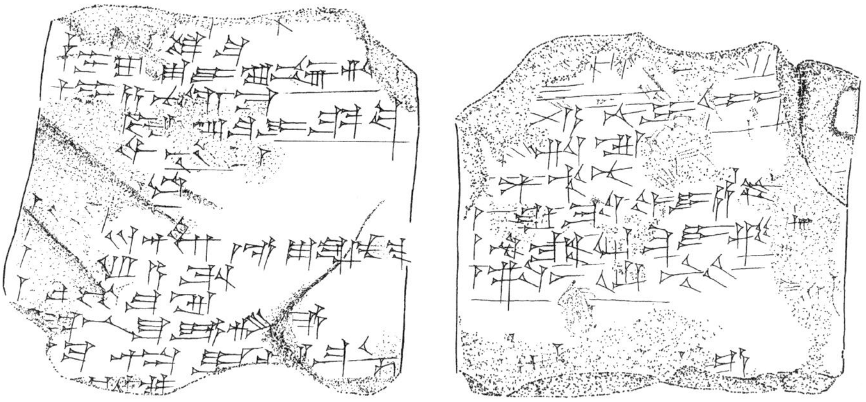

Taanach 4 (left: obverse; right: reverse)

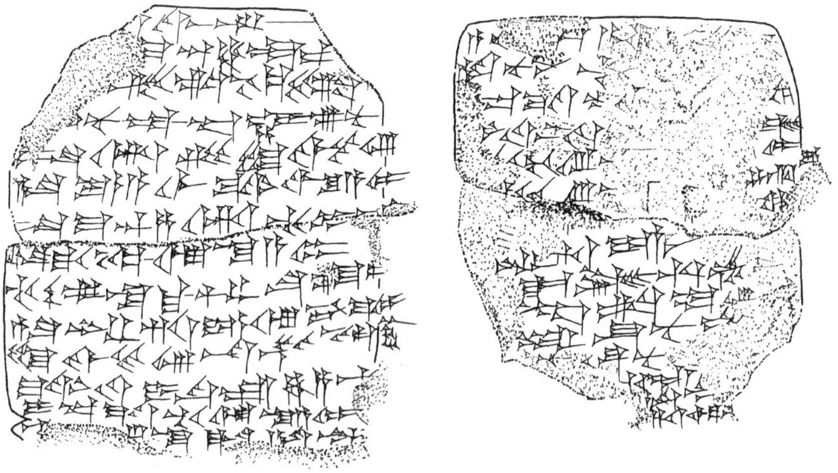

Taanach 6 (left: obverse; right: reverse)

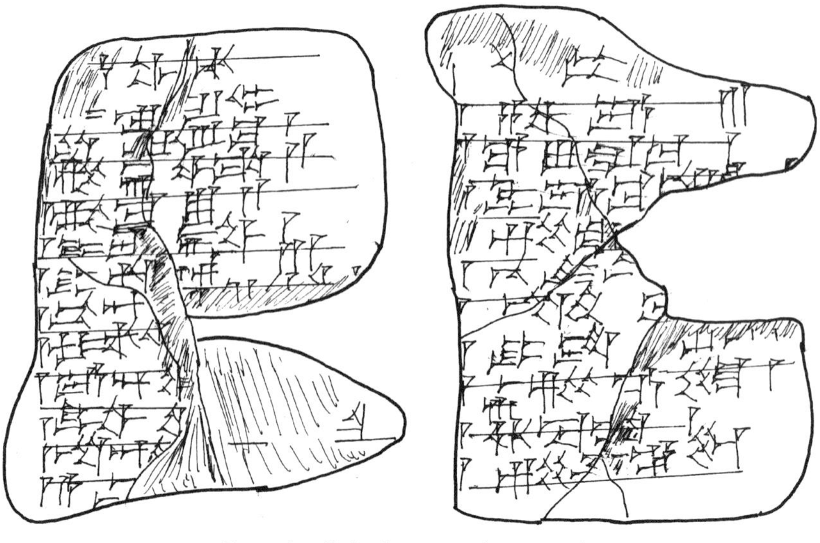

Taanach 7 (left: obverse; right: reverse)

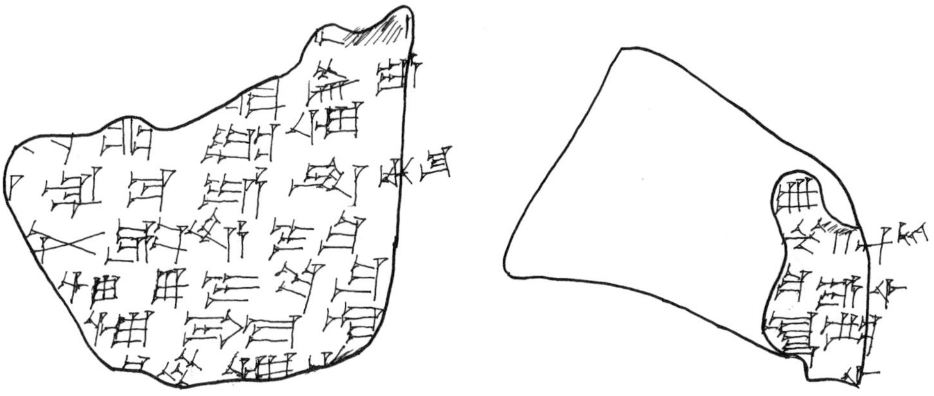

Taanach 8 (left: obverse; right: reverse)

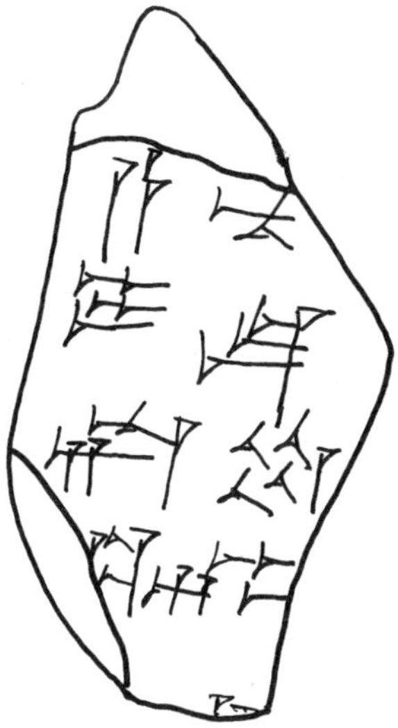

Taanach 8a

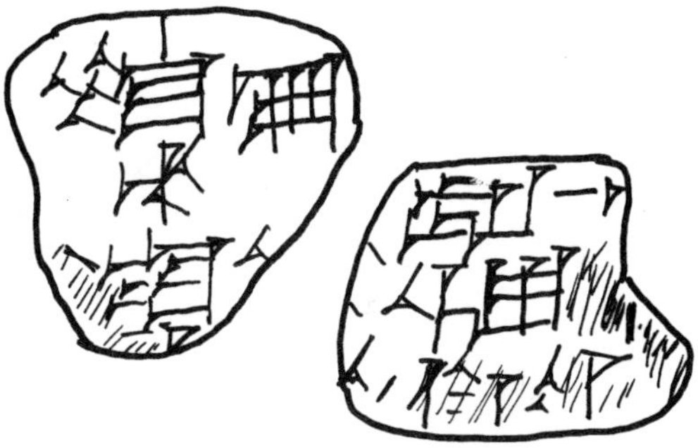

Taanach 9 (left: obverse; right: reverse)

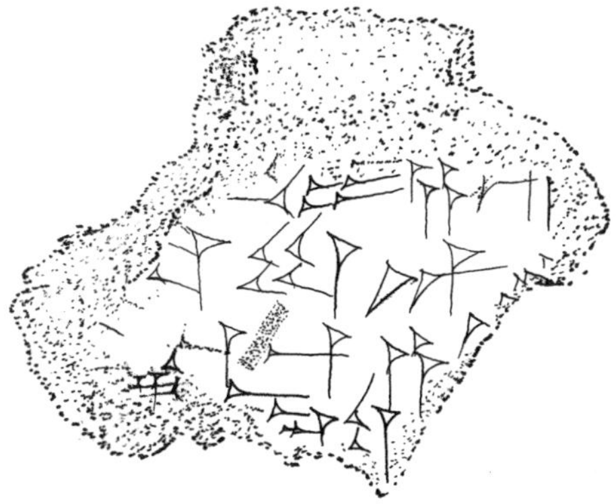

Taanach 10

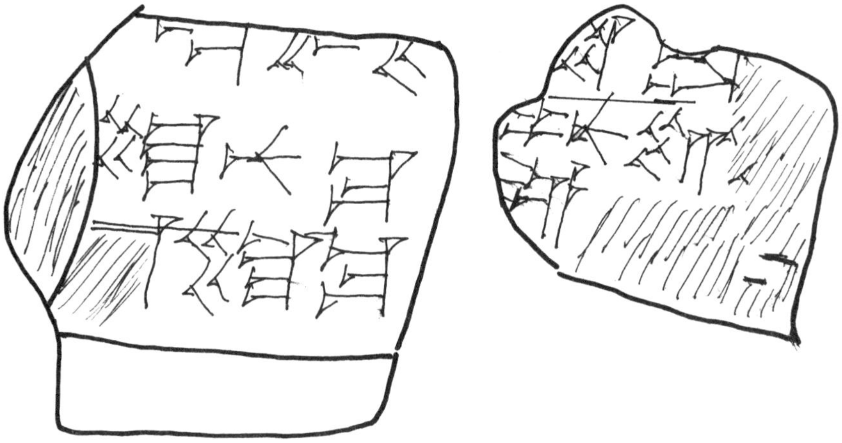

Taanach 11 (left: obverse; right: reverse)

Photographs

Aphek 1

Aphek 3

Aphek 2

Aphek 6 (left: obverse; right: reverse)

Aphek 7 (left: obverse; right: reverse)

Beth Mirsim 1 (left: impression; right: cylinder seal)

Beth Shean 1 (left: impression; right: cylinder seal)

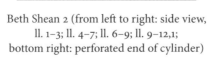

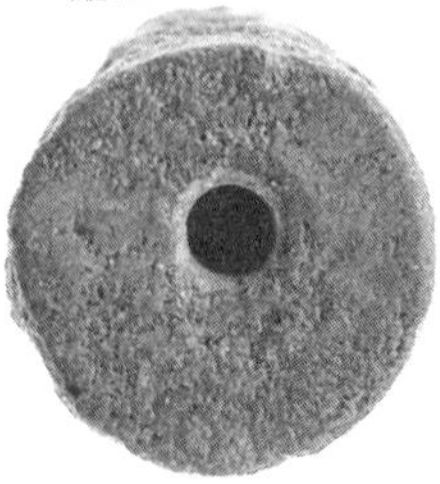

Beth Shean 2 (from left to right: side view, ll. 1–3; ll. 4–7; ll. 6–9; ll. 9–12,1; bottom right: perforated end of cylinder)

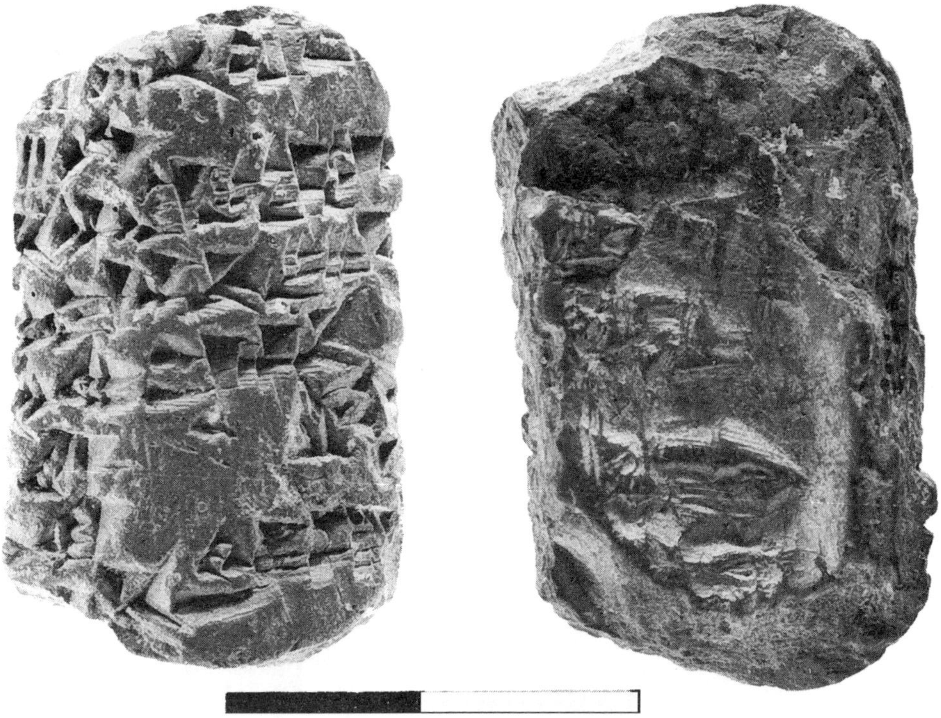

Gezer 1 (left: obverse; right: reverse)

Hazor 2 (left: obverse; right: reverse)

Hazor 3 (top: obverse; bottom: reverse)

Hazor 4

Hazor 5 (left: obverse; right: reverse)

Hazor 6 (left: obverse; right: reverse)

Hazor 7 (top left: obverse; top right: reverse; middle left: lower edge; middle right: right edge; bottom: left edge)

Hazor 8

Hazor 9 (top right: side view;
bottom left: side I; bottom right: side IV)

Hazor 10 (top: obverse; bottom: reverse)

Hazor 11 (top: obverse; bottom: reverse)

Hazor 12 (top: obverse;
middle: lower edge; bottom: reverse)

Hazor 13

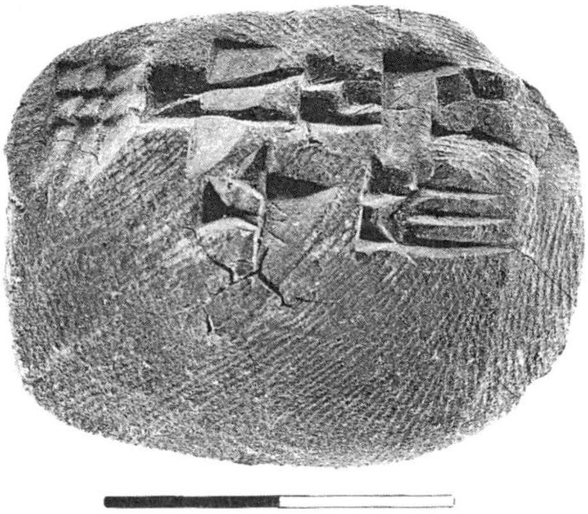

Hazor 14

Hebron 1 (left: obverse; right: reverse)

Jericho 1 (left: obverse; right: reverse)

Jericho 3 (left: impression; right: cylinder seal)

Khirbet Kusiya 1 (left: obverse; middle: reverse; right: seal)

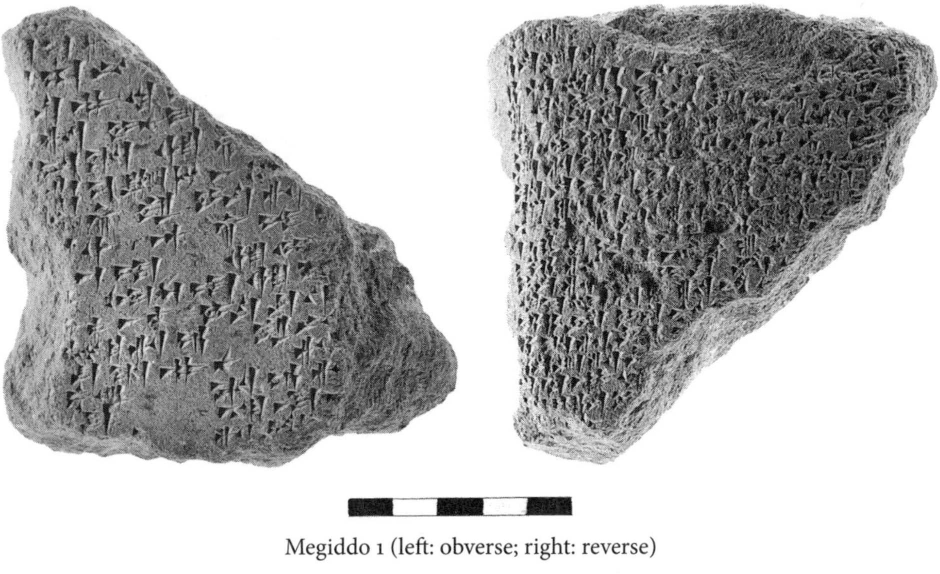

Megiddo 1 (left: obverse; right: reverse)

Megiddo 2 (left: impression; right: cylinder seal)

Megiddo 4 (left: impression; right: cylinder seal)

Megiddo 5 (top: side view;
bottom: view from above)

en-Naṣbeh 1

Sepphoris 1

Shechem 1 (left: obverse; right: reverse)

Shechem 2 (left: obverse; right: reverse)

Taanach 1 (from top to bottom: obverse; bottom edge; reverse; upper edge; left edge)

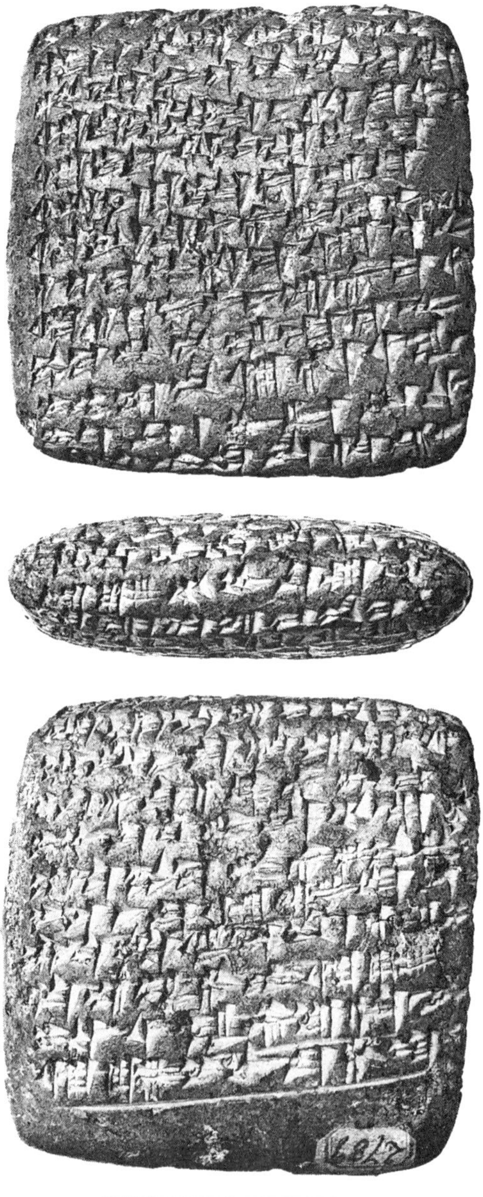

Taanach 2 (top: obverse; middle: bottom edge; bottom: reverse)

Taanach 3 (top left: obverse;
top right: reverse; bottom: left edge)

Taanach 4 (left: obverse; right: reverse)

Taanach 5 (left: obverse; right: reverse)

Taanach 6 (top left: obverse; top right: reverse;
bottom left: bottom edge; bottom right: upper edge)

Taanach 7 (top: obverse; bottom: reverse)

Taanach 9 (top: obverse; bottom: reverse)

Taanach 10

Taanach 11 (obverse)

Taanach 14 (top: obverse;
middle: lower edge; bottom: reverse)

Appendix A: New Hand Copies

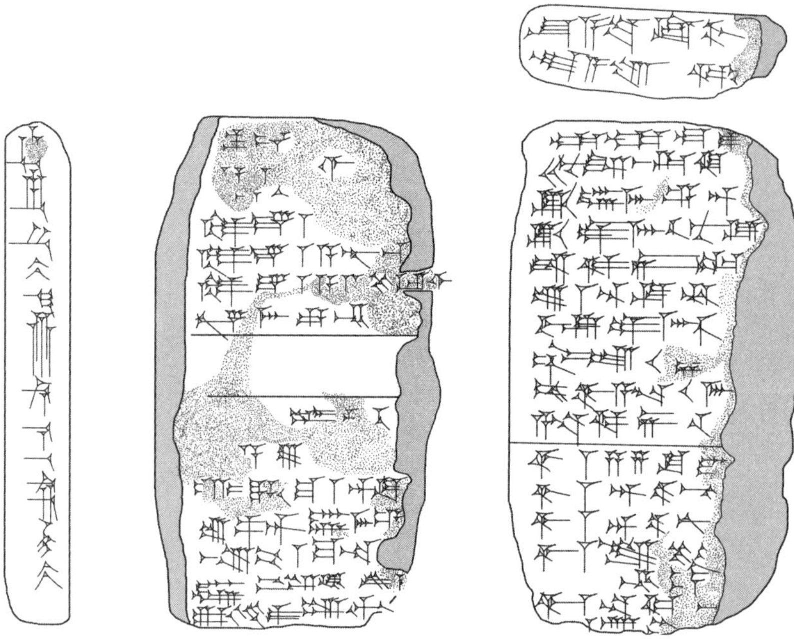

Hadid 1 (left: side; middle: obverse; right: reverse; top right: edge)

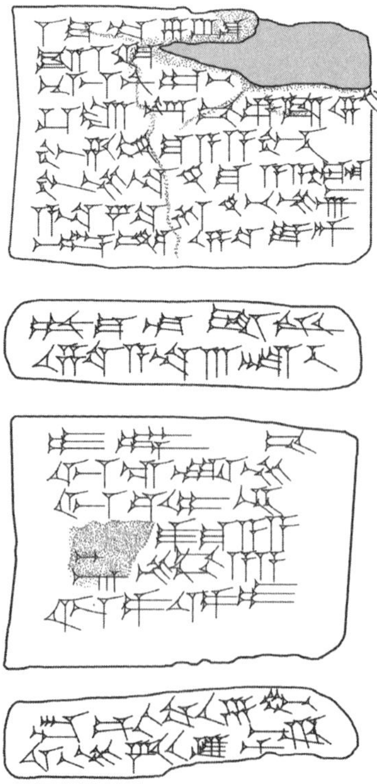

Hadid 2 (from top: obverse; edge; reverse; lower edge)

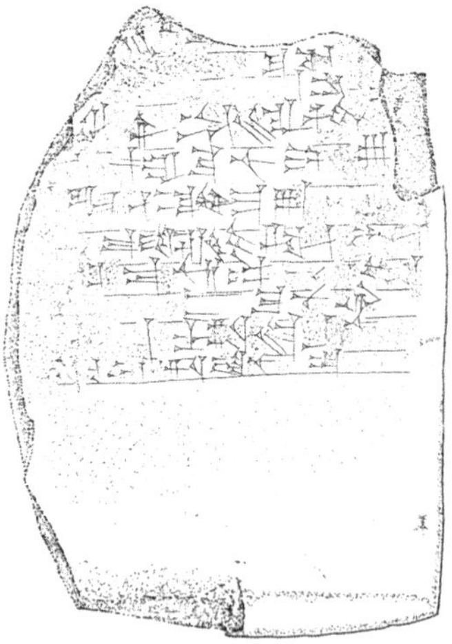

Hazor 15

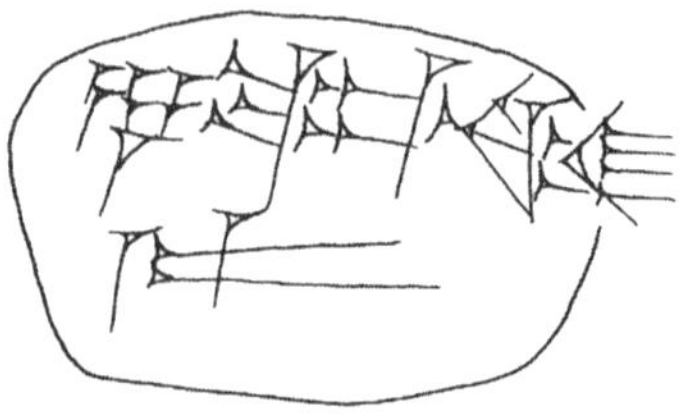

Hazor 16

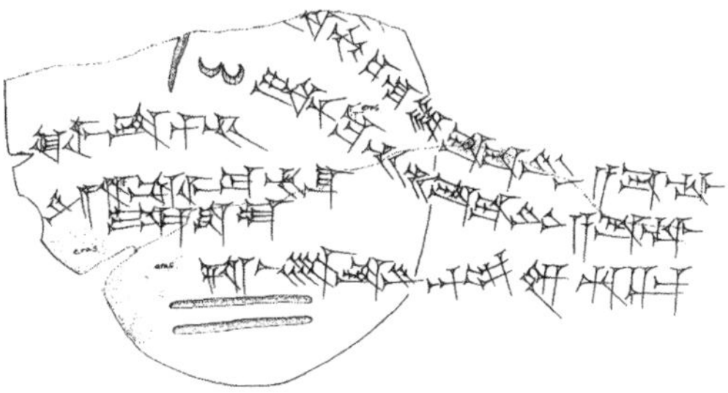

Hazor 17

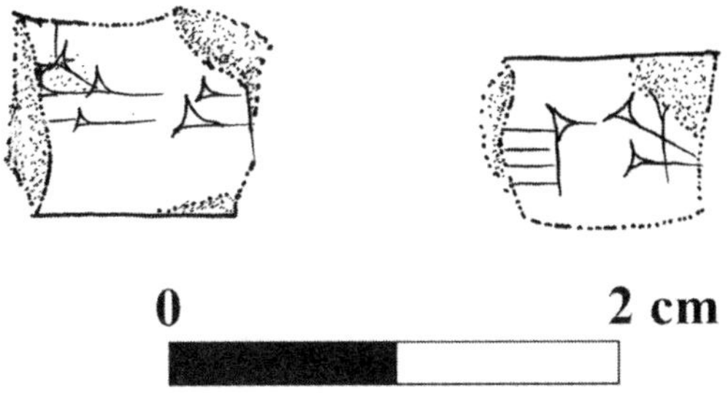

Jerusalem 2

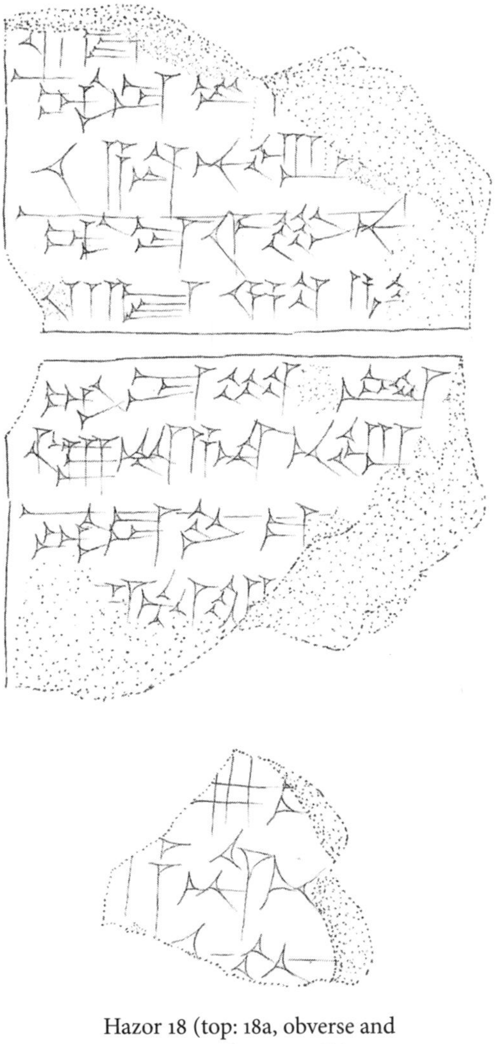

Hazor 18 (top: 18a, obverse and reverse; bottom: 18b)

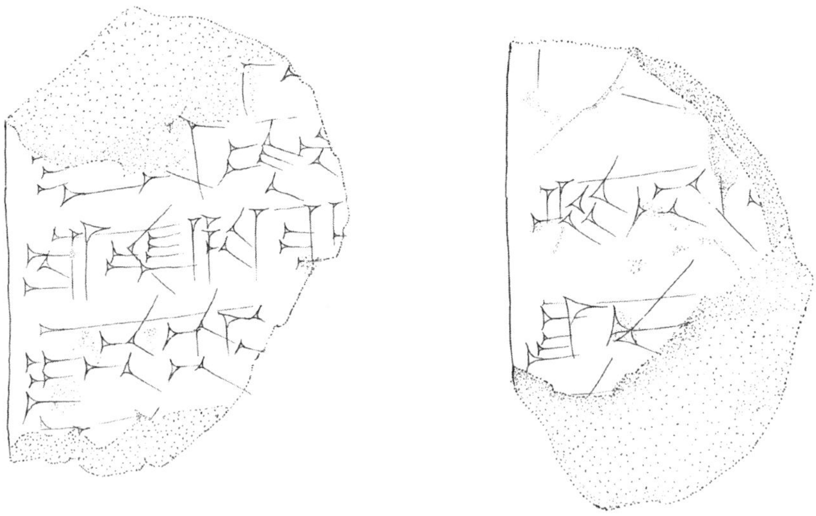

Jerusalem 1 (left: obverse; right: reverse)

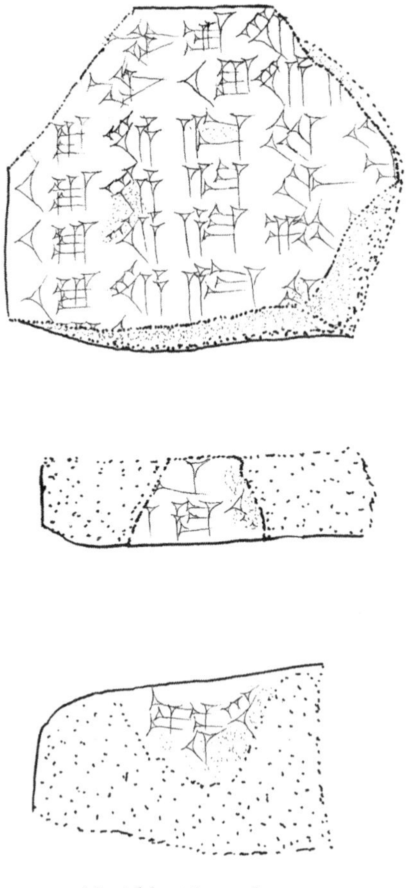

Megiddo 6 (top: obverse;
middle: lower edge; bottom: left edge)

Appendix B: New Photographs

Hazor 15

Hazor 17

Hazor 16

Hazor 18a (left top: obverse; left bottom: reverse; above: side)

Hazor 18b

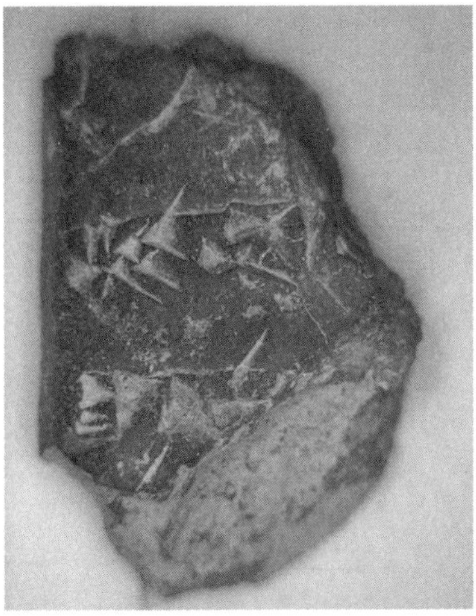

Jerusalem 1 (left: obverse; right: reverse)

Jerusalem 2